# THE STRUGGLE FOR

# BLACK EQUALITY

## 1954 – 1992.

CONSULTING EDITOR

ERIC FONER

...........................................................

🖐 *Hill and Wang*
*New York*
*The Noonday Press*

# *T*HE *S*TRUGGLE FOR *B*LACK *E*QUALITY

## 1954 – 1992

......................................................

REVISED EDITION

HARVARD
SITKOFF

LIBRARY OF CONGRESS CATALOGING-IN-PUBLICATION DATA
Sitkoff, Harvard.
The struggle for black equality 1954–1992 / Harvard Sitkoff ;
consulting editor, Eric Foner.
p.   cm.—(American century series.)
Includes bibliographical references and index.
1. Afro-Americans—Civil rights.   2. United States—Race
relations.   3. Civil rights movements—United States—History—20th
century.   I. Foner, Eric.   II. Title.   III. Series.
E185.615.S572   1993   323'.196073—dc20       92-20244 CIP

Sixteenth printing 1993

*For*
*Alexandra, Adam, Erica,*
*and Charles*

# PREFACE

........................

This book is concerned with one of the most significant developments in American history: the struggle for racial equality and justice waged between 1954 and 1992. It is designed primarily to provide a succinct narrative and interpretation of the civil-rights movement. I have, accordingly, written neither a comprehensive nor a scholarly account of the struggle. Important developments before 1954 are merely sketched; some events, organizations, and individuals that merit discussion are omitted; and topics that warrant definitive treatment are dealt with concisely. To help the reader who wishes to pursue a particular aspect of the struggle more fully, I have appended a bibliographical essay. The works listed there are also the source for all the quotations included in this account.

Some may consider it presumptuous to publish a historical analysis and synthesis of a recent and controversial subject. The limited perspective of time, the many archival sources still closed, the scarcity of solidly researched monographs, and the inherent biases of most contemporary attempts to record and evaluate the bewildering rush of events from the pathbreaking *Brown* decision of 1954 through the crescendo of violence in the late 1960s combine to make the writing of a history of the modern struggle a hazardous

task. This revised edition is sure to need further revision as perspectives continue to change and still more information becomes
available. Nevertheless, I hope it will be of use to future historians.
I am confident it will aid readers in the 1990s to develop an informed
understanding of the recent past and to come to some preliminary
conclusions and evaluations about the enduring significance of the
struggle.

The facts of history, of course, do not speak for themselves. Any
effort to describe and explain requires judgment; and no historian
can entirely escape his basic beliefs. Honesty, however, dictates that
a historian consider and test all the evidence according to the canons
of the craft, guard against personal biases, avoid forcing the past
into preconceived notions, and inform the reader of the author's
viewpoint. My perspective derives from association and identification with the movement in the early sixties. I believed then that
the struggle was confronting the United States with an issue that
had undermined the nation's democratic institutions for nearly two
hundred years, and that morality, justice, and a due concern for
the future well-being of our society necessitated an end to racial
inequality. A third of a century later, I believe it more than ever.
Moreover, given the rapidity with which the popular media have
relegated the civil-rights battles to the scrap heap of inattention and
indifference, I felt compelled to write of the strivings and sufferings
of these battles to make real the promise of democracy. I want the
reader to encounter the anguish and hope, the violence and passion,
the joy and sorrow that the fighters for freedom experienced. My
attempt to recapture the drama of the era, as well as my value
judgments, will certainly provoke disagreement. Good. At the very
least, the writing of history ought to stimulate debate and further
inquiry.

My effort to tell the story of the actions and consequences of the
black struggle for equality, like the movement itself, has truly been
a collective effort. Although a small part of the book derives from
archival research and my own participation in some of the events
narrated, this synthesis would not have been possible without the

pioneering efforts of those historians, journalists, political scientists, sociologists, and memoirists who have written on aspects of this topic. Their personal accounts and scholarly studies, discussed in the bibliographical essay, underpin this book. My intellectual debt to them is enormous. I owe much, in addition, to the many important substantive and stylistic suggestions offered by my editor, Eric Foner, and my publisher, Arthur Wang. They made the manuscript much better in every way than it would otherwise have been. I am also indebted to many of my students and friends in the movement, too numerous to name individually, who shared with me their questions and observations, and sharpened my perception of the black struggle. As always, the encouragement and inspiration of William Chafe and William Leuchtenburg have been invaluable. The flaws of content, expression, and interpretation that remain are mine alone.

H.S.

# CONTENTS

........................

# THE STRUGGLE FOR

# BLACK EQUALITY

## 1954–1992

# ONE

. . . . . . . . . . . . . . . . . . . . . . .

# Up from Slavery

There is a difference in knowing you are black and in understanding what it means to be black in America. Before I was ten I knew what it was to step off the sidewalk to let a white man pass.

MARGARET WALKER

Nourished by anger, revolutions are born of hope. They are the offspring of belief and bitterness, of faith in the attainment of one's goals and indignation at the limited rate and extent of change. Rarely in history are the two stirrings confluent in a sufficient force to generate an effective, radical social movement. They would be so in African America in the 1960s.

During the last decade of the nineteenth century, however, few African-Americans struggled hopefully. Many African-Americans resisted, often in subtle and solitary ways, at times in an organized and collective manner, transmitting from one generation to the next a tradition of black protest. But their initial efforts to continue the campaign against Jim Crow initiated by the black abolitionists failed to stem the rising crest of white racism after Reconstruction. Largely bereft of white allies, blacks fought on the defensive, trying to hold their limited gains. They lost each battle. Congress permitted the white South to reduce blacks to a state of peonage, to disregard their civil rights, and to disenfranchise them by force, intimidation, and statute. So did the Supreme Court. Writing into the Constitution its own beliefs in the inferiority of blacks, the late-nineteenth-century high court tightened every possible shackle confining the ex-slaves. Most American scholars cheered this legal counterrevolution which effectively nullified the Fourteenth and Fifteenth Amendments. It exemplified their teachings of inherent and irremediable racial differences, of blacks as the most primitive, degraded, and least civilized of the races, and of the folly of governmental tampering with local folkways. Whether appealing to scriptural or scientific evidence, to Darwinism, the gospel of Anglo-Saxonism, or the new interest in eugenics, a generation of clergymen, editors, and educators propounded the intellectual rationalizations for white supremacy.

Not surprisingly, most white Americans at the beginning of the twentieth century believed that, for the good of all, the naturally superior whites should rule over the baser races. They heard or read little to the contrary. The Southern Way had become the American Way. Even the most humanitarian reformers concerned with racial injustice counseled gradualism. Northern liberals preached the necessity of deferring citizenship for blacks until the freedmen were ready for it; they emphasized the long-term gains to be derived from education, religion, and economic uplift and denigrated strategies predicated on agitation, force, or political activity.

This total acquiescence by government officials and Northern public opinion gave the white South all the permission it needed to institutionalize its white-supremacist beliefs. First came disenfranchisement, accomplished in the 1880s mainly through fraud and force. All the Southern states felt emboldened in the next two decades to follow the lead of the 1890 Mississippi state constitutional convention in officially adopting such disenfranchising techniques as poll taxes, "grandfather clauses," literacy and "good character" tests, and white primaries. Black voter registration plummeted 96 percent in Louisiana between 1896 and 1900. The number of African-Americans permitted to vote in the new century hovered around 3,500 in Alabama, which had an adult black population of nearly 300,000; and in Mississippi, with an even larger black population, fewer than a thousand blacks voted.

Political impotency bore on every aspect of African-American life. Unable to participate in the enactment or enforcement of the law, Southern blacks became increasingly vulnerable to physical assault and murder. Over a thousand were lynched between 1900 and 1915. No records exist to tally the number beaten or tortured. Nor can one describe adequately the terror of living with a constant fear of barbarity and violence, of having your security subject to the whim of those who despise you, of having no recourse to police or courts.

The Southern states, in addition, adopted a host of statutes methodically outlawing everything "interracial." These new segregation laws expressed the white South's all-encompassing belief in the inequality of blacks. Most Southern states now formally required Negroes and whites to be born separately in segregated hospitals; to live their lives as separately as possible in segregated schools, public accommodations, and places of work and recreation; and, presumably, to dwell in the next life separately in segregated funeral homes and cemeteries. The rapid proliferation of Jim Crow laws inspired an irrational competition among Southern legislators to erect ever more and higher barriers between the races. "White" and "Colored" signs sprouted everywhere and on everything. Atlanta mandated Jim Crow Bibles in its courtrooms and prohibited African-Americans and whites from using the same park facilities, even from visiting the municipal zoo at the same time. Alabama forbade African-Americans to play checkers with whites, and Mississippi insisted on Jim Crow taxicabs. New Orleans segregated its prostitutes, and Oklahoma, its telephone booths. The lawmakers of Florida and North Carolina saw to it that white students would never touch textbooks used by African-Americans. Such edicts bolstered white power and privilege while demeaning the spirit of African-Americans.

Jim Crow, furthermore, easily led to gross inequities in the distribution of public monies for education and civic services. The eleven Southern states in 1916 spent an average of $10.32 per white public-school student, and only $2.89 per black pupil. There was one hospital bed available for every 139 American whites in the 1920s, but only one for every 1,941 blacks. And that was not all. Southern governments victimized blacks by bestial convict-leasing and chain-gang practices, and confined them to serfdom on the lowest rung of the economic ladder, doing all they could to implement the view of James K. Vardaman, who became Governor of Mississippi in 1904, that "God Almighty had created the Negro for a menial."

Alexis de Tocqueville's observation early in the nineteenth century that white Americans "scarcely acknowledge the common features of humanity in this stranger whom slavery has brought among them" remained as accurate a century later.

And blacks could do little to alter the situation. More than 90 percent of the nearly ten million African-Americans in 1910 lived in the South, three-quarters of them in rural areas, the vast majority working a white man's land, with a white man's mule and a white man's credit. Theirs was an oppressive, closed society, designed to thwart black advancement and encourage black subservience. All political and economic power remained vested in whites determined to maintain the status quo, however many black lives it cost. Daily facing grinding poverty, physical helplessness, and all the banal crudities of existence under an open, professed, and boasting racism, many blacks grew fatalistic. Segregation and discrimination came to seem permanent, immutable, an inevitable condition of life, and the majority of African-Americans succumbed to the new racial order.

But not all. Some protested by migrating. Between 1890 and 1910, nearly two hundred thousand Southern blacks fled to the North. Others returned to Africa or established autonomous black communities in the West. A few, mostly members of the tiny, Northern black elite, continued the struggle they had inherited from the black abolitionists and from the inspiring vision of equal rights nourished by the Civil War and Reconstruction. They spoke out for racial justice in such organizations as the Afro-American Council, Monroe Trotter's National Equal Rights League, Ida B. Wells's Antilynching League, and the Niagara Movement. Yet few blacks heard their pleas, and fewer whites heeded their demands. These small communities of resistance and struggle in the early twentieth century, lacking adequate finances, political leverage, influential white allies, access to the major institutions shaping public opinion and policy, and the support of large numbers of blacks, could do virtually nothing to alter the course of American life and thought. As Willie Brown lamented in his blues:

*Can't tell my future, I can't tell my past.*
*Lord, it seems like every minute sure gon' be my last.*
*Oh, a minute seems like hours, and hours seem like days.*
*And a minute seems like hours, hour seems like days.*

The ascendancy of Booker T. Washington at the turn of the century epitomized both the widespread despair of blacks and the powerlessness of the handful of blacks actively fighting against racial injustice. Although he worked covertly to diminish disenfranchisement and Jim Crow, Washington publicly emphasized the necessity of accommodation, conciliation, and gradualism. "The best course to pursue in regard to civil rights," he lectured to blacks, "is to let it alone; let it alone and it will settle itself." When the British author H. G. Wells criticized Jim Crow while on a visit to the United States, Washington answered back: "The only answer to it is for colored men to be patient, to make themselves competent, to do good work, to give no occasion against us." A spokesman for the emerging black middle class, he counseled all blacks to lift themselves up by their own bootstraps. Too few, however, even

had boots, and in the years before his death in 1915, Washington's
nostrums failed abysmally to alleviate the plight of blacks.

The National Association for the Advancement of Colored People, organized in 1910, fared no better. Declaring its purposes to
be "to promote equality of rights and eradicate caste or race prejudice . . . to advance the interests of colored citizens; to secure for
them impartial suffrage; and to increase their opportunities for
securing justice in the courts, education for their children, employment according to their ability; and complete equality before the
law," the interracial NAACP relied on litigation as the chief means
to those ends. Despite two victories at the Supreme Court, which
declared unconstitutional the grandfather clause and city ordinances
mandating residential segregation, the association's goals remained
an impossible dream during its first quarter of a century. It could
not destroy the edifice of discrimination, lessen the rampant prejudice everywhere in the nation, or deter the mushrooming ghet-
toization of blacks. Because of continuing white indifference and
black impotency, the NAACP could do nothing to affect the racial
policies of Southern governments or to compel the necessary corrective actions by the national government.

Indeed, no black leader or organization or strategy could stem
the tide of discrimination and segregation in the first third of the
twentieth century. Powerlessness fostered frustrations. Defeat bred
disillusionment. Blacks in the 1920s squabbled among themselves
more than they assailed their oppressors.

Certain harbingers of change nonetheless appeared. Most
stemmed from the mass migration of blacks to the cities and to the
North. Between 1910 and 1920 the "Great Migration" brought
more than half a million blacks northward, and another three-
quarters of a million blacks fled from the boll weevil and the lynch
mob in the 1920s. Some who followed the North Star looking for
the Promised Land found hell instead: educational and residential
segregation, dilapidated housing milked by white slumlords, discrimination by labor unions and employers, brutality by white policemen, and liquor and narcotics the only means of escape. Yet,

for most, the Northern urban ghetto meant surcease from permanent tenantry, poverty, disease, and ignorance, and the first step into the mainstream of the industrial labor force.

Northern Negroes, unlike their Southern brethren, could vote. In 1928, for the first time in the century, an African-American was elected to Congress. Other blacks won local offices in Chicago, Cleveland, Detroit, New York City, and Philadelphia, and the votes of African-Americans became a factor in election results. Politically, the African-American in the North began to command attention. The bonds of hopelessness of the rigid caste system of the Black Belt less and less characterized all of black America.

Hope sprouted also from the seeds of spiritual emancipation planted by the literary movement of the 1920s that African-Americans labeled the Harlem Renaissance, the Black Renaissance, and the New Negro Movement. Whether celebrating the racial chauvinism of African-Americans, affirming their identification with Africa, or decrying lynchings and racial oppression, poets and novelists of color sought to free themselves from white symbols and images and to write in their own idiom. By focusing white America's attention on blacks, by awakening the pride of African-Americans in their race and folk traditions, and by militant protests and demands for civil rights, the New Negro articulated the possibility of change brought about by migration.

So did the NAACP. Led by W. E. B. Du Bois, the brilliant black editor of its monthly journal, *The Crisis*, the NAACP publicized the hostility of organized labor to blacks, railed against disenfranchisement, and demanded that Congress enact an anti-lynching bill. Despite repeated rebuffs, the NAACP kept aloft the banners of racial equality, and gradually gained adherents. Its branches enabled local African-American leaders to acquire organizational skills and to develop networks of resources. Most important, its tactic of loudly complaining at each manifestation of racism slowly eroded the myth that Southern whites and black accommodators had forged: that blacks were content, even happy, with the status quo; that they did not consider the rights and duties of citizenship vital to black interests; and that they preferred the separation of the races to association with whites.

And so did Marcus Garvey's movement for racial pride and self-determination. Garvey convinced millions of blacks to believe in their ability to shape their destiny. A true visionary, he aroused African-Americans to affirm their Africanness and urged the redemption of Africa from European control. A master showman, Garvey dramatized the extreme plight of African-Americans and the desperate necessity of change. An intuitive psychologist, he radicalized the powerless by instilling in them a sense of their potential power. And as a persuasive teacher, the Jamaican leader convinced masses of Negroes that white racism and not black failings explained their lowly status.

In the 1930s, these stirrings began to innervate the struggle for black equality. The proponents of civil rights no longer stood alone. They fought alongside radicals pressing for class unity unhampered by racial divisions, labor leaders wanting strong unions, ethnic and political minorities desiring greater security for themselves from a strong central government that would protect constitutional rights, and liberals battling Southern opponents of the New Deal. African-Americans also benefited from the new ideological consensus emerging in the academic community that undermined racism by accentuating the influence of environment and by downplaying innate characteristics. It stressed the damage done to individuals by prejudice and the costs to the nation of discrimination. It demolished the stereotype of the African-American as a contented buffoon. Intellectually, white supremacy was now on the defensive.

The New Deal's substantive and symbolic aid to African-Americans further stimulated hope for racial reforms. With some success, the New Deal insisted on equality of treatment in its relief programs. President Franklin D. Roosevelt appointed over a hundred blacks to administrative posts, and the number of African-American federal employees tripled in the 1930s. The Roosevelt Administration began the desegregation of federal rest rooms, cafeterias, and secretarial pools. A host of government publications and conferences made explicit the federal government's responsibility for issues of human rights. Never before, moreover, had a First Lady and so many high-level government officials been associated so closely with civil-rights groups. On a wide variety of racial issues, prominent whites legitimated the aspirations of blacks. This was especially true of Roosevelt's appointees to the Supreme Court. Their decisions in the late 1930s increasingly made the African-American less a *freedman* and more a *free man*. ✗

Nevertheless, the basic conditions of life for most blacks barely changed in the thirties. Civil rights had begun to emerge as a major national concern but disenfranchisement and discrimination remained the rule, and the "job ceiling" kept blacks in the lowest-paid positions. The majority of whites, enslaved by fear, ignorance, and prejudice, favored neither desegregation nor equal opportunities for blacks. And most blacks, still plagued by poverty and powerlessness, could not yet battle the inequities destroying them.

That changed during the Second World War. The ideological character of the war and the government's need for the loyalty and manpower of all Americans stimulated blacks to demand a better deal. Many responded with a militancy never before seen in black communities. Membership in the NAACP multiplied nearly ten times, to a half a million. The Congress of Racial Equality, organized in 1942, experimented with nonviolent direct action to challenge Jim Crow; and A. Philip Randolph attempted to build his March-on-Washington Committee into an all-black mass protest movement. In 1941, his threat of a massive black march on Washington, combined with the growth of the African-American vote and the exigencies of the defense effort, led Roosevelt to issue Executive Order 8802. The first Presidential directive on race since Reconstruction, it established the President's Committee on Fair Employment Practices and prohibited discriminatory employment practices by unions and companies with government contracts or engaged in war-related work. The FEPC and the desperate labor shortage caused by the draft and booming war production resulted in some two million blacks gaining employment in defense plants and another two hundred thousand entering the federal civil service. By 1945, black membership in labor unions had doubled to 1,250,000.

Still other barriers crumbled during the war. The army integrated its officer-training program and the marines and navy opened their ranks to blacks for a variety of duties other than messmen. Liberals repeatedly emphasized that the practices of white supremacy impeded the war effort and brought into disrepute the stated war aims of the United States. And over seven hundred thousand blacks pulled up stakes in the South to find a new home outside Dixie. By the end of the war, blacks had gained enough from the expansion in jobs and income, from service in the armed forces, and from the massive urbanization of the African-American population to foresee an assault on white supremacy, and such African-American veterans as Harry Briggs of South Carolina and Medgar Evers of Mississippi came home to enlist in the battle.

But the renewed campaign for black equality would proceed slowly and haltingly at first. In part, the Second World War muted black protest. While discrimination in defense employment and in the armed services had stimulated militancy early in the war, the prolonged involvement of the United States in what it viewed as a war for survival dampened that militancy. Winning the war as speedily as possible with the least possible loss of American lives overrode all other concerns. Few took kindly to anything that threatened that goal, such as a war against racism at home. The nation demanded unity not division, consensus not conflict. Accordingly, few black leaders after 1942 flirted with any tactic or strategy that might remotely be considered to harm the war effort, and the belligerence of blacks dramatically decreased. The race riots in 1943, particularly in Detroit and Harlem, further frightened the black leadership, causing it to concentrate on reducing black assertive behavior of any kind. "Good Conduct" campaigns and the control of racial rumors took precedence over actively combatting segregation and discrimination. A poll by the Pittsburgh *Courier* in the midst of the war showed 71 percent of African-Americans opposed to a March on Washington to protest discrimination, a sharp turn from the mood of 1941. So did the fact that every major civil-rights spokesman and Negro newspaper denounced A. Philip Randolph's 1943 call for civil disobedience against Jim Crow, and that CORE's efforts to involve large numbers of blacks in militant direct action came to naught. While the war brought revolutionary changes in American life that would eventually make possible a successful black campaign for racial justice, in the short run it hampered the growth of mass black protest.

In part, the very steps taken toward racial justice after a half a century of deteriorating race relations beguiled civil-rights leaders. They chose, in the words of a popular song of the day, "to accentuate the positive, eliminate the negative." With pride they ballyhooed the increasing number of "Negro firsts," listing the advances made by individual blacks. Their loud cheers for Jackie Robinson's crossing the color line in major-league baseball drowned out their quiet grumbling at the black Brooklyn Dodger not being allowed to stay in the same hotels as his white teammates and at the overwhelming extent of segregation remaining throughout professional and amateur sports. They made far more of the honors accorded Dr. Julian Perry, the renowned black scientist, than of the news of firebombing of his home by whites who would not accept the presence of an African-American in their neighborhood. Indeed, while African-American spokesmen confidently counted on the benefits to be derived from the migration of blacks northward, the white trek to the suburbs of the North became an exodus. At the close of the 1950s, whites outnumbered blacks in the suburbs by a ratio of more than thirty-five to one. A new color line, just as effective as the old, still kept the United States two nations—separate and unequal.

The Negro press, similarly, went to great lengths to publicize the jump in the number of blacks registered to vote in the South, from 250,000 in 1940 to over a million in 1950, but downplayed the fact that three out of four adult blacks in Dixie still could not vote. Headlines trumpeted the election of blacks to the governing councils of Richmond and Nashville in 1948 and 1951. Yet hundreds of counties deprived blacks of any voice in government whatsoever, and blacks throughout the South remained politically powerless. In scores of articles and speeches, moreover, the leadership of civil-rights organizations played up the Negro vote in the North as the "balance of power," and credited it with providing the margin of victory for Harry Truman in 1948. After the election, however, President Truman refused to press Congress to enact civil-rights legislation and did nothing to implement the Supreme Court's 1950 decision against segregation in interstate commerce. Nevertheless, the NAACP's balance sheet in race relations that year highlighted signs of progress and optimistically concluded: "Some might call these mere straws in the wind, but they do indicate the direction in which the wind is blowing."

The widespread anticipation of even greater progress in race relations further muffled African-American protest. Basic changes in American society gave blacks hope that discrimination and segregation would soon be overcome. None was more important than the elephantine growth of the American economy. The Gross National Product rose from $206 billion in 1940 to $285 billion in 1950, and then to nearly $400 billion in 1955. The number of civilian jobs increased from 54 million at the end of World War II to 60 million in 1950, to 63 million in 1955. Personal expenditures leaped in these same years from $122 million to $195 million to $257 million. This spectacular rate of economic growth made possible an increasing income for blacks, their entry into industries and labor unions previously closed to blacks, and a gain in occupational status as the constant shortage of workers necessitated a slackening of restrictive promotion policies. Between 1940 and 1960, the median income of African-Americans more than doubled. The huge growth of the economy, moreover, meant that the advancement of blacks did not have to come at the expense of whites, thus undermining perhaps the most powerful source of white resistance to black progress.

The effect of economic changes on race relations was particularly marked in the South. The rapid industrialization of Dixie after 1940 ended the dominance of the cotton culture. With it went the need for a vast black underclass of unskilled laborers. Power began to shift from rural areas to the cities, and from tradition-oriented landed families to the new officers in absentee-owned corporations who reckoned segregation to be a costly anachronism. Industrialization also accelerated urbanization and the migration to the South of millions of white-collar employees and their families who had little stake in the perpetuation of the rural color-caste system. The "New South," many prophesied, would be far more concerned with profits and economic expansion than with outdated racial mores. Industry required a broadly educated labor force and markets unhampered by racial divisions.

In addition, changes in the economy radically affected black migration. The mechanization of cotton production pushed blacks off the farms and the lure of jobs pulled them to the cities. Over a million would leave the South in the 1940s, and another million and a half in the fifties. This mass migration fundamentally altered the configuration of the race problem. It became national in scope. No longer affecting only one region, it could not now be left in the hands of Southern whites. It also both modified the objective conditions of life for blacks and changed their perceptions of goals and tactics. Freed from the confines of a rigid caste system, subject to urban formative experiences, and congregated in numbers large enough to foster group consciousness and solidarity, African-Americans developed new norms and beliefs. Aggression could be turned against one's oppressor rather than against one's self, more employment and educational opportunities could be secured, and political power could be mobilized. The promise of a better world in the next one would not suffice. The urban black would not wait for his rewards until the afterlife, and enfranchisement promised all in this life that religion did in the next. The New Deal and the Second World War, moreover, had corroded the doctrines of localism and decentralization which had blocked hope for a federal effort to guarantee blacks either civil rights or economic opportunity.

The new prominence of the United States as a world power further presaged black advancement. During World War II, millions of Americans became aware for the first time of the danger of racism to national security. Japan focused on the United States' racist treatment of nonwhites as the core of its propaganda campaign to win the loyalty of the colored peoples of China, India, and Latin America. Each lynching and race riot was publicized by the Axis as proof of the hypocrisy of President Franklin Roosevelt's Four Freedoms. The costs of racism went even higher during the Cold War. The Soviet Union undercut American appeals to the nations of Africa and Asia by highlighting the ill treatment of blacks in the United States. Rarely in the first two decades after the Second World War did a plea for civil rights before the Supreme Court, on the floor of Congress, or emanating from the White House, fail to emphasize the point that white racism adversely affected American relations with the nonwhite majority of the world. The rapid growth of independence movements among the world's colored peoples had special significance for African-Americans. They proved the feasibility of change and the vulnerability of white supremacy, while at the same time aiding African-Americans to see themselves as members of a world majority rather than as a hopelessly outnumbered American minority.

The further decline in intellectual respectability of racist ideas also convinced blacks that the winds of change blew their way. The excesses of Nazism and the decline of Western imperialism combined with internal developments in various academic disciplines to discredit the pseudo-scientific rationalizations once popularly accepted as the basis for white supremacy. Books and essays attacking racial injustice and inequality, epitomized by Gunnar Myrdal's *An American Dilemma*, dominated discourse on the subject.

These fundamental transpositions made it easy to believe that continued progress would be automatic, that just a bit more legal action or political pressure would suffice to usher in a new era in race relations. The demise of Jim Crow would necessitate neither struggle nor sacrifice, neither radical strategies nor disruptive tactics. This faith, obviating the need for mass black direct action, also reflected the conservative American mood after World War II. After more than a decade of rapid, bewildering change, and exhausting battles against the Great Depression and the Axis, the vast majority wanted surcease. Most Americans yearned for stability. They desired harmony. The fear of increasingly rapid social change hampered support for anything thought extremist, even reformist.

White supremacists, moreover, played on the obsessive American fear of Communism to discredit the civil-rights cause. They equated challenges to the racial status quo with un-Americanism, and missed no opportunity to link the black struggle with Communist ideology and subversion. In the heyday of red-baiting after World War II, these tactics worked. Most civil-rights groups avoided direct action. Their leadership opted for a conservative posture to avoid even a hint of radicalism. When a small interracial band of pacifists and socialists from the Congress of Racial Equality and the Fellowship of Reconciliation journeyed throughout the upper South to test compliance of a Supreme Court ruling against segregation in interstate travel, the Negro press barely reported the news, and other civil-rights organizations shunned the 1947 Journey of Reconciliation. The following year they opposed A. Philip Randolph's call for civil disobedience to protest Jim Crow in the armed forces. With undue haste, the civil-rights leadership condemned the pro-Soviet remarks of Paul Robeson, a controversial black singer and actor, and disassociated themselves from the Marxist stance of W. E. B. Du Bois. The fear of McCarthyism so inhibited blacks that they failed to use the Korean War as a lever for racial reform, as they had World War II. At mid-century, direct action had ceased being a tactic in the quest for racial justice.

That suited the NAACP hierarchy. Never entirely at ease with the black mass actions during the New Deal and early war years, the NAACP became less a protest organization and more an agency of litigation and lobbying after World War II. No longer fearing that competition from more combative black groups would overshadow the NAACP, its branches in the South concentrated on voter registration, while those in the North endeavored to secure fair-employment and fair-housing ordinances. By 1953, twelve states and thirty cities had adopted fair-employment laws of varying effectiveness. Median black-family income rose from $1,614 to $2,338 between 1947 and 1952. As a percentage of median white-family income, black earnings jumped from 41 percent in 1940 to 51 percent in 1949, and to 57 percent in 1952. That year, nearly 40 percent of blacks were engaged in professional, white-collar, skilled, and semi-skilled work, double the proportion of 1940. The life expectancy of blacks increased from 53.1 years in 1940 to 61.7 years in 1953, compared to 64.2 and 69.6 for whites, and the proportion of black families owning their homes went from 25 percent to 30 percent in the forties. Meanwhile, the proportion of blacks aged five to nineteen enrolled in school leaped from 60 percent in 1930 to 68.4 percent in 1940, to 74.8 percent in 1950. That figure still lagged behind the 79.3 percent of whites in school, but the gap had narrowed dramatically. And the number of blacks in college had soared from about 27,000 in 1930 to over 113,000 in 1950.

Such gains apparently justified the NAACP's approach and secured its hegemony in race relations. The national office and legal staff at midcentury marshaled all their resources for a courtroom assault on de jure school segregation. Many blacks believed integrated education to be the main route to racial equality. No other African-American protest group put forth an alternative strategy of social change. By 1954, all the hopes of blacks rested on the success of the NAACP litigation. It had become an article of faith that a Supreme Court decision ruling school segregation unconstitutional would cause the quick death of Jim Crow in America.

The first major crack in the edifice of school segregation had come in 1938, when the NAACP won a Supreme Court ruling which held that an out-of-state scholarship to a black Missourian wishing to study law at the University of Missouri denied that student the equal protection of the laws guaranteed by the constitution. The Court declared that Missouri could not exclude blacks from its law school when it offered African-Americans only out-of-state tuition grants as an alternative. Hoping to make segregation so prohibitively expensive that the South would dismantle its biracial system because of the financial burden, the NAACP launched a series of suits seeking complete equality in facilities governed by the separate-but-equal rule. Then, emboldened by the strides made by blacks during the Second World War, the NAACP's Legal Defense and Education Fund, led by Thurgood Marshall and based on a foundation of scores of courageous African-American plaintiffs, shifted from skirmishes on the inequality of separate facilities to a direct attack on segregation itself. Marshall hoped his strategy would force the Court to overrule *Plessy*, the 1896 opinion that declared segregation no infringement on civil rights if the states provided blacks with separate accommodations equal to those given to whites. Marshall's work resulted first in three unanimous decisions on a single day in 1950 which demolished the separate-but-equal façade. The high court struck down Jim Crow on railway dining cars in the South; it ruled that if a state chose not to establish an equal and separate school for blacks, then it could not segregate blacks within the white school; and, lastly, the tribunal so emphasized the importance of "intangible factors" in determining the equality of separate schools that separate-but-equal no longer seemed possible. Although the Supreme Court held that it was not necessary to reexamine *Plessy* to grant relief to the three black plaintiffs, the 1950 decisions made the end of segregated schooling for students at all levels a near-certainty.

Working closely with the grassroots leadership of the local chapters, Marshall began to coordinate a series of lawsuits in 1951 charging segregated education with being discriminatory per se, even if the facilities were equal. In Clarendon County, South Carolina, the NAACP sued in the name of several black schoolchildren, and in Prince Edward County, Virginia, they represented black high-school students. In New Castle County, Delaware, and in the District of Columbia, Marshall filed suits on behalf of both elementary and high-school black students. And in Topeka, Kansas, the NAACP argued the case of Oliver Brown, who sought to enjoin enforcement of a state law that permitted cities to maintain segregated schools, which forced his eight-year-old daughter, Linda, to travel a mile by bus to reach a black school even though she lived only three blocks from an all-white elementary school. Risking their jobs and lives, the plaintiffs persisted, and on December 9, 1952, the Supreme Court heard oral argument on all five cases, combined and docketed under the name of the petitioner listed first—Oliver Brown. Unexpectedly, the NAACP was aided by the Truman Administration, which, in its last days, filed a brief as a friend of the Court arguing against the constitutionality of segregation.

The Supreme Court initially divided on the question of overturning *Plessy*. After several months of discussion, two justices changed their mind, creating a slim majority in favor of the NAACP's contention. Now the question became whether the justices in the minority could be likewise persuaded. To that end, the Court voted for a reargument. It asked the litigants to prepare answers to questions pertaining to the intentions of the framers of the Fourteenth Amendment, the power of the Court to abolish segregation in the schools, and, if the tribunal did have such a right and chose to exercise it, whether the Supreme Court could permit gradual desegregation or did it have to order an instant end to segregation. While the lawyers revised their briefs, Chief Justice Fred Vinson died suddenly in the summer of 1953. The new President, Dwight D. Eisenhower, appointed California Governor Earl Warren to fill the vacant post. Vinson had sought to avoid ruling on *Plessy*, and in all likelihood, two other justices would have voted with him, resulting in either a further postponement on the constitutionality of school segregation or a seriously split decision.

Following the reargument, which began on December 7 and lasted for three days, the nation waited for what commentators predicted would be a historic decision. But for half a year the Court remained silent. Behind closed doors, the bickering and bargaining continued. A clear majority of the justices wanted to void segregation in the schools and to reverse *Plessy*. Two justices held out, and Warren kept postponing the decision, hoping he could gain their concurrence. Above all, the Chief Justice wanted the Court's ruling to be unanimous. Anything less on a social issue so sensitive, on a political question so explosive, would destroy the chance for full compliance by Southern whites. So, patiently, Warren beseeched and compromised. Finally, early in May, the two dissenters gave the Chief Justice their assent.

By Monday, May 17, 1954, the Supreme Court ruling on school segregation had been so overdue that many forgot its imminence. The morning's newspapers gave no hint that a decision would be announced. Most journalists in Washington speculated on the consequences of a French loss of Dien Bien Phu in Vietnam, on the outcome of the Army–McCarthy hearings, and on the chances for more rain. Even those reporters seated in the ornate chamber of the Supreme Court did not anticipate that the segregation decision would be announced when the Court convened at noon.

After forty minutes of routine business, the Chief Justice leaned forward and began to read: "I have for announcement the judgment and opinion of the Court in No. 1—*Oliver Brown et al. v. Board of Education of Topeka*." Warren traced the paths that led the cases to the Supreme Court and reviewed the history of the Fourteenth Amendment, finding it "inconclusive" in relation to school segregation because public education, particularly in the South, had barely developed in the 1860s. "Today," the Chief Justice continued, "education is perhaps the most important function of state and local governments." Since it is the key to opportunity and advancement in American life, public education "is a right which must be made available to all on equal terms." On this premise, he came to the nub of the matter: "Does segregation of children in public schools solely on the basis of race, even though the physical facilities and other 'tangible' factors may be equal, deprive the children of the minority group of equal educational opportunities?"

Warren paused. "We believe that it does." Buttressed by a footnote citing several contemporary studies on the psychological effects of segregation, the former governor contended that the separation of black children "from others of similar age and qualifications solely because of their race generates a feeling of inferiority as to their status in the community that may affect their hearts and minds in a way unlikely ever to be undone." He ended in a rising voice. "We conclude that in the field of public education the doctrine of 'separate but equal' has no place. Separate educational facilities are inherently unequal. Therefore, we hold that the plaintiffs and others similarly situated for whom the actions have been brought are, by reason of the segregation complained of, deprived of the equal protection of the laws guaranteed by the Fourteenth Amendment."

Blacks shouted hosannas as they heard the news. They hailed Marshall, the black lawyer who had used the white man's laws before an all-white Supreme Court to win a verdict voiding segregation. Their jubilant leaders vied in choosing superlatives to laud the decision. *Brown* would be the precedent for declaring unconstitutional any state-imposed or enforced segregation. African-Americans in pursuit of full citizenship rights now had not only morality on their side but the law as well. Surely, most rhapsodized, a new day in race relations had dawned. *Brown* promised a truly equal education for black children in integrated classrooms throughout the nation. More, it offered the real beginning of a multiracial society. Robert Williams of North Carolina, who would later urge African-Americans to get guns to assert their due, remembered: "My inner emotions must have been approximate to the Negro slaves' when they first heard about the Emancipation Proclamation. . . . I felt that at last the government was willing to assert itself on behalf of first-class citizenship, even for Negroes. I experienced a sense of loyalty that I had never felt before. I was sure that this was the beginning of a new era of American democracy." *Brown* heightened the aspirations and expectations of African-Americans as nothing before had. It *proved* that the Southern segregation system could be challenged and defeated. It *proved* that change was possible. Nearly a century after their professed freedom had been stalled, compromised, and stolen, blacks confidently anticipated being free and equal at last.

Little in the next year shook this faith. Few Dixie politicians rushed to echo Mississippi Senator James O. Eastland that the South "will not abide by nor obey this legislative decision by a political court." Most educators foresaw scant difficulty in putting the court ruling into effect. According to a *New York Times* survey of school officials, none thought "that the threats to abandon the public school system would be carried out. . . . No one expected any violence or any real crisis to develop." Several hundred school districts in the border states (Delaware, Kentucky, Maryland, Missouri, Oklahoma, and West Virginia) and in states with local option on segregation (Arizona, Kansas, New Mexico, and Wyoming) quickly and peacefully integrated their classrooms, as did the District of Columbia at President Eisenhower's direction.

Then, on May 31, 1955, the momentum stopped. Just fifty-four weeks after the Supreme Court had taken a giant stride toward the demise of Jim Crow, it stepped backward. Its implementation decision on the *Brown* ruling rejected the NAACP's plea to order instant and total school desegregation. The justices, instead, adopted the "go slow" approach advocated by the Justice Department and by the attorneys general of the Southern states. The Court assigned the responsibility for drawing up plans for desegregation to local school authorities and left it to local federal judges to determine the pace of desegregation, requiring only that a "prompt and reasonable start toward full compliance" be made and that desegregation proceed "with all deliberate speed." Acknowledging the potential for difficulties, the Supreme Court refused to set a deadline and authorized delays when necessary. For the first time, the Supreme Court had vindicated a constitutional right and then deferred its exercise.

However much the Warren Court foresaw the endless round of further litigation and obstruction this invited, circumstances dictated the decision for gradualism. It was the price of unanimity in *Brown v. Board of Education*, the compromise needed to keep two justices from dissenting. Warren deeply believed that a divided Court on so sensitive an issue "would have been catastrophic," that only a unanimous desegregation decision stood a chance of public support.

He accepted gradualism to allay the fears of those justices who worried that the Court's inability to enforce a momentous ruling would discredit the judicial process. The compromise also reflected the unpopularity of *Brown* in the South. Public-opinion polls showed more than 80 percent of white Southerners opposed to school desegregation, and the Supreme Court hoped to head off resistance to the law of the land by permitting the change to be piecemeal. To order immediate school desegregation, the Court reckoned, would force most Southern politicians to take up the cudgels of defiance to federal authority, an action only a tiny minority had taken to date. The Justices sought to contain the rebellion, since they could not count on the other branches of the federal government.

No help would come from the White House. President Dwight D. Eisenhower refused to endorse or support the *Brown* ruling. Covetous of the votes of white Southerners and wedded to a restrictive view of Presidential authority, Eisenhower stated that he would express neither "approbation nor disapproval" of *Brown v. Board of Education*. He lumped together those who demanded compliance with the Court decision and those who obstructed it, publicly denouncing "extremists on both sides." To one of his aides, Eisenhower emphasized: "I am convinced that the Supreme Court decision set back progress in the South at least fifteen years. . . . It's all very well to talk about school integration—if you remember you may also be talking about social *dis*integration. Feelings are deep on this. . . . And the fellow who tries to tell me that you can do these things by force is just plain nuts."

Eisenhower preferred change as a result of education, rather than coercion. But he would not educate. The President rejected pleas that he tour the South seeking compliance, or call a conference of Southern moderates, or appeal on television to the nation for understanding. He simply did not favor school desegregation, much as he had never approved desegregation of the armed forces. Eisenhower regretted he had ever appointed Earl Warren to the Supreme Court, calling it "the biggest damfool mistake I ever made." And the titular head of the Democratic Party, Adlai Stevenson, barely differed on this issue from his GOP rival. Stevenson asked that the white South be "given time and patience," rejected the idea of using federal troops to enforce court-ordered desegregation, and opposed all proposals that would bar federal aid to schools maintaining segregation.

To be sure, no danger existed in the mid-fifties that Congress would legislate to speed desegregation. A conservative coalition of Midwestern Republicans and Southern Democrats controlled both the House of Representatives and the Senate, guarding against any infringement on states' rights. Not content merely to stonewall any move to support *Brown*, Southern congressmen mobilized in 1956 to fight against what Senator Richard Russell of Georgia termed "a flagrant abuse of judicial power" and what Virginia Senator Harry Byrd called "the most serious blow that has been struck against the rights of the states." On March 12, 1956, 101 members of Congress from the South signed a "Declaration of Constitutional Principles" asking their states to refuse to obey the desegregation order. Labeling *Brown* "unwarranted" and "contrary to the Constitution," the Southern manifesto proclaimed that the Supreme Court possessed no power to demand an end to segregation, that only a state, and not the federal government, can decide whether a school should be segregated or not, and that the states would be in the right in opposing the Court's order.

The manifesto, along with Eisenhower's silence and the Supreme Court's paradoxical "deliberate speed" ruling, ushered in an era of massive resistance to the law of the land in the eleven states of the Old Confederacy. Defiance of the Court and the Constitution became the touchstone of Southern loyalty, the necessary proof of

one's concern for the security of the white race. With the overwhelming support of the South's white press and pulpit, segregationist politicians resurrected John C. Calhoun's notions of
"interposition" and "nullification" to thwart federal authority.

White supremacists first resorted to stalling, doing nothing until
confronted with a federal-court injunction. This forced black parents and NAACP attorneys to initiate individual desegregation suits
in the more than two thousand Southern school districts. Usually,
the black plaintiffs faced economic intimidation by the local white-
power structure; often they risked physical harm; always, they encountered repeated postponements due to crowded court dockets
and motions for delay by school authorities. After years of harassment to the plaintiffs, mounting legal costs to the NAACP, lost jobs,
mortgages foreclosed, loans denied, and incalculable psychological
damage to blacks due to threats and fear, school authorities would
finally come up with a plan for the most limited, token desegregation.

Then black schoolchildren had to face the horrors of racist resistance. In one school district after another, segregationists forced
young African-Americans to walk a gantlet of hate, fear, and ignorance, to pass by rock-throwing mobs and pickets shrieking "Nigger! Nigger! Nigger!" They pressured white teachers to ignore or
persecute the black students, and encouraged white children to
torment and threaten their new black classmates. " 'If you come
back to school, I'll cut your guts out!' could be heard in the halls,"
recalled a Tennessee high-school teacher. "Eggs smashed on their
books, ink smeared on their clothes, in the lockers, knives flourished
in their presence, nails tossed in their faces and spiked in their seats.
Vulgar words constantly whispered in their ears." The harassment
proved too much for some blacks. They reenrolled their children
in segregated schools; they moved to other towns and states. But
more and more blacks endured the hatred and persisted in their
struggle for dignity and equality.

To frustrate such black courage, segregationists pressed for new
laws to obstruct integration. "As long as we can legislate, we can

segregate," said one white supremacist, and the Southern states rushed pell-mell to enact more than 450 laws and resolutions to prevent or limit school desegregation. Some acts required schools faced with desegregation orders to cease operation; others revoked the license of any teacher who taught mixed classes; still more amended compulsory-attendance laws, so that no child could be required to enroll in an integrated school, and provided for state payments of private-academy tuition, so that districts could abolish their public-school system rather than desegregate.

Of all the legislative tactics of massive resistance, none proved more successful than the pupil-placement law. Theoretically, it guaranteed each child "freedom of choice" in the selection of a school. Local authorities could not consider race in assigning pupils to particular schools. But they could accept or reject transfer applications on such criteria as, in the Georgia law, "the psychological qualification of the pupil," "the psychological effect upon the pupil of attendance at a particular school," and "the morals, conduct, health and personal standards of the pupil." Invariably, school boards assigned black and white children to different schools. In 1958, moreover, the Supreme Court upheld the constitutionality of the pupil-placement laws, which were nondiscriminatory at face value but which actually maintained school systems as rigidly segregated as those which the justices had struck down four years earlier.

To frustrate blacks further, most of the Southern states also passed measures to hound and harass the NAACP, which had almost singlehandedly carried the campaign for school desegregation. Various laws required the NAACP to make public its membership lists, made membership a cause for dismissal of public-school teachers and state employees, charged the association with committing "barratry" (the persistent instigation of lawsuits), and made it a crime for organizations to cause trouble by attacking local segregation ordinances. By 1958 the NAACP had lost 246 branches in the South, and the South's percentage of the NAACP's total membership had dropped from nearly 50 percent to just about 25 percent. In time, the Supreme Court struck down all the anti-NAACP laws, but for several years the association was forced to divert energy, money, and talent away from the desegregation battle to the fight for its own survival.

Not content with legal measures of obstruction, hostile segregationists preached violent resistance. Virulent rabble-rousers, often with the approval of the South's respected spokesmen, stirred up the region's whites to attack blacks insisting on their constitutional rights. The Ku Klux Klan revived. Zealots across the South organized new klaverns, donned their white hoods and robes, and burned crosses to terrorize blacks. Too respectable to join the low-status KKK, thousands of middle-class whites rushed to enroll in the White Citizens' Councils, the National Association for the Advancement of White People, and the American States Rights Association. They wore no masks but proved just as determined as the Klan to defy *Brown* and enforce racial orthodoxy, by intimidation if possible and by insurrection if necessary. Together, the KKK, the Councils, and a host of local vigilante committees brought riots and violent demonstrations to the South at the start of the school year each September.

Their lawless behavior, often directed at young children, outraged millions of Americans who did not live in the South. Most Northerners cared little about school desegregation in Dixie and considered the NAACP too militant. Nevertheless, they were shocked at the news headlines of schools being dynamite-bombed and the televised scenes of hate-filled white mobs. Time and again in the decade ahead, such racist extremism would discredit the cause of the white South and force a majority of otherwise unconcerned citizens to demand that the federal government act to preserve order. It happened first in Little Rock.

A New South city, Little Rock appeared an unlikely battleground in the fight over school desegregation. It had a racially moderate mayor, congressman, and newspaper, and a governor not known to be a race-baiter. Several other Arkansas communities had peacefully begun to desegregate, as had the state university, and, after a bit of stalling, Little Rock's school board acceded to a federal court order to admit nine blacks to Central High, a school with some two thousand white students, as the first step toward integration. A model of gradualism and deference to the whites of Little Rock, the desegregation process would take eight years to complete. Indeed, the only vocal opposition to it came from the local NAACP, which denounced the process as too token and too slow.

In 1957, however, the winds of resistance howled. A storm of racial demagoguery swept the South. Politicians shouted defiance of the Supreme Court and vied in pledging unyielding opposition to *Brown*. Some vowed they would go to jail rather than desegregate; some swore they would die rather than permit integration. Those who counseled moderation customarily came in second and, like George C. Wallace in Alabama, promised: "They outniggered me that time, but they'll never do it again." In Arkansas, Governor Orval Faubus believed he faced a difficult fight for reelection. But he found the answer to his ambitions in the political climate. He would campaign as the preeminent defender of white supremacy. He would "outnigger" his racist opponents. He would obstruct the federal court order in Little Rock.

On September 2, the evening before Arkansas schools were to reopen, Faubus went on television to announce that it would "not be possible to restore or to maintain order if forcible integration is carried out tomorrow," despite the fact that no Little Rock officials then anticipated trouble. He ordered a National Guard contingent to Central High School. Ostensibly, their mission was to prevent violence. But when the nine black students sought to enter the school on September 3, the guardsmen barred their way. "Governor Faubus has placed this school off limits to Negroes," announced a National Guard spokesman. The federal district court in Arkansas again insisted that desegregation begin and ordered the governor to show cause why he should not be enjoined from interfering with the school board's plan. When the black students prepared to enter Central High the following day, a milling crowd of angry whites shouted: "Niggers. Niggers. They're coming. Here they come!" The guardsmen once again barred the African-Americans seeking to enroll in Central High. The authority of the federal government and of a state had directly clashed. National attention now focused on President Eisenhower, who was constitutionally required to enforce the law of the land.

Eisenhower had no desire to do so. He had never offered leadership on racial matters. He considered *Brown* a mistake. His belief in the limits of federal power and his fondness for states' rights combined to make the President highly reluctant to intervene in Little Rock. "You cannot change people's hearts merely by laws," he told a press conference that week, adding a grave remark about the white South's concern for the "mongrelization of the race." The general believed Dixie ripe for Republicanism. He had won four Southern states in 1952, and five in 1956. Looking ahead to 1960, Eisenhower was determined to avoid any action that would reestablish the Democratic grip on the mass of white Southern voters. Purposefully, he would do nothing to rally public opinion behind desegregation. Yet he could not ignore Faubus's defiance of a federal court order, and television had made Little Rock the focus of national attention. To give the appearance of action without really acting, Eisenhower met with the governor on September 14. Both politicians talked truce and temporized.

On September 20, the federal district court repeated its order to the governor to stop interfering with school desegregation in Little Rock. Predicting bloodshed, Faubus withdrew the National Guard from Central High and left the state. However, several of the governor's henchmen, adept at mobilizing mob violence, remained in Little Rock. By early Monday morning, September 23, over a thousand shrieking white protesters surrounded the high school. Racists from across the South had flocked to the city to prevent the blacks from entering the school. While white students sang "Two, four, six, eight, we ain't gonna integrate," the mob jeered "Niggers, keep away from our school. Go back to the jungle." Over and over the crowd reassured itself: "The niggers won't get in." Suddenly someone roared: "They've gone in!" "Oh, my God!" a woman cried.

"The niggers are inside!" "They're in!" others screamed. "They're in!" "The niggers are in our school." Some began a new chant: "Come on out! Come on out!" Groups of white students exited from Central High to shouts of approval, stimulating louder importuning, and more white students left the school. The mayor, fearful of violence, ordered the nine blacks withdrawn.

That evening President Eisenhower appeared on television to denounce the "disgraceful occurrence" at Little Rock. Aware that the unruly segregationist mob had riveted world attention on Little Rock, he issued a proclamation directing those who had obstructed federal law "to cease and desist." But an even larger mob milled about Central High the next morning and school board officials dreaded inflaming the howling protesters by forcing the entry of the nine blacks. Eisenhower responded by federalizing the Arkansas National Guard and dispatching a thousand troops of the 101st Airborne Division to Little Rock. The next morning, with fixed bayonets, the paratroopers dispersed the crowd and led the black students into Central High School. Armed troops remained in the school for two months, escorting the nine blacks to their classes. Then the President replaced the paratroopers with federalized Arkansas guardsmen, who continued to patrol Central High for the rest of the year.

Southern extremism had forced Eisenhower's hand. Not to have acted, he ruefully told a Southern senator, would have been "tantamount to acquiescence in anarchy and the dissolution of the union." As a last resort he dispatched federal troops to uphold national supremacy, defend Presidential authority, and enforce the law of the land. In so doing, Eisenhower became the first President since Reconstruction to use armed troops to protect African-American citizens and their constitutional rights.

Also in 1957, Congress enacted civil-rights legislation for the first time since Reconstruction. This further bolstered black aspirations. More a symbolic milestone than an act to increase black registration, Congress formally declared illegal the disenfranchisement of African-Americans.

Attorney General Herbert Brownell began early in 1956 to press President Eisenhower to propose a civil-rights bill. Whether or not Congress passed it, Brownell argued, such a proposal would highlight the North–South split in the Democratic Party and bolster the image of the party of Lincoln with Northern black voters. A former chairman of the Republican National Committee, Brownell knew that, in 1956, blacks constituted about 5 percent of the voters in fourteen states which held 261 electoral votes. Brownell also sensed the widespread dissatisfaction with the Democrats among blacks, who blamed the party of Byrd and Eastland for the massive resistance to desegregation. The opportunity now existed, he pleaded with the President, to end the black allegiance to the Democrats that had been firm since 1936.

Eisenhower demurred. "I personally believe if you try to go too far too fast in laws in this delicate field that has involved the emotions of so many millions of Americans," he said at a press conference, "you are making a mistake." Eisenhower had his eyes on the votes of Southern whites resistant to change. He wanted to make the Republican Party of limited government the new home of conservative Southern states' righters and decided not to support any civil-rights legislation before the 1956 election. Democratic congressional leaders sighed with relief. The last thing they wanted on the eve of a Presidential contest was a divisive intra-party squabble on civil rights.

Immediately after the election, however, Eisenhower requested suffrage legislation and the Senate majority leader, Democrat Lyndon Johnson of Texas, agreed to work for its passage. Unwilling to accept continued Democratic stalling on civil rights, Harlem's congressman, Adam Clayton Powell, Jr., had bolted to Ike in 1956 and brought tens of thousands of black votes into the GOP column. The President had a substantially increased proportion of the black vote over 1952, winning black majorities in at least a score of cities. This caused Republicans looking ahead to an even better record in black communities in 1960, especially Vice-President Richard Nixon, to press Eisenhower to support civil rights. At the same time, the popularity of Republicanism among African-Americans in 1956 frightened Northern Democrats. They were determined to win back the black votes the GOP had gained; they believed that enacting civil-rights legislation was the only way to do it. Democratic liberals would no longer sacrifice their own political needs in deference to those of their Southern brethren. Johnson, meanwhile, sought both to hold the Democratic Party together and to foster his own Presidential aspirations. He thought he could do so by fashioning a moderate civil-rights act, one not odious enough to alienate his Southern backing yet significant enough to enable him to shed his reputation as a Southern white supremacist.

The politics of expediency, not surprisingly, produced a compromise bill. The forces fighting for and against civil rights each gained a little and gave up a bit, as did Democrats and Republicans, liberals and conservatives, Northerners and Southerners. Steering a middle course between reform and reaction, Eisenhower and Johnson won enactment of a mild bill palatable to most. The 1957 civil-rights act authorized the Justice Department to seek injunctions against interference with the right to vote and established a Commission on Civil Rights empowered to investigate, appraise, and report. The law ignored the issue of segregation and barely reduced the resistance to black voting by Southern election officials or the intimidation tactics of vigilante groups opposed to black enfranchisement. Still, most civil-rights proponents argued that a half loaf is better than no bread at all. "Roy, if there's one thing I have learned in politics," Senator Hubert Humphrey confided to Roy Wilkins of the NAACP, "it's never to turn your back on a crumb." Wilkins agreed, but changed the metaphor: "If you are digging a ditch with a teaspoon, and a man comes along and offers you a spade, there is something wrong with your head if you don't take it because he didn't offer you a bulldozer."

After three years of registration drives which added fewer than two hundred thousand blacks to the voting lists, an increase of just 3 percent, the NAACP again demanded suffrage legislation, and the dynamics of election-year politics again resulted in an emasculated civil-rights act. The 1960 palliative authorized the courts to appoint federal referees to safeguard voting rights and made it a federal offense to obstruct court orders by violent means. Too weak to have any real impact on Southern voting, the measure still signified the growing strength of the civil-rights alliance.

All these initial, halting, partial moves by the federal government to assist the cause of black equality resulted in intensifying the struggle. They produced among blacks both expectations that Jim Crow could soon be eliminated from American life and a growing rage toward all temporizing. Cumulatively they generated a determination that segregation and discrimination, however wrong and unconstitutional, would cease only when blacks themselves acted militantly enough to guarantee that end.

By enacting civil-rights legislation for the first time since 1875, Congress did much to legitimatize black aspirations for first-class citizenship. The termination of a Southern filibuster after 125 hours in 1960 encouraged blacks to believe that racial justice could be attained within the constitutional framework. The two voting-rights acts inspired African-Americans to attempt to register and to insist on other rights. But the patent weakness of the measures convinced them that they still did not have effective political power. Legislation, moreover, needed to be implemented to produce real change, and neither the Justice Department nor the federal judges in the South evinced much enthusiasm to utilize the two laws to promote black voting. In the 1960 elections, less than one in four eligible blacks could vote in the South. Disappointed, African-Americans questioned the legislative tactics of the NAACP, which placed a premium on neither provoking the black masses nor embittering the white majority, and the preference of Roy Wilkins for a quiet, diplomatic campaign rather than "the kind that picks a fight with the sheriff and gets somebody's head beaten."

The crisis at Little Rock similarly engendered black faith and frustration. Eisenhower's use of federal force to protect black rights inspired confidence that Southern extremism would not be tolerated. Bolstering such assurance, some 90 percent of the whites outside the South questioned in a Gallup poll stated that Eisenhower had been right in sending troops to Little Rock. Still further buoying blacks, the Supreme Court convened a special session in 1958 to deal with Little Rock and ruled that the threat of white violence could not justify a refusal to desegregate. "The constitutional rights of respondents," the Court declared, "are not to be sacrificed or yielded to violence and disorder. . . . Law and order are not here to be preserved by depriving the Negro children of their constitutional rights." But the Supreme Court could not transform its lofty aims into reality; most Northern whites lost interest after the crisis subsided; and President Eisenhower refused ever again to enforce the school-desegregation decision. In addition, the whites of Little Rock replaced moderate Congressman Brooks Hays with a militant segregationist and opted to close down all the public high schools rather than accept token integration. It would take two years and another federal-court edict to reopen them, and by 1964 still only 123 black children out of a total African-American registration of nearly seven thousand students would be attending desegregated schools in Little Rock. Arkansas whites, meanwhile, swept Faubus back into the statehouse by a landslide and kept reelecting him until he retired in 1967. The use of federal forces had made him a folk hero to segregationists. Stung by the resurrection of the Lost Cause, the leader of the desegregation struggle in Little Rock expressed the mood of determination seeping throughout black America: "We've got to decide whether it's going to be this generation or never."

More than anything else, *Brown v. Board of Education* and its aftermath stimulated black hope and anguish. For much of the first half of the twentieth century, blacks had accepted the leadership of the NAACP in their struggle for equality and had followed the association in relying upon litigation and legislative lobbying to eradicate racism. By 1954, many African-Americans believed that the overturning of *Plessy* in the school cases would rapidly undermine the whole Jim Crow system.

But it did not happen. "Colored" and "White" signs remained over drinking fountains and rest rooms from one end of the South to the other. Southern blacks could not sit down next to a white and be served a hamburger or a cup of coffee. Drivers continued to demand that blacks stay in the back of the bus. Worse, African-Americans still attended schools that were both squalid and segregated. In 1960, only one-sixth of one percent of the black students in the South went to a desegregated school. By 1964, just two percent of the black children in the South attended integrated schools, and none at all in the two Southern counties involved in the *Brown* decision.

Disenchantment thus tempered the euphoria with which blacks greeted the Supreme Court's ruling on May 17, 1954. *Brown v. Board of Education*, Eisenhower's employment of federal troops to curtail racist extremism, and the passage of two civil-rights bills undoubtedly prepared the way for a more massive and militant phase of the black struggle. They gave legitimacy to the quest for equality. Each raised the aspirations of blacks and inspired blacks to insist on the full rights of citizenship. The repeated heroism of the black men, women, and children engaged in the school-desegregation battle, moreover, broke the shackles from many chained black minds. Yet disenfranchisement and segregation remained the rule in the South. The White Citizens' Councils continued to flourish and dominate state governments. In the North, suburbanization encouraged the growth of a racially segmented society. Automation and recessions would lead to a tripling of black unemployment in the 1950s. Summing up the halting progress of those years, the NAACP's Roy Wilkins observed: "President Eisenhower was a fine general and a good, decent man, but if he had fought World War II the way he fought for civil rights, we would all be speaking German today." African-Americans could no longer expect automatic progress. Their reliance on legalism and on white politicians diminished. Anger and hope gave rise to a new sense of urgency. Bitterness mixed with confidence stimulated a yearning to widen the scope of the struggle. And an amalgam of impatience, indignation, and buoyancy readied the black struggle for new protest leaders and strategies.

·······················

# TWO

# THE CRADLE ROCKS

> I think people were fed up, they had reached the point that they
> knew there was no return. That they had to do it or die. And
> that's what kept it going. It was the sheer spirit for freedom,
> for the feeling of being a man or a woman.
>
> JO ANN ROBINSON

Mrs. Rosa Parks said no. Her feet hurt. Politely yet firmly, the forty-
two-year-old brown-skinned seamstress said no a second time.
Some black passengers on the bus, fearful for Parks's safety, and
their own, shook their heads; others exclaimed "Lawd, Lawds,"
expecting a violent reprisal. The driver sternly insisted again that
she move back and give up her seat to a standing white man. That
was the law. Parks held fast. Weary after her long hard day of
holiday-season work at the men's alteration shop of the Montgomery Fair department store, she wanted to remain seated for the rest
of her ride. On that fateful first of December 1955, Parks demurred
again, defying the canons of white supremacy.

"Are you going to stand up?"

"No."

"Well, if you don't stand up, I'm going to have you arrested."

Parks paused. Although she considered herself in the vanguard of the struggle for racial justice—she served as secretary of the Alabama State Conference of NAACP Branches, secretary of the Montgomery NAACP, adult adviser to the local NAACP Youth Council, and had recently returned from an integrated workshop on desegregation held at the Highlander Folk School in Tennessee—she had no intention of challenging the Jim Crow laws. Yet Parks believed "that the only way to let them know I felt I was being mistreated was to do just what I did—resist the order."

"Go on," she replied softly, deliberately, "and have me arrested."

The Black Panther publicist Eldridge Cleaver would later write about that moment: "Somewhere in the universe a gear in the machinery had shifted." At the next stop, Court Square, where slaves had once been auctioned, the driver summoned police to arrest Rosa Parks for violating the municipal ordinance mandating segregation on publicly owned vehicles. Martin Luther King, Jr., would describe this as the moment when Parks had been "tracked down by the Zeitgeist—the spirit of the times. . . . She was anchored to that seat by the accumulated indignities of days gone by and the boundless aspirations of generations yet unborn." Parks recalled: "I felt it was just something I had to do."

So did other blacks. News of her defiance, circulated by the telephone network of Montgomery's black elite, transmitted a surge of determination through the community, a resolve to do something. Many looked to E. D. Nixon for leadership. President of the Alabama NAACP and a veteran member of the Brotherhood of Sleeping Car Porters, Nixon had long sought to arouse black Montgomery to a mass protest of their mistreatment. He hurried to the jail to post bond for his friend Rosa Parks. The former local head of the World War II March-on-Washington Movement, Nixon remained a disciple of A. Philip Randolph's tactics and strategy. He longed for an opportunity to organize black power and pressure through mass demonstrations. As Nixon drove Parks home, he searched for an appropriate form of direct action, maybe a strike, perhaps a boycott. He thought about what had happened in Baton Rouge, where African-Americans had boycotted that city's segregated bus system in 1953. He felt sure that the arrest of Parks was a cause blacks would rally around. "Mrs. Parks," he finally summoned the courage to blurt out, "this is the case we've been looking for. We can break this situation on the bus with your case." Both knew the risks: the possibility of violence to Parks, the certainty of losing her job. Yet both knew the time had come. "I'll go along with it," Parks answered. *Something* had to be done."

"This is what we've been waiting for!" Nixon shouted on the telephone later that night to Jo Ann Robinson, an English professor at all-black Alabama State College. Robinson, president of the Women's Political Council, the black counterpart to Montgomery's segregated League of Women Voters, agreed. Impatient with the deferential leadership of Montgomery's black ministers, Robinson's council that year had pressured white merchants into ending the segregation of public drinking fountains and the custom of not using the courtesy titles of Mrs. and Miss when billing black women. They had also forced the city to begin hiring black policemen and were demanding equal recreational facilities for black Montgomery. The council, moreover, earlier in the year, had been set to stage a boycott of the city's buses to protest the arrest of a woman who refused to give up her seat to a white. But the fact that the defendant was an unwed mother made the Women's Political Council draw back. Rosa Parks, however, was dignified, intelligent, respectable, and married. Nixon and Robinson agreed that she was the perfect symbol. They would attempt to organize a one-day bus boycott on the fifth of December to coincide with Mrs. Parks's trial.

Early the next morning, Nixon began calling Montgomery's black ministers, college professors, physicians, and civic spokesmen. "We have taken this type of thing too long already. I feel the time has come to boycott the buses," Nixon repeated to each. "Only through a boycott can we make it clear to the white folks that we will not accept this type of treatment any longer." To his surprise, many of the elite Nixon telephoned accepted his invitation to meet that evening to plan a bus boycott. Most had previously exhibited little inclination to act in concert, and even less desire to act militantly. The nearly fifty representatives of black Montgomery, mostly ministers, who gathered in the Dexter Avenue Baptist Church agreed even more unexpectedly to deliver sermons on the proposed boycott to their congregations on Sunday, to ask Negro taxicab companies to transport blacks at bus-fare cost, to cap the boycott with a city-wide meeting, and to distribute the mimeographed leaflets written by Robinson. Claiming "The next time it may be you, or your daughter, or mother," she urged African-American Montgomerians to stay off the buses in a daylong gesture of solidarity with Parks.

On Monday, December 5, in the city called the Cradle of the Confederacy, over 90 percent of the blacks who ordinarily rode the buses stayed off them. Blacks walked, joined car pools, drove wagons, rode mules. They did not ride the buses. The historic Montgomery bus boycott had begun. It would last 381 days. It would cost blacks nearly a quarter of a million dollars. Out of it would come a towering leader, a new kind of Southern black leadership, an effective strategy for social change, and a determined spirit that Jim Crow could be ended, that life could be better. Historians eventually would look back to Montgomery as the Cradle of the New Negro.

Nixon had pressing concerns that fifth of December. Following Mrs. Parks's brief trial, which expectedly resulted in a guilty verdict and a fine of ten dollars plus four dollars court costs, Nixon met on the courthouse steps with several black ministers. He feared that without active leadership, specific goals, and a committed organization the boycott would fizzle and the mass meeting would fail. Nixon suggested that an ad hoc group continue to lead the boycott until the city and bus company agreed to hire Negro bus drivers in black neighborhoods, insist that all bus drivers treat black patrons more courteously, and adopt a first-come, first-served seating system. Nixon initially had no intention of attacking the segregation ordinance confining blacks to the back of the bus. He merely proposed that those blacks seated in the rear be allowed to keep their seats. Nixon also thought the name for the new organization ought to be the Citizens' Committee. But the Reverend Ralph D. Abernathy, the young pugnacious minister of the First Baptist Church, objected. The name sounded too much like the White Citizens' Council. Abernathy suggested, instead, the Montgomery Improvement Association, adding: "Brother Nixon, now you gon' serve as president, ain'tchya?" "No," Nixon shot back, "not unless'n you all don't accept my man."

Nixon had his reasons for declining. His job as a Pullman porter frequently kept him out of town. His lack of formal education inhibited him, and he considered himself too old to be an active leader. Too many black ministers would not work with him, a legacy of old conflicts and rivalries. What we need, Nixon went on, was an intelligent, respected minister, a dynamic orator, someone who could easily find another job if the boycott failed and the white community retaliated. He further suggested that a man new in the community would be less likely to be identified with any faction of Montgomery's divided black leadership or to be a lackey of the white establishment. Nixon might also have added that his ideal candidate needed to be extraordinarily brave or naïve to be identified publicly as the leader of such an uncertain, hazardous, quixotic venture. He recommended Martin Luther King, Jr. The others agreed.

At three in the afternoon, Montgomery's black leaders met again, to prepare for the evening's mass rally. The old fears surfaced. How, some asked, could their involvement in the boycott be kept secret from the white community? Could they ban white reporters from the evening meeting? Could they forgo public forums and circulate their plans by mimeographed pamphlets and word of mouth? Enraged, Nixon jumped from his seat. "What the hell you people talking 'bout? How you gonna have a mass meeting, gonna boycott a city bus line without the white folks knowing it?" We are acting like little boys, he continued, afraid to discuss our plans in the open, wanting to pass around papers secretly. "You oughta make up your mind right now that you gon' either admit you are a grown man or concede to the fact that you are a bunch of scared boys." Silenced, the leaders rapidly agreed to an organizing committee, named the Montgomery Improvement Association (MIA), to lead a bus boycott until the city met the three demands proposed by Nixon.

Rufus Lewis nominated Martin Luther King, Jr., to the MIA presidency and in a moment the motion carried. Stunned by the speed of the maneuver, King did not decline, although he had recently turned down the presidency of the local NAACP because of the press of his pastoral duties and the new obligations of fatherhood. He could not afford the luxury of second-guessing his decision. King had less than an hour before the evening mass meeting to prepare "the most decisive speech of my life."

At first glance, neither King nor the blacks of Montgomery appeared ready for what would come. The black community seemed complacent or cowed, and King hardly fitted the mold of a fiery freedom fighter who could arouse and lead. The son and grandson of pastors of Atlanta's prestigious Ebenezer Baptist Church, "Mike" King grew up on prosperous "sweet" Auburn Avenue—the capital of the black bourgeoisie. An avid student, he skipped two grades of high school and at fifteen enrolled at Morehouse College, a branch of the Atlanta University system. He dreamed of being a lawyer or a teacher. But his father insisted that he be a minister. King obeyed, and following his graduation in 1948, he entered Crozer Theological Seminary in Pennsylvania for his Bachelor of Divinity Degree.

King, one of six blacks in a student body of one hundred, happily immersed himself in the world of ideas, particularly the philosophy of Kant, Hegel, the religious existentialists, and Walter Rauschenbusch's social gospel. He finished first in his graduating class, earning a fellowship to pursue a doctorate. In 1951 King began his course of study at Boston University's School of Theology. While in Boston, King met Coretta Scott, a graduate of Antioch College who was studying voice at the New England Conservatory of Music. They were married in 1953. Each reinforced the other's desire to remain in the North and for King to pursue a career of religious scholarship. But family ties and an attractive job offer proved too strong a lure. "Finally we agreed," wrote King in his autobiography, "that, in spite of the disadvantages and inevitable sacrifices, our greatest service could be rendered in our native South. We came to the conclusion that we had something of a moral obligation to return—at least for a few years."

King arrived in Montgomery in September 1954, aged twenty-six, to serve as pastor of the Dexter Avenue Baptist Church, "the big people's church." Its influential congregation, largely professionals and faculty members of Alabama State College, emanated a respectability and an aura of intellectualism that King highly prized. He still found the emotionalism of the traditional Negro church distasteful, and still believed in moderate, middle-class politics as the best path for Negro advancement. Quite removed from the needs and spirit of the black rank-and-file, King served on the Alabama Human Relations Council, a genteel, paternalistic organization as elitist as it was ineffectual.

Montgomery's blatant white supremacy, however, jolted King. A virulent white racism enveloped the city. It dictated its laws and mores. It poisoned white minds and destroyed the bodies and souls of blacks. The shocking contrast with what King had earlier experienced in Atlanta and Boston produced in him both a desire to change the racial situation and a belief that change was possible. He reread Gandhi and Thoreau on civil disobedience. He pondered the speeches he had heard on the application of Gandhian tactics to the race problem by Howard Thurman, dean of the Howard University chapel, and by A. J. Muste of the Fellowship of Reconciliation. In December 1955, King had not yet arrived at a definitive philosophy or strategy for racial change. But his thoughts were in flux. At the least, as he told his wife on the eve of the boycott, the continued passive acceptance of evil could only perpetuate its existence.

Beneath the placid surface of the black community in Montgomery, many had quietly come to the same realization. For some, the moment of decision came with the coupling of the 1954 Supreme

Court decision and the white vow to fight integration at any cost, or with the juxtaposition of the news of successful beginnings of school desegregation in various border cities and headlines telling of violent riots to thwart the law of the land. For others, it came in 1955 with the brazen appearance of White Citizens' Councils and the brutal murder of fourteen-year-old Emmett Till in Mississippi—purportedly for whistling at, or speaking to, a white woman. The absurdity of the fact that the days of the cotton South had ended while its racial practices continued aroused many. Blacks had become far more educated, industrialized, and urbanized than their parents' generation, yet they experienced the same racial indignities and horrors. The African-American who had seen service in an integrated unit during the Korean War, or who had lived for a while without Jim Crow in the North, or who worked on the desegregated military bases just outside the city, still faced in Montgomery a near-total system of segregation and white supremacy. It was pervasive, cruel, and humiliating.

Twice daily, for most Montgomery blacks, the Jim Crow buses served as a constant reminder of how far toward freedom they still had to travel. Blacks had to pay the driver at the front of the bus and then enter through the door at the rear, however inclement the weather. They had to stand in the crowded back of the bus while seats were empty in the white-only front section. They could do little to constrain a vicious bus driver, no matter how abusive or violent he became. Then, in the last week of November 1955, the Interstate Commerce Commission banned racial segregation in all facilities and vehicles engaged in interstate transportation. On the first of December, Rosa Parks said no. Could they now do less? The trend of the law seemed unmistakable. The Parks incident had unified the black community, for a while at the least. Perhaps . . . Maybe . . . The time had come to force Montgomery to change.

When King returned for the evening rally, Montgomery blacks had filled every seat in the Holt Street Baptist Church and stood shoulder to shoulder in the blocks surrounding the church. More than four thousand stood outside to listen to the loudspeakers,

demonstrating the commitment and solidarity they had shown by
staying off the buses. Seemingly with one voice they sang "Onward
Christian Soldiers." In unison they shouted that "like a mighty
army" they would march against the citadel of Jim Crow. Unanimously they voted to boycott the buses until they gained their three
demands. Then the crowd grew silent. Dr. King began to speak.

King quietly recounted the arrest of Rosa Parks. He reviewed the
many injustices blacks had endured on Montgomery buses. The
murmurs of "Amen" grew louder and King suddenly brought his
audience to a fever pitch.

There comes a time when people get tired. We are here this
evening to say to those who have mistreated us so long that
we are tired—tired of being segregated and humiliated, tired
of being kicked about by the brutal feet of oppression. We
have no alternative but to protest. For many years, we have
shown amazing patience. We have sometimes given our white
brothers the feeling that we liked the way we were being
treated. But we come here tonight to be saved from that patience that makes us patient with anything less than freedom
and justice.

"We are impatient for justice"—King moderated his tone—"but
we will protest with love. There will be no violence on our part."
He preached persuasion, not coercion. He dwelt on the transforming power of love. "Love must be our regulating ideal. . . . If we
fail to do this our protest will end up as a meaningless drama on
the stage of history, and its memory will be shrouded with the ugly
garments of shame." "Let no man pull you so low as to make you
hate him," he quoted Booker T. Washington. The "Amens" swelled
again. "If you will protest courageously"—King built to a
crescendo—"and yet with dignity and Christian love, when the
history books are written in future generations, the historians will
have to pause and say 'There lived a great people—a black
people—who injected new meaning and dignity into the veins of

civilization.' This is our challenge and our overwhelming responsibility." The thousands listening roared their approval. Again and
again they shouted their joyful determination. King had crystalized
their feelings. He had articulated their mood and exalted their vision. The time had come.

White Montgomery at first ridiculed the boycott. Disdainful
whites thought the fractious Negro leadership would be unable to
maintain unity, much less be competent to deal with the complicated
day-to-day operations of a city-wide boycott. They scorned the
black masses as too apathetic to stay to a course of sacrifice. A
little stalling, a bit of pressure, a few threats would surely end this
folly. "Our niggers," the contemptuous assumed, "will soon tire
out and start climbing back on the buses." Secretly, some blacks
also feared the collapse of the boycott. Memory made them doubt
the perseverance of the troops and the fortitude of their leaders.
They hoped for a speedy settlement. After all, the doubtful black
Montgomerians sought to reassure themselves, none of their three
moderate demands struck directly at segregation, and their fares
accounted for 75 percent of the Montgomery City Line revenue.

After three days of almost total black boycott, King met with
Mayor W. A. Gayle, his commissioners, and the attorneys for the
bus company. Logic and reasonableness, King optimistically believed, would prevail. He could not have been more wrong. There
would be no compromise. The whites spurned King's proposals.
They would not accept anything that might suggest a black victory
for fear that it would stimulate additional demands. They drew the
line. To underscore their adamancy, the city fathers threatened legal
action unless the black cab companies again began to charge the
prescribed minimum fares for taxis.

Disheartened, King returned to confer with the MIA. He now
realized that the matter was one of power, not reason, that "no
one gives up his privileges without strong resistance." Far more
than courtesy and comfort were involved in the bus issue, moreover,
for "the underlying purpose of segregation was to oppress and
exploit the segregated, not simply to keep [people] apart." A chas-

tened MIA turned to the organization of car pools to replace the black taxis. Over a hundred and fifty blacks volunteered their automobiles at a mass rally that evening. Within several days forty-eight dispatch and forty-two collection stations were operating with what the local White Citizens' Council groused was "military precision." The boycott continued. Black Montgomery stayed off the buses. As one elderly black woman expressed it: "My feets is tired, but my soul is rested." And another, when offered a ride so she would not have to walk: "I'm not walking for myself. I'm walking for my children and my grandchildren." The days of the boycott became weeks and then months.

The white community, no longer deriding the boycott, felt its impact. The downtown merchants claimed that they had lost a million dollars in sales due to the restricted travel of blacks. The boycott cut into the bus company's income some 65 percent, forcing it to raise fares and trim schedules. Its losses mounted daily. At the end of January, Mayor Gayle announced a "get-tough" policy. He went on television to denounce the boycott as a campaign to stir up racial strife and its leaders as "a group of Negro radicals who have split asunder the fine relationships which have existed between the Negro and white people for generations." He warned Montgomery that the blacks sought to end segregation, that "what they are after is the destruction of our social fabric." It is time to be honest and frank, Gayle concluded: "The white people are firm in their convictions that they do not care whether the Negroes ever ride a city bus again if it means that the social fabric of our community is to be destroyed so that Negroes will start riding the buses again."

An official policy of harassment began. The mayor and his commissioners ceremoniously took out memberships in the White Citizens' Council. Boycott leaders lost their jobs; others were threatened with dismissal. Car-pool drivers faced warnings that their licenses would be revoked and their insurance policies cancelled. Many were fined on trumped-up charges of speeding. Indiscriminate arrests for imaginary violations followed. The old fears resurfaced. The car pool lost many of its volunteers. Some blacks climbed back on the rear of the buses. Four days of retaliation by white Montgomery had brought the boycott to the brink of collapse. Then two policemen arrested King for speeding.

His jailing revitalized the movement. Hundreds rushed to the jail to protest, and the police gave in, releasing King on bond. Several days later, as King addressed an MIA rally, a dynamite bomb shattered the front of his house. Quickly he left the meeting to return home. When he arrived, several hundred angry African-Americans, brandishing guns, knives, rocks, and broken soda pop bottles, surrounded his house. After assuring himself that no harm had come to his wife and baby, King stepped out on his porch. Now a volatile crowd of more than a thousand blacks milled in front of the house. "Don't get panicky," King raised his arms. "Get rid of your weapons"—he quieted the crowd. "We are not advocating violence. We want to love our enemies. We must love our white brothers no matter what they do to us." He spoke of forgiveness and promise. "I did not start this boycott. I was asked by you to serve as your spokesman. I want it to be known the length and breadth of the land that if I am stopped, our work will not stop, for what we are doing is right. What we are doing is just and God is with us."

This moment—Lerone Bennett, Jr., a biographer of King and a historian of the movement, would write—"changed the course of the protest and made King a living symbol. He and other members of the boycott directorate had spoken before of love and forgiveness. But now, *seeing the idea in action*, fleshed out by pain, paid for by anguish, millions were touched, if not converted. The parable of the porch went out now over the wires of the news media and King's name became a token for almost all American Negroes."

On February 21, 1956, city officials obtained indictments against King and some one hundred other boycott participants on charges of violating a 1921 law forbidding hindrance to a business without "just cause or legal excuse." "In this state," the indictment read, "we are committed to segregation by custom and law; we intend to maintain it." Instead of seeking to avoid arrest, the black leaders

of Montgomery hurried to the police station to surrender. E. D.
Nixon arrived first. "You are looking for me? Here I am." Hundreds
of blacks gathered outside the station to applaud the leaders as they
entered. King, visiting his parents in Atlanta, declined their advice
that he not jeopardize his life by returning, and rushed to the Montgomery jail. The photograph of him with a numbered plaque hang-
ing from his neck captured national and international attention.
Statements in support of the boycott, as well as cash contributions,
poured in from all over the world.

At a mass meeting the next evening, the indicted leaders marched
between thousands of cheering men, women, and children who
overflowed the street outside the Dexter Avenue Baptist Church.
Inside, hundreds more chanted, and prayed, and pledged themselves
to "passive resistance," to shun the buses and "walk with God."
They learned a new song, to the tune of "Give Me That Old-Time
Religion," whose four stanzas proclaimed the essential elements of
their struggle: protest, unity, nonviolence, and equality.

> We are moving on to vict'ry
> With hope and dignity.
>
> We shall all stand together
> Till every one is free.
>
> We know love is the watchword
> For peace and liberty
>
> Black and white, all our brothers
> To live in harmony.

They sang "O lift me up and let me stand on higher ground," and
then grew quiet to listen to King.

"We are not struggling merely for the rights of Negroes," the
Baptist minister began, "but for all the people of Montgomery,
black and white. We are determined to make America a better place

for all people." The protest, said King, was not against a single incident but over things that "go deep down into the archives of history."

> We have known humiliation, we have known abusive language, we have been plunged into the abyss of oppression. And we decided to rise up only with the weapon of protest. It is one of the greatest glories of America that we have the right to protest.
>
> There are those who would try to make of this a hate campaign. This is not a war between the white and the Negro but a conflict between justice and injustice. This is bigger than the Negro race revolting against the white. We are seeking to improve not the Negro of Montgomery but the whole of Montgomery.
>
> If we are arrested every day, if we are exploited every day, if we are trampled over every day, don't ever let anyone pull you so low as to hate them. We must use the weapon of love. We must have compassion and understanding for those who hate us. We must realize so many people are taught to hate us that they are not totally responsible for their hate. But we stand in life at midnight, we are always on the threshold of a new dawn.

On June 4, a three-judge federal district court handed down its ruling in the case brought by four Montgomery black women to end bus segregation in the city. "We hold that the statutes requiring segregation of the white and colored races on a common carrier," the majority declared, "violate the due process and equal protection of the law clauses of the Fourteenth Amendment." The order enjoined the mayor from enforcing racial segregation on the buses, but stayed the effect of the decision until Montgomery officials appealed the case to the Supreme Court. Fearing the worst from the high court, white leaders in Alabama again fought the boycott with vengeance. The state outlawed the NAACP as a foreign cor-

poration that had failed to register; accused it of "causing irrepar-
able injury to the property and civil rights of residents," a reference
to its role in handling the federal suit against Montgomery; and
fined the association $100,000 for refusing to surrender its mem-
bership lists. Concurrently, Montgomery obtained an indictment
against the MIA on charges of operating a business—the car
pool—without a license.

"You know the people are getting tired," King confided to his
wife. "If the city officials get this injunction against the car pools
—and they will get it—I am afraid our people will go back to the
buses." The blacks of Montgomery had become dependent on the
MIA station wagons and the volunteer automobiles. Their loss
would be incalculable; the boycott without them inconceivable. At
his lowest ebb since the boycott began, King awaited the crushing
injunction. Instead, as if providentially, he received word that the
Supreme Court had affirmed the district court's ruling voiding segregation on the buses. It came, said King, "as a joyous daybreak
to end the long night of enforced segregation in public transportation." The boycott had proved that local activism could compel
intervention from the federal government.

The next night, nearly ten thousand blacks convened to end the
boycott officially. The Reverend Robert Graetz, the sole white in
the MIA hierarchy, rose to read the scripture according to Paul to
the meeting: "When I was a child, I spoke as a child, I understood
as a child, I thought as a child. . . ." He could not go on. "There
was a vast uproar," reported Lerone Bennett. "All over the floor
now, men and women were on their feet, waving handkerchiefs
and weeping." Belatedly, haltingly, Graetz ended the sentence: "But
when I became a man, I put away childish things." Not since the
Civil War had the Southern black rank-and-file protested so visibly
and volubly against Jim Crow, smashing the stereotype of an ac-
quiescent Negro content with segregation. Their numbers and courage would point the way for countless other blacks to assert their
rights militantly. That was the meaning of the 381-day struggle.

On this same night, the Ku Klux Klan, hooded and gowned,

appeared in black Montgomery. A procession of forty vehicles drove slowly through the black neighborhoods. In the past, such demonstrations had petrified the black community. They had caused African-Americans to flee and hide. "Fearing death, they played dead," King explained. But on the evening of November 13, 1956, most of black Montgomery reacted as if the Klan were truly invisible. No one ran away or dimmed their lights. Some blacks followed the Klan procession, applauding, laughing, jeering. Dumbstruck, the KKK terminated its effort at intimidation and slunk away into the night. That, too, was the meaning of the Montgomery bus boycott. "A once fear-ridden people had been transformed," King would write of the blacks who openly defied Montgomery statutes used to try to destroy the protest campaign. "Those who had previously trembled before the law were now proud to be arrested for the cause of freedom."

Shortly before 6 a.m. on December 21, 1956, King and his aides boarded a Montgomery bus and sat in the front, black next to white. Droves of news reporters and cameramen recorded the historic event, proclaiming its significance throughout the world. "For the first time in this 'cradle of the Confederacy' all the Negroes entered buses through the front door," *The New York Times* reported. "They sat in the first empty seats they saw, in the front of buses and in the rear. They did not get up to give a white passenger a seat. And whites sat with Negroes." The 381-day struggle which began as a hope for simple courtesy and convenience ended as a triumph for desegregation. And, King added: "The skies did not fall when integrated buses finally traveled the streets of Montgomery."

In preparation for this day, King had schooled blacks in the techniques and philosophy of nonviolence. The Montgomery movement had been explicitly Christian. King had quoted Jesus, not Gandhi. The tactics of the MIA had been patterned on previous examples of black protest, not on Thoreau's "Civil Disobedience." The fervor with which the MIA practiced passive resistance sprang from the religion of the Black Belt. Its strategy flowed from the pragmatic recognition that black violence in the Deep South, where whites held a preponderance of force and power, would be self-defeating, even suicidal. The heart and soul of the movement—noncooperation with evil, coupled with love and forgiveness—exemplified the Southern blacks' faith in their church and in their leaders' gospel of avoiding armed conflict.

Gradually, however, King began to construct a strategy based on Gandhian precepts. African-Americans saw films of Gandhi's nonviolent movement; songs and skits emphasized the success of passive resistance in India. A leaflet given out in every black church urged the bus protesters to "read, study and memorize" seventeen rules, among them: "Pray for guidance and commit yourself to complete nonviolence in word and action as you enter the bus. . . . Be loving enough to absorb evil and understanding enough to turn an enemy into a friend. . . . If cursed, do not curse back. If pushed, do not push back. If struck, do not strike back, but evidence love and goodwill at all times. . . . If another person is being molested, do not arise to go to his defense, but pray for the oppressor and use moral and spiritual force to carry on the struggle for justice. . . . Do not be afraid to experiment with new and creative techniques for achieving reconciliation and social change. . . . If you feel you cannot take it, walk for another week or two."

King's doctoral education in theology led him to articulate the thrust of the movement in sweeping biblical terms and grand transcendental ideas. He adapted the rhythms and rhetoric of the African-American church to discourses on the Gandhian distinctions between *agape, eros*, and *philia*. At the same time, he larded his sermons with references to the documents of American democracy, translating the African-American quest for justice into an idiom whites could understand and accept. His unique blending of traditions was accentuated by the tendency of the press to label King the *new* African-American leader or the leader of the *New* Negro. Mistakenly, yet repeatedly, the news media depicted King's Gandhian views as a wholly novel approach to racial protest. By ignoring earlier Gandhian civil-rights groups and African-American ministers, they made King and the Montgomery bus boycott even more of a watershed.

The influence of Bayard Rustin and Reverend Glenn E. Smiley furthered King's Gandhian approach. Both had come to Montgomery in February 1956 to assist the MIA. They stayed and became indispensable to King, prodding him to articulate the bus boycott in Gandhian terms and persuading him to form a regional network of African-American ministers. Rustin, the black executive secretary of the War Resisters' League, and Smiley, a white field secretary for the Fellowship of Reconciliation (FOR), were both pacifist disciples of the Mahatma and of A. J. Muste, and they took every opportunity to reinforce King's understanding of *Satyagraha*. Both, as well, were thoroughly familiar with the wartime experiences of the March-on-Washington Movement and the Congress of Racial Equality (CORE). They recalled A. Philip Randolph's insistence on the need for broad, organized, militant mass action, rather than polite pleading, to achieve racial equality, and CORE's adoption of Gandhian nonviolence to the race problem. With their assistance, King developed an ideology of disciplined, nonviolent direct action by the black masses.

King's neo-Gandhian persuasion fit the needs of the American South in the mid-twentieth century. It offered something to nearly all in an especially palatable way. King had learned in the crucible of the boycott that this form of black protest weakened the white community's resolve, unity, and readiness to retaliate with violence. It placed blame on the impersonal system of segregation, not on individual segregationists; it played on the whites' growing feeling of guilt; it forced whites to confront the plight of blacks, while assuaging the white fear of bloody reprisals. King also emphasized that the achievement of the movement's goals would result not in victory for blacks alone but in triumph for all Americans. He clothed the consequences of racial change in the garb of reconciliation and the creation of a beloved community. At the least, this disarming message from a man of God minimized virulent white opposition and made the inevitable appear a bit more acceptable.

Simultaneously, King's words energized the black community, dispelling its feelings of helplessness, insignificance, and powerlessness. He sensed the untapped wellsprings of black hostility. He understood how the resentment of white supremacy had been kept in check by a Christian tradition tabooing hatred and by an awesome fear of white violence. So King transformed the immoral into the moral: "To accept passively an unjust system is to cooperate with that system; thereby the oppressed become as evil as the oppressor. Noncooperation with evil is as much a moral obligation as is cooperation with good." He equated apathy, not protest, with sin. He bestowed legitimacy on aggression against racism, redefining it as Christian love. Moreover, by lessening the likelihood of white vengeance, by decreasing the dangers to black protesters, King increased the probability of black militancy. The possibility of violent reactions by whites remained, and King made a virtue of it by exalting black suffering as redemptive, the highest manifestation of Christianity and the surest path to triumph. Unearned suffering, he preached, amplified the self-esteem of blacks much as knowing that they were part of a larger movement, a mass movement, gave them a sense of strength they had not possessed individually.

Inspired by one woman's courage and the successful example of an African-American community challenging racism in the Deep South, the boycott accelerated the movement of the struggle from the courtroom to the streets. It proved the power of organized collective action as an effective agent of social change. It ushered in an age of open confrontation with white racism; it encouraged large numbers of African-Americans to march under King's banner and to court beatings, jailings, even death, certain in the faith that their martyrdom would hasten the victory of their cause, firm in their belief that "we shall overcome."

The bus boycott also led to the organizing of black clergymen throughout the South into a cadre of protest leaders. The Southern Christian Leadership Conference (SCLC) sprang directly out of the Montgomery movement. Indeed, even before the successful termination of the Montgomery crusade, black ministers in other cities began to plan similar campaigns of noncooperation. After visiting King in the winter of 1956, the Reverend Charles K. Steele returned home to Tallahassee, Florida, to organize a bus boycott and form an Inter-Civic Council, modeled on the MIA. In Alabama, clergymen Joseph E. Lowery of Mobile and Fred L. Shuttlesworth of Birmingham met with King to plan the bus boycotts in their respective cities. In Tuskegee, blacks led by C. G. Gomillion, who also regularly conferred with King, boycotted white merchants to fight disenfranchisement. In Georgia, the Montgomery experience produced bus boycotts in Atlanta and Savannah.

King recognized the need to capitalize on this momentum. With Steele and Shuttlesworth, he issued a call for civil-rights-minded clergymen to convene in Atlanta on January 10–11, 1957. Sixty blacks from ten states agreed on the necessity of a coordinating force for their various movements. They named themselves the Southern Conference on Transportation and Nonviolent Integration and urged African-Americans "to assert their human dignity" by refusing "further cooperation with evil." A month later, nearly a hundred black ministers attended the formal organization of the conference in New Orleans. They elected King president and Abernathy treasurer, and tried several different names before calling themselves the Southern Christian Leadership Conference. In its first official declaration, the SCLC called upon blacks "to understand that nonviolence is not a symbol of weakness or cowardice, but as Jesus demonstrated, nonviolent resistance transforms weakness into strength and breeds courage in the face of danger." Until the founding of the SCLC, the struggle for racial equality had been largely the domain of a Northern elite oriented primarily toward legal action. Now the Southern black church would become preeminent in leading black resistance to white oppression, and they would do so by preaching the virtues of massive nonviolent protest. This crucial transformation in the African-American struggle had momentous consequences. The black churches, the hub of communities in the South, provided the movement with a stable base of supporters, a leadership economically independent of white society, a national ministerial communications network, a source of financial assistance, and a place to meet, to plan, to gain faith and courage. In addition, they gave the movement a language understood by all, expressed in biblical oratory and hymns, to battle against racial oppression; and they bestowed religious sanction on that battle. They would make possible the key ingredients of the modern civil-rights movement: large masses of African-Americans engaged in disruptive protest activities and the utilization of nonviolent direct action to create the necessary pressures for social change.

But they would not do so in the next three years. The SCLC initially accomplished little and failed to spark the mass, direct-action movement needed to alter the South. Blacks scored few victories for desegregation. Indeed, momentum shifted to those in the white South who defiantly said *Never* to black calls and court orders for integration. The second half of the fifties was the high tide of white massive resistance, of white reaction and repression. Authorities in Alabama had Autherine Lucy permanently expelled after she had won a federal court order admitting her to the University of Alabama in 1956. The university would remain segregated for seven more years. Governor Orval Faubus closed the schools in Little Rock, and Virginia officials disbanded the public educational system of Prince Edward County rather than comply with desegregation. The KKK waxed and the White Citizens' Councils flourished. Crosses were burned; black churches, homes, and schools were bombed. The Southern Regional Council tabulated over two hundred acts of violence against black protesters and their allies from 1955 to 1959. The NAACP struggled just to survive. It channeled its energies and resources primarily into the effort to thwart the scores of Southern laws passed to outlaw the association directly or to hamstring its ability to function effectively. The civil-rights offensive envisioned by King seemed to many in the late 1950s more like a retreat before the forces of racism.

Not surprisingly, King's strategy of nonviolent resistance struck many African-Americans as unproductive, unbearable, even suicidal. "Are you Gandhi?" King's father asked. "The British threw him in jail. The 'Bamians and Mississippians would shoot him. Dead!" Some considered nonviolence debasing; others questioned what fundamental conditions it could change; many simply tired of turning the other cheek. In 1959, the dismissal of Robert Williams as head of the Monroe, North Carolina, NAACP rocked the association's fiftieth annual convention. Earlier in the year, Williams had organized some fifty blacks into a gun club. Armed and drilled, they repelled with gunfire a group of Klansmen threatening the home of an NAACP official. Williams then publicly advocated defensive guerilla warfare by blacks and called for the formation of rifle clubs throughout the South. The NAACP hierarchy defended the dismissal of Williams, but the deep rumblings of discontent by delegates served notice that proponents of civil rights would not indefinitely adhere to nonviolence if it proved fruitless. Near the end of the year, a two-hour television documentary, "The Hate That Hate Produced," shocked the nation with its portrayal of the Black Muslims, nearly a hundred thousand strong, rejecting Christianity and integration. The program focused national attention on Malcolm X and his fiery denunciations of all white people and their Negro stooges in the civil-rights movement. Emerging from prison in 1952 to become the head of the Nation of Islam's mosque in Harlem, Malcolm X dismissed any chance of meaningful racial change in the United States. He insisted that true African-Americans did not want "to *integrate* into this corrupt society, but to *separate* from it, to a land of our *own*, where we can reform ourselves, lift up our moral standards, and try to be godly."

Yet other blacks, mainly the young, demonstrated an impatient hopefulness. They took heart from the legal and legislative victories of the NAACP. The desegregation efforts of the federal government, however irresolute, buoyed them. They knew that national and international politics made it imperative for Washington to deal with the racial problem. They sensed that the economic, educational, and demographic changes swirling about them foretold the crumbling of the old racial order. Montgomery had made them proud and confident. They read and reread FOR's widely circulated comic book *Martin Luther King and the Montgomery Story* and King's *Stride Toward Freedom: The Montgomery Story*. They dreamed of their opportunity to act.

Returning from a nonviolent action workshop in 1958, Barbara Ann Posey decided to act. A member of the Oklahoma City NAACP Youth Council, Posey organized a sit-in which resulted in the desegregation of five stores. The idea spread to the Youth Councils in Tulsa and Stillwater, and then across the state line to NAACP youth in Wichita and Kansas City, Kansas. King and Rustin organized a Youth March for Integrated Schools that brought nearly nine thousand young blacks to Washington, D.C. The following year, the March drew twenty-five thousand. Two thousand attended a Pilgrimage of Prayer for Public Schools in Richmond, Virginia, the first such large demonstration in the Deep South to decry "massive resistance" to school desegregation. Black students in Charlotte, North Carolina, protested being barred from state ceremonies which welcomed whites, while their counterparts in Marion, South Carolina, desegregated an ice-cream stand after a successful boycott. Also in 1959, African-American students began a sit-in in Durham, North Carolina, and CORE members in Miami, Florida, sat-in at a W. T. Grant's lunch counter and started a drive to desegregate the beaches of that resort city. None of these actions attracted national press coverage. None led to new organizations or leaders. None sparked a nationwide movement.

Yet together they revealed a new mood of restiveness, compounded of hope and anger. The charismatic young preacher who imparted a more moral and militant quality to the movement and the nonviolent, direct action campaign by the mass of ordinary black Montgomerians that rocked the Cradle of the Confederacy had together made an extraordinary impression on African-Americans, especially black middle-class youth. Disappointed with the NAACP's inability to provide immediate relief from the yoke of discrimination and oppression, they yearned to take to the streets. They bitterly decried the lack of racial progress in the late 1950s, yet optimistically believed that by using the strategy fashioned by Martin Luther King in Montgomery they could topple Jim Crow, quickly and throughout the South. King's prediction to the annual convention of the Fellowship of Reconciliation in mid-1959 that the coming years would witness mounting black "direct action against injustice without waiting for other agencies to act" defined their propensity. His thundering peroration to the FOR—"We will not obey unjust laws or submit to unjust practices"—adumbrated their cause.

# THREE

# BIGGER THAN A

# HAMBURGER

By appealing to conscience and standing on the moral nature
of human existence, nonviolence nurtures the atmosphere in
which reconciliation and justice become actual possibilities.

STUDENT NONVIOLENT COORDINATING
COMMITTEE STATEMENT OF PURPOSE

"We don't serve Negroes." This common retort, like the daily in-
dignity of having to board a Jim Crow bus, stung and humiliated
blacks seeking to eat in Dixie's restaurants and lunch counters.
Such segregation was usually a matter of custom or tradition; sometimes it was required by statute or city ordinance; in either event,
blacks throughout the South and the border states could not sit
down and eat alongside white diners.

"We don't serve Negroes here," the waitress responded to Joseph
McNeill on January 31, 1960, at the bus terminal in Greensboro,
North Carolina. He had heard it before. It always hurt. Now it
particularly rankled. That night in his dormitory at North Carolina
Agricultural and Technical College, McNeill, a physics major, emo-
tionally recounted the incident to his roommate, Ezell Blair, Jr.,

and to fellow freshmen Franklin McCain and David Richmond. The four young men often sat together for hours discussing the racial situation. They all resented the snail's pace of desegregation in the South. The countless subterfuges employed by the white South to evade the *Brown* decision, to disfranchise African-Americans, and to continue to discriminate against blacks, deeply angered them. They were not content to wait forever for the courts and the white South to grant them rights they felt were their due. They had frequently expressed their desire to act. The moment had arrived.

"We've talked about it long enough, let's do something." "But what can we do?" Suddenly the room grew quiet. No one spoke. Then McNeill answered his own question: "Let's have a boycott. We should go in and ask to be served and sit there until they do." They decided to go to the local Woolworth store and request service at the lunch counter. "We'll stay until we get served." "Well, you know that might be weeks, that might be months," Blair wondered aloud. "That might be never." Suddenly pounding the dresser, McCain asked, "Are you guys chicken or not?" That did it. They would give one another courage and take their chances.

The next afternoon the four freshmen walked into the downtown Greensboro five-and-dime store. They bought some school supplies, then took seats at the "white only" lunch counter, and asked for coffee and doughnuts. "I'm sorry," came the anticipated reply of the waitress, "we don't serve colored in here." "I beg to disagree with you," Blair responded politely, showing the receipts for their purchases. "We've in fact already been served; you've already served us at a counter only two feet from here." Dumbfounded, the waitress hurried off to get her manager. "Fellas," he tried kindly, "you know this is just not the way we do business. Why don't you go on back to your campus?" The students explained what they called their "passive demand for service" and promised to remain until they could eat where they sat. By then, other customers in the store had crowded around the lunch counter. One white woman patted them on the back, saying, "Ah, you should have done it ten years ago. It's a good thing I think you're doing." "Nasty, dirty niggers," another white rasped, "you know you don't belong here at the lunch counter." A black dishwasher, fearful of losing her job and of what might happen to the young blacks, reprimanded them: "That's why we can't get anyplace today, because of people like you, rabble-rousers, troublemakers. . . . This counter is reserved for white people, it always has been, and you are well aware of that. So why don't you go on out and stop making trouble?" The four students would not be moved. "By then," McCain recalled, "we had the confidence of a Mack truck." They remained seated until the store closed, and vowed to repeat their demand the next day.

By the time they returned to their campus, a local radio station had flashed the news. Word spread. The college was a beehive of activity. The four students now knew they were not alone. That evening they met with about fifty student leaders and formed the Student Executive Committee for Justice. They voted to continue the boycott "until we get served," and agreed on ground rules for new volunteers. The protesters would remain passive, never raise their voices, never indulge in name-calling. Their movement would be one of nonviolence and Christian love.

On Tuesday, February 2, twenty-three A & T students and four black women from Bennett College sat-in with Blair, McCain, McNeill, and Richmond at the Woolworth lunch counter. None was served. They just sat. Wednesday morning the students occupied sixty-three of the sixty-six lunch-counter seats. On Thursday, they were joined by three white students from the Women's College of the University of North Carolina campus in Greensboro and scores of sympathizers from A & T and Bennett. They overflowed Woolworth's and began to sit-in at the lunch counter in the S. H. Kress store down the street. Greensboro became national news. Over three hundred young blacks demonstrated on Friday. Even more jammed Greensboro's lunch counters the next day. City officials, seeking to end the protest, decided that the time had come to negotiate. Although not a single black had received a cup of coffee at the lunch counters, nearly 1,600 students, flushed with victory, attended a mass rally Saturday night. They would cease demonstrating to allow an agreement to be settled.

But, as would happen time and again all over the South, the white leadership of Greensboro, unable to gauge the depth of black determination, was unwilling to compromise. Whites resisted all pleas for change. They insisted on preserving the status quo. So pressure had to be applied anew. On April 1, the sit-ins resumed. White officials now offered the blacks a plan for partial desegregation of the lunch counters. The Student Executive Committee for Justice rejected the offer. Tokenism was no longer acceptable. Greensboro merchants and officials tried another tack, arresting forty-five students on trespass charges on April 21. This enraged the already fired-up black community of Greensboro, provoking a massive boycott of targeted variety stores. After profits had dropped by more than one-third, Greensboro's white leaders grudgingly acceded. Six months after the four freshmen sat-in at Woolworth's, Greensboro blacks could sit down at a lunch counter and be served a cup of coffee.

Greensboro, moreover, inspired sit-ins all over the South. The actions taken by Blair, McCain, McNeill, and Richmond initiated the student phase of the black struggle. The Greensboro "Coffee Party" made direct action the vogue. By April 1960 the tactic had spread to seventy-eight Southern and border communities; some two thousand students had been arrested. By August 1961, according to the Southern Regional Council, more than 70,000 blacks and whites had participated in sit-ins and three thousand had been jailed. It was a watershed. Race relations in the United States would never be the same. The lunch counters in Greensboro had joined the buses of Montgomery, Gandhi's salt marshes, and Thoreau's Walden Pond as focal points in the quest for justice through nonviolent civil disobedience.

First within North Carolina, then to neighboring states, the spark ignited in Greensboro spread like a brushfire, building on the indigenous support nurtured by decades of African-American protest. On February 8, 1960, sit-ins began in Durham and Winston-Salem.

"We want to put justice in their business," explained the chairman of the student movement from Winston-Salem Teachers College. "We believe it is morally wrong, as well as un-Christian, to maintain segregated facilities. We will continue to use the nonviolent approach because we believe non-violence is not the weapon of the weak and the coward; it is the weapon of the strong and the brave." In both cities it would take the arrests of students, the mobilization of the adult community, boycotts by blacks, and the support of white faculty and students from Duke University and Wake Forest College before desegregated lunch-counter service would begin.

On Tuesday, February 9, about 150 black students from Johnson C. Smith University began sit-ins against white-only eating facilities in Charlotte. "It's a manifestation of the unrest among this generation of students. It comes from their desire to dramatize the injustices of the Negro's position," stated one divinity student. "It is part of their feeling about the schools, the vote—civil rights in general." Another student leader expounded on the demonstrations as a "means of expressing something that has been in our hearts for a long time." Again, arrests and a "Don't buy where you can't eat" campaign had to precede desegregation in Charlotte.

Two days later, without leadership, planning, or organization, high-school students staged sit-ins in High Point and Portsmouth, Virginia. The Portsmouth police turned their dogs loose on the young blacks. "Our struggle is not an easy one," their spokesman said, "but we know we are not alone and we plan to continue in accordance with our common ideal: equality for all through nonviolent action." A news broadcast reported that black students at Shaw University and St. Augustine College in Raleigh would not follow the Greensboro example. That sparked the rebellion of black young people there to do just that. Dissatisfaction with the racial situation in this capital city ran high. Not a single Raleigh public school had yet started to desegregate. To enjoy an evening out, black students had to enter the local movie theater, owned by the mayor, through a "colored" side door, sit in the "owl's nest," and then walk ten blocks to a Negro restaurant for a Coke. Now, irritated at being pictured as docile by the white establishment, the blacks from Shaw and St. Augustine planned and executed a series of sit-ins at Raleigh variety stores. Over forty would be arrested for trespassing before the mayor established an interracial committee to deal with desegregation.

On Lincoln's birthday, students in Nashville and Tallahassee demonstrated their readiness to rebel. A small CORE group at Florida A & M, responding to a call from their national office to follow the lead of Greensboro, staged a sit-in at Woolworth's. They were joined by fifteen white supporters from Florida State University. When the waitress told the blacks, "I'm sorry, I can't serve you," all the students propped books on the counter and began to read. They stayed until the counter closed. A week later they returned. Again, they sat silently, reading. This time, the police arrested eleven students and charged them with disturbing the peace by riotous conduct and unlawful assembly. The pace of sit-ins and arrests quickened, culminating in a protest march of nearly a thousand students. On March 18, the first group of eleven arrested students introduced a militant new tactic in the movement: the jail-in. Following their trial and conviction, they chose to serve sixty-day sentences in the Leon County jail rather than pay a fine.

Writing to a friend, Patricia Stephens described the "dank and cold" cells, the inedible food, and the hopeful determination of the jailed students. "We are all so very happy that we were (and are) able to do this to help our city, state and nation. This is something that has to be done over and over again, and we are willing to do it as often as necessary. We strongly believe that Martin Luther King was right when he said, 'We've got to fill the jails in order to win our equal rights.' " The A & M junior concluded her letter simply: "When I get out, I plan to carry on this struggle. I feel I shall be ready to go to jail again if necessary."

When the sit-in leaders in Greensboro at the beginning of February 1960 asked, "What can the students in Nashville do to support students in Greensboro?" a contingent of blacks from Fisk University and the American Baptist Theological Seminary, aided by some whites from Vanderbilt University, immediately decided on massive, nonviolent direct action in Nashville. James Lawson, studying theology at Vanderbilt, had already galvanized a dedicated band of students, including Marion Barry, James Bevel, Bernard Lee, John Lewis, and Diane Nash, and they joined him in initiating the Nashville sit-ins. A confirmed pacifist who had gone to prison rather than serve in the military during the war, then a missionary in India, Lawson conducted workshops on nonviolence and drew up the sit-in rules: "Do show yourself friendly on the counter at all times. Do sit straight and always face the counter. Don't strike back, or curse back if attacked. Don't laugh out. Don't hold conversations. Don't block entrances." Lawson reminded each volunteer: "Remember the teachings of Jesus, Gandhi, Martin Luther King." On a snowy twelfth of February, forty students sat-in at Woolworth's in Nashville. They stayed for several hours, politely reading, studying, in their best Sunday clothes. Then they met with some five hundred other students in a local church to plan the next day's demonstration and to sing the spirituals and freedom songs that had started to characterize the student movement.

Each succeeding day, the number of students sitting-in grew. Tension mounted in Nashville. Violence began. White hecklers pushed lighted cigarettes against the backs of girls sitting at the counter. They beat and kicked "nigger lovers." They threw french fried potatoes and gum at the demonstrators. They spat on them and blew cigar smoke in their faces. Yet the police arrested only the protesters. Seventy-six students had been jailed by the fifth day. By early May, when the first downtown lunch counters announced an end to the color line, Nashville students had been arrested by the hundreds and had marched in protest by the thousands.

Day after day, sit-ins rocked the cities of the South. The arrest of thirty-three blacks sitting-in at the restaurant in Thalhimer's department store in Richmond on February 22 immediately provoked similar demonstrations in Petersburg, Hampton, Newport News, and Arlington. On February 23, high-school students sat-in at the Chattanooga Kress store. Students took to the streets in

Knoxville, Memphis, and Oak Ridge. Over a hundred blacks from Friendship Junior College launched sit-ins and picketed against segregation in Rock Hill, South Carolina. Demonstrations in Orangeburg, Columbia, and Sumter, South Carolina, followed within the week. More than six hundred Allen University and Benedict College students marched to the dime stores of downtown Columbia and took turns sitting-in after being refused service.

In Orangeburg, the students from Claflin College and South Carolina State College painstakingly schooled themselves in the principles and practices of nonviolence. They read King's *Stride Toward Freedom* and the pamphlet "CORE Rules for Action." They constantly asked one another: "Could each one of us trust our God and our temper enough not to strike back even if kicked, slapped, or spit upon?" A CORE staffer instructed them:

> To protect the skull, fold the hands over the head. To prevent disfigurement of the face, bring the elbows together in front of the eyes. For girls, to prevent internal injury from kicks, lie on the side and bring the knees upward to the chin; for boys, kneel down and arch over, with skull and face protected.

Over a thousand students were trained. Their first wave of sit-ins closed the lunch counters of Orangeburg on February 25. They returned the next day, and the next. On March 1, nearly a thousand blacks paraded through Orangeburg with signs reading "Down with Jim-Crow," and "All Sit or All Stand." Two weeks later, police met another mass march in support of the sit-ins with tear-gas bombs and high-pressure water hoses. Over five hundred students, knocked off their feet by streams of water, retching and temporarily blinded, were arrested. They filled the city and county jails, so the police herded more than three hundred into a chicken-coop stockade that afforded no protection against the sub-freezing weather. A photograph of those well-dressed, drenched students shivering and herded behind a wire fence appeared all over the country and throughout the world.

The sit-ins now spread southward. Thirty-five Alabama State College students demonstrated for service at the Montgomery County courthouse snack shop on February 25. When Governor John Patterson ordered the president of the college to expel any student involved in a sit-in, the campus staged a mass rally, addressed by Martin Luther King. Nearly a thousand students pledged to quit the college en masse if any expulsions followed their protest. A week later, about a hundred Texas Southern University students sat-in at the lunch counters of Houston. Mass arrests followed a series of sit-ins in the east Texas city of Marshall. Threatened with sit-ins, the managers of the variety stores in San Antonio announced the desegregation of their lunch counters on March 20. Sit-ins by high-school students quickly produced a dramatic headline in the Galveston *Tribune*: "City Lunch Counters Integrated."

More commonly, however, the sit-ins stripped the veneer of civility to reveal the savage core of white racism in the South. In Houston, a white youth slashed an African-American with a knife and three masked white men seized another black, flogged him with a chain, carved the initials of the KKK on his chest, and hung him from an oak tree. Unknown assailants stabbed a student protester in Columbia and firebombed the gymnasium of a Negro college in Frankfort, Kentucky. The KKK pistol-whipped a young demonstrator in Jacksonville, Florida. A crowd of whites in Biloxi, Mississippi, attacked blacks with clubs and chains, and wounded ten by gunfire. Jackson, Mississippi, police employed tear gas and police dogs against women and children. Acid was thrown in the face of a sit-in leader in Atlanta.

The brutality did not deter the students. Indeed, it often forged an even stronger commitment. There was no stopping them. Their parents often tried, and failed. School administrators tried, to no avail. When white officials and police tried, they succeeded only in stimulating more protests. Young Southern blacks conquered their fears, courted arrest, and each sit-in set a new standard of commitment to be matched and topped.

Their most ambitious campaign developed in Atlanta. On February 4, Julian Bond, an aspiring poet and student at Morehouse College, was relaxing at Yates and Milton's Drugstore, which functioned as an informal meeting place for Atlanta University Center students, when Lonnie King approached him with a copy of the Atlanta *Daily World*. The headline blared: "Greensboro Students Sit-In, Third Day." King, a veteran of military service and campus football hero, bluntly demanded of the influential Bond: "What do you think about it?" "Well, it's all right, pretty good stuff," Bond replied. "Don't you think it ought to happen here?" King pushed. "It probably will." King insisted: "Let's make it happen." And so they did.

They hoped to stage their first demonstration on Lincoln's birthday, sitting-in at Woolworth's, W. T. Grant's, and Kresge's simultaneously. Meetings were held with all the student leaders of Morris Brown, Clark, Morehouse, and Spelman colleges, the Interdenominational Theological Center, and the professional schools of Atlanta University. When the college administrators learned of the plan, however, they delayed the students by insisting on further consultation and more meetings. Out of these discussions came an agreement by the students to publish a clear, open statement of their aims before demonstrating. The University presidents agreed to raise the funds to publicize their manifesto.

On March 9, a full-page advertisement appeared in the Atlanta *Constitution, Journal*, and *Daily World* entitled "An Appeal for Human Rights." It began with a pledge of "unqualified support" for the student sit-ins in other cities and then proclaimed:

The students who instigate and participate in these sit-down protests are dissatisfied, not only with the existing conditions, but with the snail-like speed at which they are being ameliorated. Every normal human being wants to walk the earth with dignity and abhors any and all proscriptions placed upon him because of race or color. In essence, this is the meaning of the sit-down protests that are sweeping this nation today. . . . Today's youth will not sit by submissively, while being denied all of the rights, privileges, and joys of life. We want to state clearly and unequivocally that we cannot tolerate, in a nation professing democracy and among people professing Christianity, the discriminatory conditions under which the Negro is living today in Atlanta, Georgia—supposedly one of the most progressive cities in the South.

"We do not intend to wait placidly for those rights which are already legally and morally ours to be meted out to us one at a time," the appeal continued. It demanded an end to segregation in restaurants, movie theaters, concert halls, and other public facilities, the enfranchisement of blacks, and equitable law enforcement. It called for jobs for blacks and for equality in education, where only 4 percent of the state's expenditures for higher education went to the black colleges. It demanded equality in housing, where the blacks of Atlanta constituted over a third of the population and had to live in less than 16 percent of the city area. And it sought better health services; only 680 of the more than four thousand beds in the city hospitals could be used by blacks. "The time has come for the people of Atlanta and Georgia to take a good look at what is really happening in this country, and to stop believing those who tell us that everything is fine and equal, and that the Negro is happy and satisfied." The students ended with a promise: "We must say in all candor that we plan to use every legal and non-violent means at our disposal to secure full citizenship rights as members of this great democracy of ours."

On March 15, some two hundred students staged a well-orchestrated protest at the lunch counters and restaurants in the City Hall, the State Capitol Building, the Fulton County Courthouse, and the city's bus and train stations. Bond led the group at City Hall, where a sign announced "Cafeteria, Public Is Welcome." "What do you want?" said the manager. "We want to eat." "Well, we can't serve you here." "Well," Bond replied, "the sign outside says the public is welcome and we're the public and we want to eat." The police arrested Bond and seventy-six of his fellow students. The next day they organized the Committee on an Appeal for Human Rights to negotiate with business and civic leaders.

Interminable meetings followed. But the Atlanta leadership had no intention of compromising. They counted on the upcoming summer vacation to end the sit-in craze; they expected to go back to business as usual in the fall. The students, however, used the summer months to plan large-scale sit-ins at the major department and variety stores and to organize a boycott of the downtown merchants. "Close out your charge account with segregation, open up your account with freedom," became their slogan. With military precision, the fall campaign began. In October 1960, Martin Luther King and thirty-six students were arrested when they sat down in the Magnolia Room of Rich's department store. Even more demonstrators appeared the next day, and police arrested fifty-seven protesters. They all vowed to stay in jail and not post bond. Then the mayor arranged a sixty-day truce. The sit-ins would cease; those arrested would be released; negotiations would resume. But the merchants refused to offer anything more concrete than vague assurances to try sincerely to end segregation sometime in the future. The students considered this response unacceptable and publicly announced the resumption of demonstrations:

> We intend to do it for as long as it takes. It has never been our intention to hurt our city, the merchants or anyone else. We do want, however, to remove the hurt from the hearts of Negroes who've been hurting for over one hundred years.

The students now had the support of the Atlanta black community. Some adults began to sit-in and picket. The boycott took its toll. Day after day, hundreds of protesters marched and clogged the downtown lunch counters. Equipped with two-way radios and cars to shuttle students quickly to any store where they might be needed, the Committee on an Appeal for Human Rights kept increasing the pressure on the merchants during the winter months. In February 1961, the arrests began again. Nearly a hundred students were behind bars by February 11. Finally, the business leadership budged. They pledged that their rest-room and eating facilities would be desegregated no later than October 15. The students dropped their demand for immediate integration. On September 27, 1961, desegregation came to Atlanta.

Long before that, however, scores of other cities in every Southern state, including Mississippi, confronted impatient young blacks. As the pace of victory quickened in desegregating lunch counters, the student movement focused on eradicating other vestiges of Jim Crow and experimented with new forms of nonviolent direct action. There were "kneel-ins" in churches, "sleep-ins" in motel lobbies, "swim-ins" in pools, "wade-ins" on restricted beaches, "read-ins" at public libraries, "play-ins" in parks, even "watch-ins" in movie theaters. Other targets of racial exclusion included amusement parks, employment agencies, laundromats, and museums. These demonstrations fundamentally transformed the use of public accommodations in the border and upper South states, where by the end of 1961 nearly two hundred cities had begun to desegregate. Try as they might, however, the students scored few victories in the Deep South. There, the segregationist wall of resistance held. The sit-ins, nevertheless, accelerated a train of consequences that would soon topple Jim Crow.

These subsequent developments and the meaning of the sit-ins can best be understood through the many who demonstrated collectively. Much has already been written about specific individuals involved, about particular groups, about single cities affected. There is a continuing debate on the causes and goals of the movement. In some instances, it is argued, a charismatic student or an especially galling local incident was the vital force. In others, sit-ins materialized spontaneously without definitive provocation, leadership, or incitement.

When asked to explain their motives, sit-in participants answered in about as many ways as their number. They stated that their inspiration came from parents engaged in the struggle for racial justice, or from teachers who dwelled on the long and noble tra-

dition of Negro protest, or even from whites who urged the necessity
to demonstrate against Jim Crow. Sometimes they stressed personal
experiences. Some had served in the armed forces or had lived in
the North and found it difficult to adjust to Southern segregation.
Some knew of the sit-ins staged by NAACP youth groups or by
CORE. Many more had heard about the Montgomery bus boycott
and the doctrines of nonviolence preached by Martin Luther King,
Jr. He had spoken in Greensboro in 1958, and Ezell Blair remembered King's sermon being "so strong that I could feel my heart
palpitating. It brought tears to my eyes." The passive-resistance
movement in Montgomery stirred innumerable students, pointed
to a workable strategy, and shamed them. The bus boycotters "were
at least trying to do something," remonstrated Joseph McNeill.
"And we weren't."

"By coincidence," recalled Bernard Lee, the sit-in leader at Alabama State College, "I had just written a term paper on civil
disobedience and non-violence—had read Gandhi for it." So had
numerous others. King's popularization of Gandhi's concepts had
become a staple of black discussion groups. Many students spoke
vividly of their experience watching documentaries on the Indian
nonviolent movement in their churches and schools. Prior to the
sit-ins, some had already participated in nonviolent workshops;
some had joined CORE; and some had already been in trouble with
the law or with school authorities because of their opposition to
racism. Yet another student emotionally recollected hearing Tom
Mboya, a leader of the black liberation campaign in Kenya, speak
at Fisk University and was stirred into realizing that he was a "part
of a worldwide struggle of young black people to control their
lives." Ghana's victorious revolution for independence in 1957 had
initiated a wave of freedom movements against the African empires
of Belgium, France, Great Britain, and Portugal. In 1960, a dozen
African nations had gained independence. "We could hardly miss
the lesson for ourselves," admitted John Lewis. "They were getting
their freedom, and we still didn't have ours in what we believed
was a free country." The successful struggles of black Africans

continued both to embarrass and to inspire African-Americans. "The pace of social change is too slow," exclaimed James Lawson in Nashville. "All of Africa will be free before we attain first-class citizenship." And black author James Baldwin jeered: "All of Africa will be free before we can get a lousy cup of coffee."

However much the student analyses of the cause of the sit-ins differed, impatience was a factor in virtually every explanation. Their generation, for the most part, had been in elementary school or beginning high school when the Supreme Court ordered an end to segregation in public education. The decision thrilled them, and the bravery of the African-American students entering Little Rock's Central High School encouraged them. They believed they would finish their education in desegregated schools. John Lewis, a seminary student in Nashville who became one of the sit-in leaders in that city, recalled learning the news of *Brown* when he was fourteen. "I thought that the next year I would go to a real high school, and not the kind of training school that blacks were sent to. I thought I wouldn't have to be bused forty miles each day, past white schools, to maintain a system of segregation." But Lewis would never attend a desegregated school. Contrary to the Constitution, in defiance of numerous federal court orders, and despite a brilliant, costly, valiant campaign by the NAACP, six years after the Supreme Court outlawed segregation only 6 percent of the schools in the South had started to desegregate. Not even a beginning had been made in Alabama, Florida, Louisiana, Mississippi, and South Carolina. At this rate of compliance with the law, segregation would not be ended in their lives, perhaps not even in the lifetime of the children of the generation who sat-in.

The pace of progress in terminating disenfranchisement was equally painful. Again, despite intensive efforts by the NAACP and SCLC, despite decades of struggle for the suffrage, despite victories in the courts and in the Congress, fewer than one in four blacks of voting age in the South could register and vote in 1960. Many realized that not even their college diplomas would open the voting booth to them. Many understood that just the attempt to claim this most elementary right of citizenship entailed the risk of losing their jobs, their homes, possibly their lives.

Yet this generation of black students expected to mature in a different America. They grew up in an era of change. For the most part, they came from cities, not sharecropper shacks; their parents were professionals, industrial workers, civil servants, not farmers. They were the middle class, certainly in aspirations if not in income; and they were the legatees of previous protests. Their youth had been marked by sweeping changes in the economy, in demography, in national and international politics, and in American attitudes about race. All this had conspired to raise their aspirations, to fuel their hopes. But the promise of change far outran the reality. Massive resistance to racial equality throughout the South proved the rule. The minimal extent of enfranchisement and desegregation seemed ludicrously disproportionate to the monumental expenditures of energy, money, time, and courage. Southern blacks, no matter how wealthy or educated, still could not even have a cup of coffee with whites in public. In 1960 their patience ran out. They were unwilling to suffer the racist indignities inflicted on their parents or to wait silently.

Having a cup of coffee, sitting down, may not seem like much today, but in 1960 it epitomized the degradation of blacks induced by segregation. "Negro Americans throughout our country will be bruised in nearly every waking hour by differential treatment in, or exclusion from, public accommodations of every description," Roy Wilkins testified to Congress. "From the time they leave home in the morning, en route to school or to work, to shopping or visiting, until they return home at night, humiliation stalks them." Then the NAACP leader invited the lawmakers to imagine themselves black and planning an auto trip in the South.

How far do you drive each day? Where, and under what conditions can you and your family eat? Where can they use a rest room? Can you stop driving after a reasonable day behind the wheel or must you drive until you reach a city where relatives or friends will accommodate you and yours for the night? Will your children be denied a soft drink or an ice-cream cone because they are not white?

John Williams, a black writer, echoed Wilkins in emphasizing the demeaning nature of Jim Crow. "Nothing is quite as humiliating," wrote Williams, "so murderously angering as to know that because you are black you may have to walk a half mile farther than whites just to urinate; that because you are black you have to receive your food through a window in the back of a restaurant or sit in a garbage-littered yard to eat."

Clearly, the students sought more than the opportunity to eat where and as others ate in public places. Their worthiness and self-esteem could not be attained within the framework of compulsory segregation. They sought, accordingly, the end of Jim Crow. The lunch counter, said one student, is only a symbol that we "aren't having it any more. . . . We're trying to eradicate the whole stigma of being inferior." Those demonstrating in Chapel Hill carried signs saying: "We do not picket just because we want to eat. We can eat at home or walking down the street. We do picket to protest the lack of dignity and respect shown us as human beings." In Little Rock, students boycotting segregated stores carried signs reading: "I am wearing 1959 clothes with 1960 dignity." The students were demanding full equality in a way that could be neither misunderstood nor ignored.

That goal, and the brave, resourceful, unambiguous manner in which the students expressed it, awakened a generation of young activists. Ruby Doris Smith, a seventeen-year-old sophomore at Morehouse College, heard a rumor about the Greensboro sit-in and rushed home to watch it on the television news. "I began to think right away about it happening in Atlanta." So did John Lewis. "I had the feeling that we were involved in something like a crusade. . . . It was a sense of duty, you had an obligation to do it, to redeem the city—as Dr. King said so many times, to redeem the soul of America. . . . I will never forget it. . . . You felt that you were doing something that *had* to be done." "It made me so proud," recalled Bernard Lee in Montgomery, "I never had to think about whether to get involved." Neither did Charles McDew in Orangeburg, or Cleveland Sellers in Denmark, South Carolina. The news of Greensboro affected Sellers "like a shot of adrenalin," bringing "a burning desire to get involved." Each evening he would rush to the student union to view the news broadcasts.

> With the exception of the announcer's voice, the lounge would be so quiet you could hear a rat pissing on cotton. Hundreds of thoughts coursed through my head as I stood with my eyes transfixed on the television screen. My identification with the demonstrating students was so thorough that I would flinch every time one of the whites taunted them. On nights when I saw pictures of students being beaten and dragged through the streets by their hair, I would leave the lounge in a rage.

James Forman, a former Chicago schoolteacher doing graduate work in French, and Robert Moses, a Harvard graduate student and mathematics teacher in Harlem, had similar reactions. Staring at the pictures of the Greensboro youths, Moses was struck by the look of anger and determination in their faces. He judged it light-years away from the "defensive, cringing" expression of older Southern Negroes. "They were kids my own age and I knew this had something to do with my life," remarked Moses. And thousands less well known, but just as angry, just as proud, just as impatient, would also act. As a Charlotte student put it: "The sit-ins were a means of expressing something that had been in our hearts for a long time."

Gradually and painfully, the intrepid resolution of their children inspired and shamed the black adult community to begin to discard the passive accommodationist etiquette and to come to the aid of the students. Those who did not have to depend on the sufferance of the local white establishment for their livelihoods, in particular, raised bail money, provided legal counsel, and supported boycotts of Jim Crow stores. An intangible yet profound shift in the psychology of the black community became manifest. The sit-ins dramatically illustrated the power of individuals to shape their own history, and a renewed will to struggle for equal rights appeared. "Something wonderful is happening in this town," commented Atlanta's Martin Luther King, Sr. "The low-down Negroes are getting tired. I mean the kind of folks who just come and go like the rain. White folks have never paid them any mind, but they're tired. They just aren't going to take it like they always have before." The behavior of the students taught their elders that the way it used to be did not have to be. As Jim Crow seemed less immutable, the paralyzing feeling of fatalism diminished.

The volume of public endorsements for the sit-ins also pointed to the new mood in black America. Privately, numbers of black clergymen, school administrators, and civic spokesmen opposed the student actions. They considered the tactics too brusque, or the strategy unwise, or the time not right. For reasons that ranged from narrowly selfish to sincerely altruistic, some older blacks tried to discourage the young. But rarely did they publicly announce their opposition; and those that did recanted. Everywhere, leaders hurried to catch up with their followers, lest they be stigmatized as Uncle Toms. The sit-ins pushed the established black leadership to a new plateau of militancy.

Some white students, and their parents, also responded positively to the spirit of nonviolent militance, redemptive love, and dignity expressed by the sit-in participants. "I have a moral obligation to support this movement," said one young white woman who joined the Greensboro sit-in. The University of North Carolina *Daily Tar Heel* editorialized about the students demonstrating in Greensboro: "We hope they win. We hope they win BIG and we hope they win SOON." Student assemblies, faculty groups, and church conventions spoke out to vindicate the demonstrators. "There are many white people in the South who recognize the injustice of the lunch counter system," pronounced the Greensboro *Daily News*. "It is based on circumstances which may have made sense 100 years ago;

today it has a touch of medievalism. It smacks of Indian 'untouchables' or Hitlerian Germany's Master Race Theories.'' Florida's Governor LeRoy Collins told a statewide radio and television audience: "I don't mind saying that if a man has a department store and he invites the public generally to come in his department store and trade I think then it is unfair and morally wrong for him to single out one department though, and say he does not want or will not allow Negroes to patronize that one department." Frank P. Graham, former United States Senator and president of the University of North Carolina, added that the black protesters are "in their day and generation renewing springs of American democracy. . . . In sitting down they are standing up for the American dream."

Although such statements remained atypical in the South, many of those opposed to the student demonstrators grudgingly praised their courage and comportment. The contrast between the dignity of the blacks sitting-in and the ugliness of their opponents' tactics was repeatedly highlighted. In a widely reprinted editorial, the Richmond *News Leader* observed:

> Here were the colored students, in coats, white shirts, ties, and one of them was reading Goethe and one was taking notes from a biology text. And here, on the sidewalk outside, was a gang of white boys come to heckle, a ragtail rabble, slackjawed, black-jacketed, grinning fit to kill, and some of them, God save the mark, were waving the proud and honored flag of the Southern States in the last war fought by gentlemen. *Eheu!* It gives one pause.

The sit-ins, moreover, opened the eyes of Southern whites as nothing had before to the depth of black discontent and determination. The risks taken by so many students, and the responses of black communities, made it painfully clear that their dissatisfaction with segregation could no longer be denied or attributed merely to a handful of "outside agitators." The African-American struggle could never again be dismissed as just the doing of the Supreme Court or the

Kremlin. The nearly seventy thousand African-Americans who joined protests in 1960 utterly demolished the myth of black contentment with the status quo.

The reaction of Northern whites also proved heartening to the black students. Within a fortnight, sympathy sit-ins and pickets appeared at the lunch counters of Grant, Kress, Liggett, Walgreen, and Woolworth stores in Boston, Chicago, and New York. Students from California to Connecticut demonstrated in support of the Southern sit-ins. Their slogan: "We Walk So They May Sit." Campus groups raised scholarship money and bail funds to assist expelled or jailed blacks. The National Student Association, the National Student Christian Federation, and the Northern Student Movement, a new organization formed specifically to support the sit-in campaign, organized boycotts against the variety-store chains, helping to make lunch-counter discrimination a national issue. Eleanor Roosevelt termed the sit-ins "simply wonderful." Various labor, liberal, and religious organizations voiced their support. Even President Eisenhower responded, when queried at a press conference whether or not he approved of the sit-ins: "Now, let me make one thing clear. I am deeply sympathetic with the efforts of any group to enjoy the rights of equality that they are guaranteed by the Constitution." More pointedly, while campaigning for the Presidency, John F. Kennedy praised the sit-ins: "It is in the American tradition to stand up for one's rights—even if the new way is to sit down."

The sit-ins energized a sagging civil-rights movement and transformed African-American youths' image of themselves. Recalling the first of February in Greensboro, Franklin McCain asserted: "I probably felt better that day than I've ever felt in my life. I felt as though I had gained my manhood, so to speak, and not only gained it, but had developed quite a lot of respect for it." Such a psychological change occurred thousands of times. Each student had his own way of expressing "I became a man." And the net result of this wellspring of self-respect was a whetted appetite for further struggle. The students' new sense of their own determination and strength also intensified this impetus. An Atlanta student described a young woman from Spelman sitting-in next to her:

> The manager walked up behind her, said something obscene, and grabbed her by the shoulders. "Get the hell out of here, nigger." Lana was not going. . . . She put her hands under the counter and held. He was rough and strong. She just held and I looked down at that moment at her hands . . . brown, strained . . . every muscle holding. All of a sudden he let go and left. I thought he knew he could not move that girl—ever.

In a thousand ways the students stated that they could not be moved, spurring themselves and others to protest yet more. "City officials pointed out that we had staged nineteen demonstrations during January," one of the Rock Hill "jail-inners" commented, "and suddenly we felt sort of ashamed of ourselves that we hadn't staged thirty-one."

Success further enhanced their commitment. They showed that blacks could challenge racism in their own communities; they demonstrated that the system was not impregnable; they proved that whites could, and would, accept integrated public accommodations. This strengthened their will to press harder against remaining discriminations. It was a heady moment in the black struggle. "I myself desegregated a lunch counter, not somebody else, not some big man, some powerful man, but little me," said a proud black student. "I walked the picket line and I sat in and the walls of segregation toppled. Now all people can eat there." Each small victory convinced thousands that "Nothing can stop us now."

The formation of the Student Nonviolent Coordinating Committee exemplified this new spirit. Soon after the sit-in fever became contagious, Ella Baker persuaded the SCLC to appropriate $800 and the president of her alma mater, Shaw University in Raleigh, to make its facilities available for an Easter-weekend conference of youth leaders. Then executive director of the SCLC, but soon to be replaced by Wyatt Tee Walker, Baker feared the appetence of older protest leaders to harness and steer the students' resolve. A community organizer in New York during the Depression and a field secretary for the NAACP during the 1940s, Baker considered both the SCLC and the NAACP too cautious and self-centered and felt that they had not kept pace with the new aggressive tempo that the students had injected into the struggle. Believing that the students "had the right to direct their own affairs and even make their own mistakes," Baker sought to keep the student movement free from adult fetters. As John Lewis remembered: "She was much older in terms of age, but I think in terms of ideas and philosophy and commitment she was one of the youngest persons in the movement."

Nearly two hundred student delegates and observers answered Baker's call, and the Youth Leadership Meeting convened on April 15, 1960. Her opening address dwelled on the need for the students to develop their own independent organization, with "group-centered leadership" rather than the "leader-oriented pattern of organization" found in the NAACP and SCLC, and to transform the whole social structure, not just integrate lunch counters. "The younger generation is challenging you and me," the fifty-five-year-old Baker added, eyeing the adults present. "They are asking us to forget our laziness and doubt and fear, and follow our dedication to the truth to the bitter end." Martin Luther King, Jr., then took the podium. The sit-in movement, he declared, "is also a revolt against the apathy and complacency of adults in the Negro community; against Negroes in the middle class who indulge in buying cars and homes instead of taking on the great cause that will really solve their problems; against those who have become so afraid they have yielded to the system." King made three specific recommendations: "some type of continuing organization" to coordinate the student struggle; a nationwide campaign of "selective buying" to punish segregating variety-store chains; and an army of "volunteers who will willingly go to jail rather than pay bail or fines." Above all, King accentuated his philosophy of nonviolence, preaching the values of reconciliation and the creation of the beloved community.

"The tactics of nonviolence without the spirit of nonviolence," he expounded, "may become a new kind of violence."

"I don't dig all this," responded one student from Virginia, voicing the reaction to King's caveat felt by the majority of those at the Raleigh conference. Some of the divinity students present shared King's beliefs, but as subsequent events made clear, most blacks viewed nonviolence as a political weapon. That was the theme of James Lawson's address, which the students accepted enthusiastically. Lawson came to Atlanta a hero to young blacks because of his leadership of the Nashville sit-ins and his expulsion from Vanderbilt University for his refusal to withdraw from the protest movement. Cheered as "the young people's Martin Luther King," Lawson emphasized the tactical benefits of direct action, dramatized the eagerness of African-American students, and rebuked the NAACP and SCLC for their timidity.

In the discussions and workshops during the next two days, the young black leaders continually reaffirmed their goal of "full equality," their hope that black students had surpassed the ministry as the new driving, dynamic force in the civil-rights movement, and their insistence that litigation now take second place to civil disobedience. The most applause at the conference went to the workshop recommendation that demonstrators choose jail over bail and to the student who declared: "The greatest progress of the American Negro in the future will not be made in Congress or in the Supreme Court; it will come in the jails." The meeting ended with the establishment of a Temporary Coordinating Committee, chaired by Ed King, who had been bloodied leading the Frankfort, Kentucky, sit-ins.

The following month, fifteen student delegates met with Ella Baker, Ed King, James Lawson, and CORE's Len Holt in Atlanta. They voted not to affiliate with the SCLC or any other group but to be an independent enterprise named the Temporary Student Nonviolent Coordinating Committee. They elected Marion Barry of Nashville their new chairman and agreed to establish their headquarters in Atlanta. The students also adopted a Statement of Purpose, strongly redolent of King's rhetoric. Love and nonviolence were its central motifs. "We affirm the philosophical or religious ideal of nonviolence as the foundation of our purpose," it stated, "the presupposition of our faith, and the manner of our action. Nonviolence as it grows from Judaic-Christian tradition seeks a social order of justice permeated by love."

In October 1960, a plenary conference meeting in the Atlanta University Center dropped *Temporary* from its name and made the Student Nonviolent Coordinating Committee (SNCC—pronounced "Snick") a permanent organization. King again spoke for the philosophy of nonviolence but the students made clear their primary desire to force overdue racial change. Charles McDew, SNCC's new chairman, articulated its temper. "The sit-ins have inspired us to build a new image of ourselves in our own minds. And, instead of sitting idly by, taking the leavings of a sick and decadent society, we have seized the initiative, and already the walls have begun to crumble." A convert to Judaism because the only white religious leader to support the Orangeburg sit-ins was the town rabbi, McDew frequently quoted Hillel: "If I am not for myself, then who is for me? If I am for myself alone, then what am I? If not now, when?" The student movement would not end, McDew now promised, until "every vestige of racial segregation and discrimination are erased from the face of the earth."

Viewing themselves as no longer "temporary" demonstrators but as leaders of a revolutionary direct-action movement, the students who met in Atlanta went forth to claim their inevitable victory. With Jane Stembridge, a young white from Virginia who left her studies at the Union Theological Seminary in New York to run the SNCC office, they believed: "What happened in Greensboro, the kick-off place, can happen and is happening all across the South. People can come to an understanding, barriers can be removed, a new South can be born, and America can become an actual democracy." They presumed they could truly bring an end to race as a source of power or privilege, of status or entitlement.

Burning with idealism and impatience, "Ella's children" emblazed the fight for equality their parents had kindled. The students would no longer accept the presence of a single black child in a formerly all-white school as a major triumph. Tokenism was out. As Baker then wrote, "the current sit-in and other demonstrations are concerned with something bigger than a hamburger. . . . The Negro and white students, North and South, are seeking to rid America of the scourge of racial segregation and discrimination—not only at lunch counters but in every aspect of life." They wanted racial equality, and they wanted it fast. Convinced that civil disobedience provided the fastest and most effective route to desegregation, black youth insisted that the focus of the struggle be nonviolent direct action in the streets, not legal skirmishes in the courtroom. Moreover, the students assumed that their elders had wasted too much energy on fund-raising, public relations, and bureaucratic minutiae. They distrusted too much structure. Wishing to "stay loose," to remain spontaneous, to stress improvisation, the young blacks judged themselves by the maxim of Bob Moses: "Go where the spirit say go and do what the spirit say do."

Although the sit-ins had achieved only a shallow breach in the South's deeply fortified caste system, the black students did not consider the possibility of failure. They took pride in their lack of professionalism. They boasted that three-quarters of SNCC's first forty fieldworkers were under twenty-two years of age. They laughed away the hindrance of having a budget of only $14,000. They exuded faith in themselves and in the promise of America. None doubted that their spirit of nonviolent militance and redemptive love would ultimately make manifest the essential righteousness of the United States. Spiritedly, they sang "Keep Your Eyes on the Prize" and "I'm Gonna Sit at the Welcome Table." Their lyrics stated their goal: "I'm so glad segregation got to go / I'm so glad integration on its way." The fervor with which they vocalized "We Shall Overcome" augmented their conviction. Originally a spiritual sung by slaves and known as "I'll Be All Right," reworked by striking tobacco laborers in the 1940s, it was then rearranged by Guy Carawan of Tennessee's Highlander Folk

School in the late 1950s. "Deep in my heart"—the young SNCC workers would sing—"I do believe"—each clasping the hand of persons on either side—"That we shall overcome some day." Forming a human chain, swaying in unity, some hummed and others intoned: "We'll all go to jail. . . . We are not afraid. . . . We'll walk hand in hand." Their voices swelled: "Black and white together. . . . We *shall* overcome." The ritual expressed the creed and the certainty of SNCC in 1960. Few could imagine the anguish, frustration, and violence of the years ahead.

## FOUR

· · · · · · · · · · · · · · · · · · · · · · ·

# THE LONG JOURNEY

The voice I have now I got the first time I sang in a movement meeting, after I got out of jail. I did the song, "Over My Head I See Freedom in the Air," but I had never heard that voice before. I had never been that me before. And once I became that me, I have never let that me go.

BERNICE JOHNSON REAGON

In 1961 and 1962 the movement for racial justice paid a fearful price in anguish and pain for minimal gains. Civil-rights workers learned that victory was not inevitable, that white resistance in the Deep South could hold firm. Consequently, new tactics and strategies evolved. The idea of changing hearts and minds gave way to confrontation politics that would induce federal intervention. SNCC led the way, augmented by the revitalized Congress of Racial Equality.

On March 13, 1961, James Farmer, CORE's new national director, issued a call for volunteers to conduct freedom rides through the South to test racial discrimination in interstate-travel terminals. Three months earlier, the Supreme Court in *Boynton v. Virginia* had extended its 1946 prohibition against segregation in vehicles engaged in interstate travel (*Morgan v. Virginia*) to include all terminal accommodations. Two CORE field secretaries, assisting students in the sit-in movement, discussed the court ruling and wondered how they could test the decision. At the February CORE national council meeting, they proposed a Freedom Ride. Farmer, who had just taken office that month, enthusiastically supported the idea and the council quickly approved the plan. "Our intention," the national director stated, "was to provoke the southern authorities into arresting us and thereby prod the Justice Department into enforcing the law of the land." CORE craved a crisis, Farmer later admitted. "We were counting on the bigots in the South to do our work for us."

Farmer had been chosen to invigorate CORE. A charismatic leader of commanding physique and Shakespearean diction, Farmer considered himself an "action man." The son of the first Negro to earn a Ph.D. degree in Texas, Farmer studied for the ministry at Howard University but refused ordination in 1941. "I did not see how I could honestly preach the gospel of Christ in a church that practiced discrimination." Living in a Gandhian ashram in Harlem, Farmer went to work for a variety of struggling pacifist and socialist groups, including the Fellowship of Reconciliation, where he served as race-relations secretary from 1941 to 1945. Believing that legal battles alone could not win the fight against Jim Crow, he helped to form CORE in 1942 and pioneered in the development of nonviolent direct action against racial injustice. After the war he became a union organizer, a youth secretary in the League for Industrial Democracy, and then program director of the NAACP. There he languished. None of his plans for bold, mass demonstrations came to fruition. The cautious NAACP leadership quietly filed away all his proposals for direct action. Having to watch from the sidelines as the student movement, practicing techniques he had devised, spread through the South particularly galled the ambitious Farmer. He longed for prominence in the thick of the action. Chafing at the bit, Farmer jumped when CORE offered him the lead post early in

1961. Though poor in finances, membership, and influence, CORE sought a dynamic leader who could make it a major power in the civil-rights movement. And Farmer considered CORE's interracial, truly dedicated believers, committed to nonviolent direct action, an ideal group to steer into the vanguard of the surging campaign against segregation and discrimination.

CORE consciously modeled its 1961 Freedom Ride on the 1947 Journey of Reconciliation. Organized by Bayard Rustin and George Houser, of CORE and the Fellowship of Reconciliation, the 1947 train and bus trip to fifteen cities in Kentucky, North Carolina, Tennessee, and Virginia sought to publicize the *Morgan* decision and to inspire blacks to practice the rights they had won in the courts. Eight blacks and eight whites met in Washington, D.C., for a weekend of sessions on the philosophy and tactics of nonviolence. They staged socio-dramas, acting out the roles of bus drivers, policemen, "hysterical segregationists," and protesters. Their journey began on April 9. It ended April 23. Most Americans never heard of it. With few arrests and little violence, the Journey of Reconciliation received scant attention in the press. No one even fancied the possibility of coverage by television, then in its infancy.

The 1961 ride, however, would have far-reaching consequences. Farmer's plan, like the earlier one in 1947, envisioned an interracial group to challenge Southern segregation and to demonstrate the extent to which the South disobeyed the law of the land. Like the Journey of Reconciliation, it would begin with training sessions on nonviolence in Washington, D.C. But there the similarities ended. The Freedom Ride would test Jim Crow in terminal restaurants, waiting rooms, and rest rooms, not merely the seating aboard buses. It would force the issue in the heart of the Deep South. But the real target would be the Administration in Washington. "We put on pressure and create a crisis," Farmer confided, "and then they react."

In April, CORE, "following the Gandhian technique," informed Washington of its intent to commit civil disobedience. It wrote to President John F. Kennedy, to the Justice Department, to the FBI, and to the bus companies involved. CORE received not a single reply. On May 4, seven blacks and six whites, split into two interracial groups, left Washington on a Greyhound and a Trailways bus. Four were CORE staff members, including Farmer and James Peck, a white pacifist who had been on the Journey of Reconciliation. Slowly they made their way southward, from Richmond to Petersburg to Lynchburg, ignoring, without incident, the signs reading "White" or "Colored" over lunch counters and toilets. At some stops, local blacks told them that such signs had just been removed.

Arriving in Charlotte on May 8, Charles Perkins strolled into the Union bus-station barbershop, reserved for whites only, and climbed into a shoeshine chair. When refused service, he remained seated. Minutes later he was arrested for his "shoe-in." On the basis of the *Boynton* decision, Perkins won an acquittal on May 10. The day before, however, violence erupted for the first time. At the Greyhound station in Rock Hill, South Carolina, John Lewis started to enter a white waiting room. Already a veteran of five arrests for his sit-in activities, the twenty-one-year-old had volunteered for the Freedom Ride because, "at this time, human dignity is the most important thing in my life." He had decided "to give up all if necessary for the Freedom Ride," Lewis wrote on his application, "that Justice and Freedom might come to the Deep South." As Lewis approached, recalled Farmer, "several young white hoodlums, leather jackets, ducktail haircuts, standing there smoking . . . blocked the door and said, 'Nigger, you can't come in here.' He said, 'I have every right to enter this waiting room according to the Supreme Court of the United States in the Boynton case.' They said, 'Shit on that.' He tried to walk past, and they clubbed him, beat him, and knocked him down."

Several then began slugging Albert Bigelow, a former naval commander who turned pacifist out of revulsion over his World War II experiences. Not until one of the women with them had been pushed to the ground did the police intervene. They did not make any arrests, but allowed all the riders to enter the white waiting room unmolested. In Winnsboro, thirty-seven miles to the south, however, police arrested Peck and Henry Thomas, a black student, for attempting to eat at a white luncheonette. Without incident, the Freedom Riders then tested facilities in Sumter, Camden, Augusta, and Athens, before arriving in Atlanta on May 13 to regroup for the dangerous journey into Alabama and Mississippi.

Mother's Day, May 14, the Freedom Riders curved along U.S. 78 into the heart of the Black Belt. When the Greyhound bus arrived in Anniston, Alabama, an angry mob surrounded it. Armed with blackjacks, iron bars, clubs, and tire chains, they smashed windows and slashed tires. Only the arrival of the police made it possible for the bus to escape. The mob pursued in cars. Six miles out of town, the bus tires went flat. The mob again beat on the bus, denting its sides. An incendiary bomb sailed through a broken window. "Sparks flew and a dense cloud of smoke immediately filled the bus," CORE field secretary Genevive Hughes remembered. "The smoke became denser and denser, becoming completely black. I crouched and figured I was going to be asphyxiated." Some passengers tried to get out the door, but the mob held it shut from the outside. "Hey, the bus is gonna explode," somebody yelled, and the door opened. While the mob beat the exiting riders, the bus burst into flames, slowly turning into a charred metal skeleton. Local hospital personnel refused to treat the Freedom Riders cut by flying glass or overcome by smoke inhalation, and only an armed caravan of cars from Birmingham, led by the Reverend Fred Shuttlesworth, succeeded in extricating the wounded.

An hour later, the Trailways bus pulled into Anniston. Eight whites jumped aboard and demanded that the black students move to the formerly segregated rear section. They refused. The whites forced them back with punches and kicks. Peck and Walter Bergman, a sixty-one-year-old retired professor, tried to persuade the whites to desist. The hoodlums set upon them, pummeling them to the floor. A blow on the head left Bergman close to death and permanently brain-damaged. The violence had only begun.

When the Trailways bus parked at its terminal in Birmingham, a mob of about forty whites lined the loading platform. The police had been warned to expect trouble, yet not a single law officer was in sight. Police Commissioner T. Eugene "Bull" Connor had promised the KKK fifteen unmolested minutes to attack the riders, whom he wanted beaten until "it looked like a bulldog got ahold of them." According to an eyewitness account by a CBS reporter, the white "toughs," who had been waiting all day, "grabbed the passengers into alleys and corridors, pounding them with pipes, with key rings and with fists." Peck, knocked unconscious, required fifty-three stitches. Still, the Freedom Riders wanted to continue. They decided to travel as a single contingent on the next lap, from Birmingham to Montgomery. But no bus would accept them. Asserting that he could not protect "this bunch of rabble-rousers," Alabama Governor John Patterson advised the CORE contingent to "get out of Alabama as quickly as possible." Stranded, frightened, the Freedom Riders reluctantly boarded a special flight to New Orleans arranged by the Justice Department. On May 17, the CORE-sponsored Freedom Ride disbanded.

Telephoning Shuttlesworth in Birmingham, Diane Nash informed the minister: "The students have decided that we can't let violence overcome." SNCC would continue what CORE began: "The ride must not be stopped. If they stop us with violence, the movement is dead." Tersely adding, "We're coming," Nash hurriedly recruited a handful of sit-in veterans in Nashville for the trip to Birmingham. A new phase of the Freedom Ride began.

On the outskirts of Birmingham, police met the bus carrying the SNCC volunteers and escorted it to the terminal, where eight black and two white Freedom Riders were arrested and put in "protective custody." The students went on a hunger strike. Around midnight the next day, Police Commissioner Connor drove the students, against their wishes, some 150 miles to the Tennessee–Alabama line. There they managed to call Diane Nash for a car to take them right back to Birmingham, and directly to the Greyhound bus station. But no driver would make the trip to Montgomery with the Freedom Riders. The students just sat on the bus-station benches and waited, singing freedom songs. Eighteen hours later, now augmented by fresh volunteers from Atlanta and Nashville, twenty-one Freedom Riders boarded a Greyhound for Montgomery early on the morning of May 20.

The two-hour ride went without incident. "There were police cars all round the bus, and helicopters flying over head," recalled a young black woman from Atlanta. "But when we got inside the Montgomery city limits, it all disappeared. . . . There was not one policeman around." The "moment that we arrived in that station, it was the strangest feeling to me," John Lewis remembered. "It was really weird. It was an eerie feeling. There was a funny peace there, a quietness. . . . Complete silence. There were no cabs around that you could see. You couldn't see any other buses. Not anything. We stepped off the bus and . . . people just started pouring out of the station, out of buildings, from all over the place. White people. . . ." At that very moment, John Doar, second in command to Burke Marshall in the Civil Rights Division of the Justice Department, put through a call to the Attorney General from his post across the street from the terminal. "The passengers are coming off," Doar reported. "A bunch of men led by a guy with a bleeding face are beating them. There are no cops. It's terrible. It's terrible. There's not a cop in sight. People are yelling, 'Get 'em, get 'em.' It's awful."

"Get those niggers," a woman cheered the mob of nearly three hundred venting its fury on students and newsmen with lead pipes and baseball bats. They clubbed John Lewis to the ground and smashed his head with a wooden soda crate, leaving him with a brain concussion. While lying in a pool of blood, Lewis was handed a state-court injunction forbidding integrated travel in Alabama.

Another group of whites grabbed James Zwerg, a white exchange student from the University of Wisconsin attending Fisk University. They stomped him into the hot tar of the pavement and smashed him in the face with his suitcase. While one of the mob pinned Zwerg's dazed head between his knees, the others took turns at socking the white Freedom Rider and kicking out his teeth. As some white adults held children on their shoulders to view the beating, others chanted, "Kill the nigger-loving son of a bitch."

Not a single policeman had arrived yet, and the swarming crowd grew to over one thousand. White ruffians broke one black boy's leg. They poured inflammable liquid on another and set his clothes afire. They slapped and chased the two white women Riders, who begged a motorist for help. "You deserve what you get," he replied. "I hope they beat you up good." "Come on, I'll help you," another driver offered, "I'm a federal man." As John Siegenthaler, the President's emissary to the Governor of Alabama, tried to get the women in his car, several whites slugged him from behind, knocking him unconscious. While people milled around, he lay on the sidewalk for nearly twenty-five minutes before the police finally drove him to a hospital. They left Jim Zwerg bleeding and in a state of shock, his spinal cord injured, for over two hours before getting him medical attention. Montgomery's Police Commissioner stated: "We have no intention of standing guard for a bunch of troublemakers coming into our city." That night a badly mauled Zwerg spoke to a television reporter from his hospital bed: "We will take hitting. We'll take beatings. We're willing to accept death. But we are going to keep coming until we can ride anywhere in the South to anyplace else in the South, as Americans, without anyone making any comment."

The mob violence and callous indifference of Alabama officials combined to make the Freedom Ride page-one news throughout the world. Banner headlines and photographs of the burning and bloodshed played up the white South's brutality and crude defiance of the law. The Communist press harped on the theme that rampant racism "exposed" the "savage nature of American freedom and democracy." Editorials in Africa and Asia stressed that the federal government's compromising with racial discrimination would make it impossible for the United States "to sell to the outside world, especially the non-white world, that she stands for equality of all men." Non-Communist European papers deplored America's racial prejudice for encouraging anti-colonial and anti-Western feeling. And almost without exception, the American news media expressed its horror and disgust at the violence against the Freedom Riders.

Even the Alabama Associated Press Association condemned "the breakdown of civilized rule" in that state.

The Kennedy Administration belatedly decided that the time had come when it must act. Private phone calls to Alabama authorities to secure safe passage for the Freedom Riders would no longer suffice. The President and Attorney General Robert Kennedy considered the international prestige of the Administration to be threatened. They could no longer tolerate either the deliberate failure of local authority to preserve civil peace or the open defiance of federal law. Yet they still sought to walk the tightrope between, as the Kennedys viewed them, the unreasonable militants on both sides. They believed Jim Crow to be wrong. They hoped to better the life of African-Americans—but slowly, and at the proper time. They thought demands for freedom *now* to be just as irresponsible as calls for segregation forever. In 1961, the Kennedys saw the struggle against racism as a conundrum to be managed, not a cause to be championed.

"Tell them to call it off. Stop them!" had been the President's initial response to the Freedom Ride. The fervor of the young blacks clashed with his own calculating approach to political problems. He prided himself on being pragmatic, tough-minded. Idealists and romantics annoyed him. Quixotic crusades interfered with his careful plans and cautious timetables. Only in the battle against Communism did he think the United States should "pay any price, bear any burden, meet any hardship, support any friend, oppose any foe." The President's education, moreover, reinforced his lack of passion and cool detachment regarding civil rights. Like most in his generation, he had been taught that radical Reconstruction was a mistake, that the solution to the race problem required moderation, not coercion. He believed in using the absolute minimal amount of force in this sensitive matter. "I don't think we would ever come to the point of sending troops," Kennedy confided to an aide just a month before the Freedom Ride began.

Politics also strengthened that resolve. Kennedy's victory in the 1960 election, won with a plurality of scarcely 100,000 votes out of some 69 million cast, made him particularly solicitous of the white South's ballots. Nixon had received a majority of its vote and Kennedy did not want that to happen again in 1964. The Democratic margin in both House and Senate, moreover, had been cut in the 1960 elections, forcing the President to curry favor with the Southern Democrats. He needed their votes for his legislative program. Therefore, Kennedy refused to aid the liberals in their effort to eliminate the filibuster; he appointed segregationists to lifetime federal judgeships in the South; he delayed issuing his promised Executive Order to end racial discrimination in federally assisted housing for nearly two years (despite an "Ink for Jack" drive that swamped the White House with thousands of fountain pens); and he remained aloof from the bills introduced to carry out the Democratic Party's 1960 campaign pledge on black rights. The President, said his press secretary, "does not think it is necessary at this time to enact civil rights legislation." Perhaps most important, Kennedy feared that the race issue would "divide the American people at a time when the international scene required maximum unity." Foreign affairs was his primary concern and he shunned potentially divisive domestic matters. Preparing to meet with Khrushchev early in June, the President considered the Freedom Riders an unnecessary burden. But the savagery of Alabama whites forced him to act.

On May 20, President Kennedy called on Alabama officials to "meet their responsibilities," stated that the United States "intends to meet its," requested that Alabama citizens and visitors alike refrain "from any action which would in any way tend to provoke further outbreaks," and ordered the Attorney General "to take all necessary steps." Robert Kennedy then announced that the Justice Department would seek to enjoin the KKK and National States Rights Party from interfering with peaceful interstate travel, and that a contingent of U.S. marshals under the command of Deputy Attorney General Byron White would be sent to Montgomery "to assist state and local authorities in the protection of persons and property and vehicles." Governor Patterson protested the moves as unconstitutional and unnecessary.

While the Kennedys acted, Martin Luther King rushed to Montgomery to urge on the stalled Freedom Ride. After conferring with representatives of CORE and SNCC, King announced a mass rally for May 21, sponsored by the Montgomery Improvement Association. A crowd of over twelve hundred crowded into Ralph Abernathy's First Baptist Church, more than twice its capacity. In a park across the street, an even larger mob of whites gathered, bent on trouble. Without any police to stop them, they began beating up blacks standing in front of the church. Some whites charged into the church to fight. Others threw stones and bottles. Firebombs and stench bombs hurtled through the windows. African-Americans in the church sang the old hymn of refuge "Love Lifted Me" to maintain their courage, but the smoke and the heat and the fright caused some to panic. Suddenly, recalled James Farmer, "the marshals materialized. . . . It seemed almost fictional . . . the marshals confronting the mob." Armed with nightsticks and tear-gas cannisters, their pistols hidden, the marshals formed a skirmish line to protect the church. They barely could. Then the governor declared "qualified martial rule," and ordered the National Guard and state troopers to reinforce the marshals. While they dispersed the mob, the troops ordered those inside the church to stay put and not attempt to leave until the next morning.

Undaunted, King, Farmer, and the Nashville student leaders announced the next day that the Freedom Ride would be resumed despite the continued threats of violence. CORE, SCLC, and SNCC established a Freedom Ride Coordinating Committee and rejected Attorney General Kennedy's call for a temporary cessation of the Rides to provide a "cooling-off period." "We had been cooling off for a hundred years," Farmer announced. "If we got any cooler we'd be in a deep freeze." Another activist added: "Had there not been a cooling-off period following the Civil War, the Negro would be free today. Isn't ninety-nine years long enough to cool off, Mr. Attorney General?" When Robert Kennedy said that racial turmoil would embarrass the President in his meeting with Khrushchev, Abernathy retorted: "Doesn't the Attorney General know that we've been embarrassed all our lives?" Even NAACP head Roy Wilkins urged black college students returning home at the end of the school year to "sit where you choose on a nonsegregated transportation basis" and to use terminal facilities "without discrimination." Additional volunteers for the Ride, meanwhile, arrived in Montgomery from Atlanta, New York, New Orleans, and Washington, D.C.

Escorted to the Trailways bus station by National Guardsmen on May 24, a bruised and bandaged corps of twenty-seven readied for the Freedom Ride to Jackson, Mississippi, and more danger. They all ate in the "white" dining room and then departed in two heavily guarded buses. Three airplanes and two helicopters flew reconnaissance overhead while motorized National Guard units scouted the road ahead and patrol cars escorted the shiny red-and-white buses. As they passed the sign "Welcome to the Magnolia State," Mississippi troopers and guardsmen took over the task of safely conveying the Riders to Jackson. To keep up their morale, the two whites and twenty-six blacks aboard sang with forced gaiety:

> Hallelujah, I'm traveling
> Hallelujah, ain't it fine,
> Hallelujah, I'm traveling
> Down Freedom's main line.

All the students wrote the names and addresses of their next of kin on notes which they shoved in their pockets or bosoms. "Everyone on the bus," said a Rider, "was prepared to die."

Determined that there be no violence, the Kennedys made a deal with Mississippi Senator James Eastland. In exchange for there being no mob violence in Jackson, the federal government would not contest the arrests of the Freedom Riders. Mississippi would be allowed to uphold segregation by making arrests as long as it prevented mobs from maintaining Jim Crow by violence. When the two buses reached the terminal in Jackson, police, state troopers, and National Guardsmen appeared everywhere and not a single group of white bullies could be seen. All twenty-seven Riders were quickly arrested when they tried to enter the "white" cafeteria and rest rooms, and they were found guilty, fined, and given two-month suspended sentences.

Farmer now announced that all would go to jail rather than pay the fine, and he urged other volunteers to keep violating Jackson's unconstitutional segregation ordinance until they filled the jails to overflowing. By the end of the summer, over a thousand persons had participated in Freedom Rides. Most were young African-Americans, and they soon extended the movement to segregated railroad and airport facilities. By creating a crisis, the Riders forced the federal government to act. The Attorney General petitioned the Interstate Commerce Commission to issue rules prohibiting racial discrimination in interstate facilities, a move supported by the Secretary of State as vital to our conduct of foreign affairs. On September 22, the ICC announced that interstate carriers and terminals must display signs stating that seating "is without regard to race, color, creed or national origin," effective November 1. The ICC also banned interstate carriers from using any terminal which practiced segregation. Although some towns in the Deep South initially evaded the order, CORE proclaimed at the end of 1962 that the battle of interstate travel had been finally won.

Beyond the removal of "White" and "Colored" signs in the terminals of the South, the Freedom Rides resulted in a complex combination of gains and losses for the civil-rights movement. They demonstrated that victory in the Deep South was possible; yet they intensified the fervor of white resistance. In 1960, Mississippi had been the only Southern state where there had been no sit-ins and Alabama had effectively used its state powers to wreck the student protests. Federal orders required both to begin integration in 1961. That outcome, and the method of its achievement, gave new strength to the KKK and similar groups and new life at the polls to the most hard-core segregationists. Rabble-rousers like Alabama's George Wallace, profiting from the politics of confrontation,

came to the fore. The Rides also underlined the benefits and dangers
of federalism, the involvement of the Executive Branch, and the
creation of crisis situations. When the Freedom Riders aroused a
torrent of public sympathy, as they did after Birmingham and Montgomery, the federal government acted to protect them and to end
the violation of federal law. But when, as in Jackson and other
cities where the Riders met little or no violence, Southern officials
engaged in peaceful defiance of the federal courts, the Kennedy
Administration condoned the mass arrests of American citizens for
attempting to implement a constitutional right clearly promulgated
by the United States Supreme Court. Such behavior reinforced the
urge of movement leaders to court white violence in the South to
trigger the Administration into enforcing federal law. It also spurred
segregationist officials to hamstring demonstrators in protracted
legal battles and to prevent violence, and thus forestall federal action. The reluctance with which the Kennedys entered the fray,
moreover, made them eager to influence, even manipulate, movement strategy. They did not want to have to fight again at a time
and on a battlefield not of their choosing.

The Freedom Rides also rejuvenated the black-rights struggle
while they tarnished its image. CORE quickly grew in membership,
income, staff personnel, and stature, challenging King, the NAACP,
and SNCC to press ever more vigorously for racial change and to
engage in ever more provocative direct action. Rivalry, often bitter,
among the civil-rights groups intensified as they each sought the
financial support of a finite number of Northern white liberals.
James Farmer recalled the "competition for the same headlines,
same news stories, and for the same buck. That was the big thing:
the same buck. And that meant competition for a number of bloodied heads to be shown on the same front pages of the same newspapers. Because that produces money." The increasingly audacious
form of the protests, in turn, highlighted the role of young African-
Americans in the movement, and induced yet more black youth to
generate the "creative tension" that might provoke the white violence necessary to force the intervention of the reluctant Kennedys.

To a far larger extent than any previous protest, the Freedom Rides also enlisted whites and non-Southerners in direct action. The Rides exposed to the nation the crudity of Southern racism. They revealed the ugly face of brutal mobs and the official connivance with violence. That appalled most whites. But their indignation did not last long. The absence of tumult was what they really cared about. Although a majority of whites approved of ending segregation in interstate travel, over two-thirds of those questioned in public-opinion polls disapproved of the Freedom Rides on the grounds that they "were causing too much trouble." In the South, particularly, the role of "outsiders" in the Rides revitalized the hoary myth of "uppity Northern niggers" and radical white agitators being responsible for the black demand for equal rights. In contrast to the images of long-suffering Montgomery bus boycotters and idealistic sit-in students, many news reporters described the Freedom Riders as aggressive, unkempt nuisances "invading" the South and provoking violence.

Finally, the impact of jail, the physical and psychological brutality encountered by the Riders, both enhanced and corroded the spirit of the black struggle. Even those who had been briefly imprisoned during the sit-ins were shocked by what they had to endure in the maximum-security wing of Mississippi's Parchman Penitentiary: the repetitious rounds of questioning and beatings, the pain of battery-operated cattle prods, the terror of wrist-breakers, and the sounds of friends groaning and crying; the back-breaking work in the fields from sunup to sundown, the execrable food, and the filthy cots in bug-infested cells; the capricious denial of cigarettes, reading materials, and showers; and the dreaded time in the sweatbox or solitary confinement for refusing to play Uncle Tom to the guards. Jail broke some. It strengthened others. Some became demoralized and dropped out. Others deepened their commitment and left jail to become full-time movement personnel. They went to work for SNCC, SCLC, and CORE changed men and women. Most had lost their faith in the ability to alter white attitudes and feelings. Most

no longer believed that the South could be converted or even shamed
into responsibility.

The themes of reconciliation and the beloved community
preached by Martin Luther King, Jr., had little relevance to many
who had suffered in the jails of Mississippi. They believed that
power alone counted, that only power could induce change. The
Freedom Rides had proved to them that Jim Crow's demise depended on the enforcement powers of the federal government. Accordingly, they searched for the lever that would move the Kennedy
Administration into a firm alliance with the proponents of racial
equality. Their protracted discussions while in jail often centered
on just what tactics and strategy could make the federal government
an unequivocal ally of the black struggle.

With the desegregation of interstate travel facilities accomplished,
moreover, all the major protest leaders agreed that the time had
come to set new priorities. They had to decide where the energies
released by the sit-ins and Freedom Rides could now be utilized,
where the new troops enlisted in the movement, especially the students choosing to become full-time civil-rights workers rather than
return to school in the fall, could best be deployed. The Southern
Regional Council (SRC) for several years had been urging a voter-
registration campaign in the South. Some of the liberal foundations
which funded the SRC had also been concerned about encouraging
black voting. Shortly after the Freedom Rides began, the Justice
Department informally communicated to the SRC its interest in
helping the civil-rights movement attack black disenfranchisement.
On the day after the bus burning at Anniston, Robert Kennedy
made the same point to Roy Wilkins. Later in the month, the Attorney General lobbied Martin Luther King, Jr., on the matter.

On June 16, Robert Kennedy met with representatives of CORE,
SCLC, SNCC, and the National Student Association. He and his
aides argued that the vote held the key to change in the South and
that registering blacks would be far more fruitful than further demonstrations. The Justice officials dangled the financial support of

the Field and Taconic Foundations and the Stern Family Fund before the financially-pressed movement personnel. They also implied protection for the voter applicants and civil-rights workers against the anticipated reprisals by Southern whites. Timothy Jenkins of Howard University, a vice-president of the NSA, recalled the principal assistant to the President on racial affairs assuring those at the meeting "that if necessary in the course of protecting people's rights to vote, that the Kennedy Administration would fill every jail in the South." Martin Luther King left the meeting believing that they had been guaranteed "all steps necessary to protect those rights in danger."

During the June 1961 meeting of SNCC, Jenkins, caustically critical of the "pain and suffering school" within the organization, proposed that the students shift their emphasis from demonstrations to voter registration. It precipitated bitter wrangling, splitting the group. Marion Barry and Diane Nash led the faction insisting that nonviolent direct action continue to be SNCC's primary strategy. They looked forward to larger and more sensational confrontations to desegregate public facilities, to gain equal employment opportunities for blacks, and to maintain the momentum generated by the sit-ins and Freedom Rides. They feared that an interminable registration effort, resulting neither in major new gains nor in dramatic news coverage, would diminish support for the movement and let the "white establishment off the hook." Furthermore, the fact that the plan emanated from the White House heightened the students' suspicions. James Forman, SNCC's executive secretary, saw it as a clever ploy by the Administration to use "the energies of black students to help line up Southern black voters for the Democratic party." Diane Nash feared that the financial support offered would put the Kennedys "in control of the Southern black movement." Most agreed with the hulking Lawrence Guyot that the scheme was "to stop public demonstrations"—to "get the niggers off the streets." Robert Kennedy had already called on civil-rights leaders for a "cooling-off period," and this suggestion to divert the militancy of the movement smacked of another way to accomplish that. They no longer would defer the black dream of freedom to the President's desire for orderly change and civic peace.

Another faction acknowledged the political benefits to Kennedy but insisted that the struggle for racial equality would profit the most from enfranchising African-Americans. Led by the "three Charlies"—Jones, McDew, and Sherrod—these students saw the vote as the lever for liberation. They considered black political strength in the South a prerequisite for the mass of blacks to exercise the rights granted them and for the liberalization of Congress, a step vital to the passage of social and economic legislation necessary for black advancement. Why not take the money and federal protection offered, they argued, and develop the power of blacks to correct injustice themselves, to destroy racist institutions, to control their own destinies. To their mind, voter registration would be less cathartic than direct action, but ultimately far more constructive. At the least, the "three Charlies" indicated, a sizable increase in African-American voters in the South might lead to an alliance between the federal government and the movement.

The debate within SNCC seethed throughout the summer of 1961, and came to a head at the August staff meeting. Neither faction would back down. Both angrily voiced proposals to disband SNCC and to resign. Indeed, some, like Lonnie King of Atlanta, did quit because of disgust at the Administration's manipulation of the movement. Then James Forman broke the impasse. Elected by the students to assume the post of SNCC's executive director, the thirty-three-year-old former Chicago schoolteacher had the respect of both sides. All viewed him as a thoughtful man of uncompromising militancy and total commitment to SNCC. Forman insisted that the effort to encourage people in the Black Belt to set aside their fears would inevitably interlock voter registration and direct action. To persuade blacks to register and face oppressive white power would indeed be direct action. He described registration work "as a tool by which consciousness might be aroused, politicized, and organized." Forman also predicted that SNCC's activities would bring white retaliation, and the resulting violence "would create more exposure and thereby more consciousness." To appease those inconsolably committed to boycotts and demonstrations, SNCC formally adopted Ella Baker's suggestion of two divisions within the organization: Direct Action Projects led by Diane Nash, and Voter Registration headed by Charles Jones.

CORE followed suit. The same debate had split its ranks. But at its September convention, CORE accepted Farmer's contention that direct action and voter registration were "not mutually exclusive" and approved a registration campaign in the Deep South. CORE and SNCC joined with the NAACP, SCLC, and the Urban League in a new Voter Education Project (VEP). Funded at $870,000 by the Stern Family Fund and the Taconic and Field Foundations, and scheduled to last two and a half years, the SRC-administered VEP formally began work in April 1962.

Bob Moses and SNCC, characteristically, initiated a voter registration project in rural Mississippi prior to any official resolution. Moses, soft-spoken and bespectacled, had majored in philosophy at Hamilton College and continued to study the pacifism of the Quakers, the Existentialism of Camus, and the spiritual mysticism of Zen Buddhism. In July 1960 he set out for Mississippi, and there met Aimzie Moore, a tough World War II veteran who ran a gasoline station and headed the local NAACP. Moore convinced Moses to concentrate his energies on Mississippi and to translate Ella Baker's ideas into a campaign to register disfranchised African-Americans. A year later, the intense Moses arrived in McComb, a city of thirteen thousand in southwest Mississippi, where in 1960 fewer than two hundred African-Americans were registered to vote out of an adult black population of more than eight thousand. In two adjoining counties, Walthall did not have a single one of its twenty-five hundred blacks of voting age registered, and Amite claimed one—but as Charles McDew commented: "We haven't been able to find him." Moses, with the help of local high-school students and the backing of C. C. Bryant, the local NAACP head, began canvassing, going door-to-door to convince McComb blacks that SNCC would totally back their attempts to register. After a week, John Hardy of the Nashville student movement and Reggie Robinson of Baltimore arrived in McComb to assist Moses. And then other SNCC activists, who now referred to themselves as field secretaries, such as Marion Barry and Bob Zellner, a white Southerner, left Parchman Penitentiary and drifted into McComb.

What happened in the next two months in these Delta counties set the pattern for voter-registration efforts in the rural South throughout 1962 and 1963. On August 7, a SNCC Voter Registration School opened in Pike County, the first in the history of Mississippi. Moses patiently explained the complexities of registering to vote in the Magnolia State; he struggled to inspire courage and build morale. A dozen or so blacks attempted to qualify to vote in the first few days. On August 10, one of the blacks who had tried to register was shot at by a white. Attendance at the Voter Registration School plummeted. Moses had to rebuild. Five days later he accompanied three blacks from Amite to register at the county seat, Liberty. None qualified.

On the drive back to McComb, a highway patrolman flagged the blacks over to the side of the road. Referring to Moses as the "nigger who's come to tell the niggers how to register," the patrolman arrested the SNCC organizer on a charge of impeding an officer in the discharge of his duties. Two weeks after that, Moses again drove several blacks to the registrar's office in Liberty. Billy Jack Caston, cousin of the sheriff and son-in-law of State Representative Eugene Hurst, met them at the door and smashed Moses across the head, opening a wound that required eight stitches to close. Undaunted, Moses filed assault-and-battery charges against Caston—the first time in Amite's history, and probably Mississippi's, that a black man legally contested the freedom of a white to beat him at will. During the farce of a trial, however, the sheriff informed Moses that he better leave the county before the "not guilty" verdict if he wanted to escape mass assault.

That same week, in McComb, Marion Barry formed the students too young to vote into the Pike County Non-Violent Movement for a direct action campaign. On August 26, two of the youths sat-in at the lunch counter of the local Woolworth's—another first in the history of the county. They were arrested and sentenced to thirty days in jail. Nearly two hundred McComb blacks then attended a protest meeting, and on August 30 a sixteen-year-old girl and five other high-school students sat-in at the lunch counter of the local bus station. For their "breach of peace" the students were expelled from school; the young men also were given eight-month jail sentences, and the young woman a term of one year in a state institution for delinquents.

The fear of Delta blacks began to turn to terror on September 5. As Moses and Travis Britt, a student from New York City, started toward the registrar's office in Liberty with four blacks, a clerk ordered them outside, where a belligerent group of whites awaited them. The white men accosted the "niggers from New York" for daring that they "could come down here and teach people how to register to vote." They then beat and kicked Britt into semiconsciousness, and threatened to kill the blacks if they did not immediately "get the hell out of town."

Two days later, John Hardy, who had set up the first voters' school in Walthall County, accompanied some black residents to register in Tylerstown. John Q. Wood, the registrar, would not let them apply. When Hardy heard this, he walked into Wood's office to introduce himself. He never had the opportunity. Wood instantly pulled a gun out of his desk and ordered Hardy to leave. As the Nashville student started to walk out, Wood smashed him on the back of the head. His head bleeding profusely, Hardy staggered out of the courthouse. He went to the county sheriff to report what had happened. The sheriff arrested Hardy for inciting to riot and breach of the peace, and he threatened to beat Hardy within an inch of his life if he dared complain. In due time, the Justice Department intervened on Hardy's behalf. But it would take until April 1963 before the county dropped the charges against the SNCC organizer. Long before that, the damage had been done.

The accumulating incidents, recalled Robert Moses, "just about cleaned us out. The farmers in both those counties were no longer willing to go down. . . . There wasn't much we could do." To make matters worse, four men fishing in the Big Black River on September 13 discovered the remains of an unidentified black man whose body had been stuffed into a cloth sack and weighted down with rocks. Then, said Moses, "the boom lowered on September 25; Herbert Lee, a Negro farmer, was killed in Amite County." Lee, an NAACP member, had been actively assisting Moses. On that fateful morning, Lee's truck had been tailgated by Mississippi State Representative Eugene Hurst as he drove into Liberty to gin his cotton. When Lee stopped his truck, Hurst approached him with his gun drawn. They argued. Suddenly Lee was dead, a .38 bullet in his brain. "This was the story that three Negro witnesses told us on three separate nights as we went out, in Amite County," said Moses, "tracking them down, knocking on doors, waking them up in the middle of the night." On the afternoon of Lee's death, however, a coroner's jury ruled that Hurst killed in self-defense. The local symbol of white political power was never booked, charged, or tried, but one of the Negro witnesses, two years later, was killed by a shotgun blast. To complete the reign of terror, McComb police arrested over a hundred high-school students and a dozen SNCC activists on October 4, when they sought to march through town to protest the slaying of Lee and the expulsion of their classmates. At the sentencing of Moses and his colleagues, a judge warned the black townsfolk: "Those of you who are local residents are like sheep being led to the slaughter. If you continue to follow the advice of outside agitators you will be like sheep and be slaughtered."

Through it all, and with worse to come, SNCC refused to be run out of Mississippi. Despite the stark terror of living unprotected in a completely hostile environment, the young activists endured, and gradually built a movement by recruiting young Mississippi blacks such as Hollis Watkins and Curtis Hayes, June Johnson, and Dorrie and Joyce Ladner. They kept canvassing, holding literacy and citizenship clinics, and accompanying applicants to the courthouse, never knowing when they might be jailed, whipped, killed; they always suspected that the hatred they encountered would explode into savagery. The volunteers had to suffer excessive pain and anguish for their belief in, and hope for, American democracy. Threatening phone calls plagued them. Vicious beatings became commonplace. Night riders ransacked their homes and offices, riddled them with bullets, set them ablaze. Truckloads of whites holding loaded shotguns and pistols tailgated their cars. Patrolmen apprehended them for every imaginable offense. To survive, SNCC's cadre learned to live with unrelenting tension. "It was always there," wrote Cleveland Sellers, "always stretched like a tight steel wire between the pit of the stomach and the center of the brain."

The brave young SNCC workers, such as the white Jack Chatfield and Bob Zellner, and the African-American Willie Peacock and Charles Jones, subsisted in the face of abuse and death but could not remain unscathed. The anxiety that never slackened took its toll. "The whole uncertainty of the thing" left its scars, said one volunteer. "You would be taking someone down to register, and you would simply be trailed by two cars of whites. Maybe they would do nothing, but you would never know. Maybe they would get out and whip you. Maybe they wouldn't." SNCC's Sellers listed some of the consequences of such strain: ulcers, migraine headaches, constipation, nervous twitches. Packs of cigarettes and vials of Miltowns were consumed daily to counter the physical and emotional strains. A volunteer in the Delta campaign recalled the nightmare of always "wondering whether someone was going to sneak in and dynamite you or fire-bomb your home. Always checking your car before you got in it, because you were worrying about whether someone stuck a piece of dynamite under it. Always making sure your tires were in good condition, because you never know, you may have to race up the road at night." The grinding, omnipresent dread changed SNCC, further eroding its faith in nonviolence, in the decency of the federal government, in the American dream.

But SNCC barely changed the political landscape in Mississippi or anywhere else in the rural Deep South, at first. The Voter Education Project recorded 688,800 blacks qualifying to vote for the first time in the South between April 1, 1962 and November 1,

1964, a jump from 26.8 to 38 percent of the potential black registrants. Almost all the increase, however, came from the urban and upper South. In Mississippi, the proportion of black voters rose from 5.3 percent to just 6.7 percent. Indeed, the VEP, having spent more money in Mississippi with fewer results than in any other state, decided in 1963 to pour no further funds into the Delta campaign. Without the promised federal assistance, the movement had been stymied by dilatory registrars, economic intimidation, and a calculated reign of jailings and violence.

Intransigent registration officials mastered tactics of harassment and delay. To suit their purposes, they changed registration dates and procedures at will; they administered literacy and understanding tests arbitrarily; they forced blacks to wait interminably, to return time and time again. Not uncommonly, the office walls of registrars sported Confederate flags and signs proclaiming "Support Your Citizens' Council." Those blacks not yet discouraged by the foregoing had to face the derision of whites gathered near the courthouse and the hostile stares of sheriffs and deputies, ominously taking their pictures or noting their names. "Who do you work for?" was frequently the first question an angry registrar asked a black attempting to enroll, underlining the price to be paid for daring to exercise this right of citizenship. Blacks who worked for whites and tried to register lost their jobs. Landowners evicted tenants from their plantations. Black farmers found banks refusing to extend them credit, merchants refusing to sell them supplies, ginners refusing to process their cotton, and grain-elevator operators refusing to store their grain. Still other blacks who sought to vote were removed from the welfare rolls and denied the federal surplus commodities due them. Indeed, in Greenwood, Mississippi, the effort of a few to respond to SNCC's exhortations to register led county officials to discontinue the distribution of surplus food to twenty thousand blacks.

To underscore the threat, local officers perverted the law to shackle black activists and voter applicants. They peremptorily arrested civil-rights workers for traffic violations, trespassing, vagrancy, and whatever else they could conjure. The fact that few convictions were ultimately upheld did not matter, wrote one lawyer, since the "primary effort is to use arrests and threats of arrests, costly bail, to hamstring voter registration." Such harassment forced CORE out of Monroe, Louisiana, and doomed its most concerted voter-registration campaign in Plaquemine in Iberville Parish. It had the same effect when used against local residents. In nearby Clinton, police arrested twelve blacks, who wrote a letter to the mayor respectfully requesting the establishment of a biracial committee, on charges of intimidating a public official. Just outside Greenwood, fifty-eight blacks who left a meeting in a church into which smoke bombs had been tossed and marched to the Itta Bena sheriff's house to ask for police protection for voter registration were all arrested, tried, convicted, and sent to prison on charges of disturbing the peace. Farther to the north, a Clarksdale black who had the temerity to wear a CORE "Freedom Now" T-shirt was arrested for parading without a permit. In Americus, Georgia, following the arrest of three hundred blacks demonstrating for voter registration, three SNCC and one CORE volunteer were charged with attempting to incite insurrection, a crime which carried the death penalty.

Violence by both law-enforcement officers and white terrorists capped the effort to stifle black enfranchisement. An SCLC worker in Alabama testified to being arrested for canvassing for voter registration. After the worker was kicked and beaten, the local police chief "got out a brand new [electric cattle] prod and applied it to me several times, but I took it. I began to get weaker and dizzy, but I tried to take it. Then when he put it to my genitals, I said to him, 'What about your God?' He stopped, but he threatened to put the Klan on me. . . . For about two days I was in a daze as a result of the prod treatment given me by the police chief." Arrested in Winona, Mississippi, fifteen-year-old June Johnson of SNCC later recalled: "I had on a beautiful pink dress and a black scarf around my head. Then the next thing I knew, I didn't have anything on. They had torn my clothes off. And they just started beating me. With billy sticks, fists, kicking me, stomping me on the floor." Then they did the same to Fannie Lou Hamer and to Annelle Ponder of SCLC. When SNCC's Lawrence Guyot came to Winona to check on the prisoners, the sheriff "said 'I got 'em. What you gon' do about it?' I said, 'All I want to do is find out what the charges are so we can raise the money to get them out. . . .' He said, 'You get the fuck out of here.' " Guyot walked to his car and the sheriff followed. " 'Nigger, what you causing all these problems?' and hit me in the mouth. . . . And then he just beat on me till he got me in the jail and just kept beating on me. One guy was a prizefighter, and he just stood me up to the wall and just beat on me, and then they used guns." Nine policemen worked him over, forced him to take all his clothes off and threatened to burn his genitals and pierce them with a sharp stick. After some four hours, "they called in a doctor and they said, 'Well, can he take any more?' And he said, 'Well, I'm not going to be responsible if you do.' " They charged Guyot with attempted murder.

With the connivance of those entrusted to uphold the law, white toughs wrecked a voter-registration campaign in a town midway between Greenwood and Jackson. They firebombed and dynamited several cars and homes, threatened the life of a black minister, set afire a new community center, and beat up the voting-rights volunteers working in the town. In Greenwood, while the police broke up peaceful marches to the courthouse and unleashed snarling dogs on black demonstrators, local whites blasted their shotguns at SNCC cars and offices and put them to the torch. This violence against the effort to enfranchise blacks, largely unnoticed by the nation and unhindered by the federal government, continued until the Mississippi Freedom Summer of 1964, when at least thirty homes were bombed, thirty-five churches burned, eighty persons were beaten, and there were more than thirty shooting incidents, and six known murders. A SNCC organizer in Georgia summed up the reasons for the failure of the registration effort in the rural Deep South: "How does one get it across to the people that we are not alone, when all around them white men are killing and getting away? Not only getting away, but in many cases promoted. . . .

How do you push a meeting when they tell you, 'I might be killed, my house may be burned, I may be fired from my job.' "

Only a significant federal presence in the rural Deep South might have saved the voter-registration program. It was promised. It was necessary. It never materialized. The Justice Department politely accepted all the phone calls it received from civil-rights volunteers in the field, respectfully replied to all movement correspondents, promptly conferred with black leaders when they requested it, but continued to maintain that the system of federalism tied its hands. "Careful explanations of the historic limitations on the federal government's police powers," admitted Robert Kennedy, "are not satisfactory to the parents of students who have vanished in Mississippi or to the widow of a Negro educator shot down without any reason by night riders in Georgia." Yet his Department of Justice insisted that it could not intervene unless local authorities proved wholly incapable of upholding law and order or defied a specific federal court order. A sign in the SNCC office read:

> There is a street in Itta Bena called Freedom,
> There is a town in Mississippi called Liberty,
> There is a department in Washington called Justice.

Only Mississippi's Governor Ross Barnett in 1962, in the realm of desegregated education, gave the Kennedy Administration the unimpeachable grounds that it required before it would act. Defying federal court orders directing the admission of James Meredith, the grandson of a slave and an air-force veteran of eight years, to the state university, Barnett announced a doctrine of interposition redolent of John C. Calhoun. President Kennedy met this challenge to his constitutional authority by sending several hundred federal marshals to the campus of Ole Miss to guarantee Meredith's admission. When they were met by a rioting mob chanting "2-4-1-3, we hate Kennedy," the President dispatched army troops and federalized the state National Guard. Two died and 375 were injured in the all-night melee. Many applauded Kennedy's stand and ac-

cepted it as evidence of his concern for racial justice. Indeed, the
brutality of diehard segregationists to deny one lone African-
American an education had begun to make J.F.K. think that he
needed to exercise more positive leadership in racial matters.

But civil-rights leaders, knowing the hundreds of unlawful acts
by white supremacists that the Kennedy Administration did nothing
about, viewed the matter differently. They saw Kennedy as a tem-
porizer and manipulator, devoid of any true sense of moral urgency
concerning the race issue. He would act when it suited his needs,
not the movement's. He would act the hero in the victory at Ole
Miss but remain on the sidelines during the really fundamental
attempt at racial change in Albany, Georgia.

In that Black Belt city of southwest Georgia, segregationist officials proved impervious to nonviolent direct action when the federal
government chose not to enforce the constitutional rights of African-Americans. Beginning in November 1961, with the efforts of
SNCC's Charles Sherrod and Cordell Reagon to register African-
American voters in southwestern Georgia, much as Bob Moses was
doing in the Delta, and lasting for more than a year, thousands of
Albany blacks marched, boycotted, and sat-in to win the franchise
and the desegregation of public facilities. It was the first attempt
to mobilize an entire African-American community in the Deep
South to protest the totality of white racism. Day after day, blacks
crossed the Harlem side of Oglethorpe Avenue to confront hard-
core segregation, and night after night they held mass meetings to
sing the freedom songs, taught them by Bernice Johnson, Charlie
Jones, Rutha Harris, and Cordell Reagon, that nurtured hope and
transformed them into courageous soldiers for freedom.

Over a thousand spent time in jail. "I felt it was necessary to
show the people that human dignity must be obtained even if
through suffering or maltreatment," said Bertha Gober after being
arrested for defying segregation at the bus station. "I'd do it again
anytime," continued the diminutive student. "I feel that I have
gained a feeling of decency and self-respect, a feeling of cleanliness
that even the dirtiest walls of Albany's jail cannot take away from

me." Similar sentiments buoyed countless others who sacrificed and suffered. They developed a sense of commitment and camaraderie that would sustain them in future campaigns. Yet at the end of 1962 only the merest handfuls of blacks could vote in "Bad" Baker, "Dangerous" Dougherty, or "Terrible" Terrell counties, and an Albany African-American still could not get a cup of coffee at a downtown lunch counter. The local schools, bus terminal, and municipal library and swimming pool remained as segregated as ever.

The first city-wide campaign of massive civil disobedience failed to achieve its objectives because the Kennedy Administration never acted against white Albany's clear violations of federal law. The Kennedy brothers, wanting calm so that the moderate Democrat Carl Sanders might triumph over his extremist opponents in the 1962 gubernatorial contest, chose not to intervene as long as Albany's segregationists could keep the peace. And that Chief of Police Laurie Pritchett did masterfully. He countered the nonviolence of the Albany movement by literally creating a police state to suppress protest and maintain order. Pritchett filled the jails with black demonstrators. But because he kept his violence hidden from the cameras and prevented white mobs from running amuck, and because federal authorities allowed him to maintain the fiction that the arrests of protesters had nothing to do with race—that they were for "disorderly conduct" or "parading without a permit"—Pritchett was hailed by the national media for his professionalism. Consequently, the public lost interest, and the Kennedys never sent federal marshals to Albany, or applied pressure to the city fathers, to insure African-Americans their constitutional rights. In the absence of tumult, few whites demanded intervention by the federal government. Even the arrests of Martin Luther King in Albany had failed to arouse a national commitment to end Jim Crow. Justice mattered less than order.

The collapse of the Albany movement proved to segregationists that police action "to keep the peace" could be their most effective instrument of oppression. Albany gave the leadership of white resistance a renewed confidence that, if they minimized outrageous public disorder, they could use local force in defiance of the law. "Albany," Pritchett beamed, "is as segregated as ever." Conversely, SNCC field secretary Martha Norman took heart from the level of participation and dedication by Albany's African-Americans: when they marched to the courthouse by the hundreds "they said, 'We're going for broke. We're not worried about oppression, we're not worried about our jobs, and we *really* aren't worried about our lives.' They were the first to do such," she recalled. "Their numbers and seriousness served notice that the South could no longer maintain its system of racial oppression—because that's all they had to uphold it, the threat of arrest, of beatings, of economic reprisals. When Albany, Georgia, citizens went to the courthouse, they announced that these threats weren't going to work anymore." To the main strategists in the movement, the lesson of Albany, as well as that of the Freedom Rides and the Mississippi voter-registration campaign, was the necessity for dramatic crises of greater disorder. Justice for African-Americans would be achieved neither through persuasion of Southern whites nor through peaceful protest. Sweeping, coercive civil-rights legislation was indispensable. And that would come only when blatant, horrifying white violence had aroused a national consensus to demand a forceful federal response.

# FIVE

........................

# WE SHALL OVERCOME

I don't know how many of you would be able to write a history book. But you are certainly making history, and you are experiencing history. And you will make it possible for the historians of the future to write a marvelous chapter. Never in the history of this nation have so many people been arrested for the cause of freedom and human dignity.

MARTIN LUTHER KING, JR.


Martin Luther King's determination to provoke a confrontation in Birmingham in 1963 resulted in a massive wave of nonviolent action—"the Negro Revolution." Birmingham decisively changed both the nature of the struggle for racial justice and white attitudes toward civil rights. After more than twenty thousand blacks were jailed in hundreds of demonstrations, King's action eventuated the passage of the most comprehensive anti-discrimination legislation in American history.

The decision to launch a campaign to end segregation in Birmingham had been reached in a three-day strategy session conducted by the SCLC at its retreat near Savannah at the end of 1962. The motives were both personal and political, practical as well as philosophical. Albany weighed heavily on King and his aides. Malcolm X had said "the civil rights struggle in America reached its lowest point" in Albany, and many in the movement agreed. Albany brought into the open doubts about King's leadership and disillusionment with the established techniques of protest. The head of the SCLC wanted desperately to prove that nonviolence could still work, that "you can struggle without hating, you can fight without violence." King also believed it imperative to demonstrate his own courage and effectiveness, to dispel rumors that he was a reluctant and losing crusader. His reputation and SCLC's importance necessitated a daring, dramatic effort, especially since 1963 would be the year of the one hundredth anniversary of the Emancipation Proclamation.

King realized the need for some decisive achievement to rekindle the morale and momentum of the freedom struggle. Social movements require victories for sustenance, and civil-rights gains had not kept pace with the rising expectations of blacks. Despair mounted in 1962, and King feared that if the movement faltered, blacks would turn to leaders like Malcolm X, who mocked nonviolence and had nothing but scorn for "integration"—a word, Malcolm said, "invented by a northern liberal." Gaining converts, and far more sympathizers, Malcolm dismissed the aspirations of civil-rights leaders as fantasy and condemned their conciliatory style as debasing. "Our *enemy* is the *white man*," he insisted as he preached black nationalism, stressing that blacks must take control of their own livelihoods and culture "*by any means necessary.*" Proudly, Malcolm accepted the label of extremist. "The black race here in North America is in extremely bad condition. You show me a black man who isn't an extremist and I'll show you one who needs psychiatric attention!"

Worried that blacks would flock to extremists like Malcolm X if he did not succeed, King decided that the time had come to force Kennedy's hand. The President's policy of trying to show concern for blacks while at the same time avoiding action to inflame the white South, said King, had brought the movement nothing but delay and tokenism. By 1963, thirty-four African nations had freed themselves from colonial bondage, but more than two thousand school districts remained segregated in the South. Only 8 percent of the black children in the South attended class with whites. At this rate of progress, civil-rights leaders moaned, it would be the year 2054 before school desegregation became a reality, and it would be the year 2094 before blacks secured equality in job training and employment. Kennedy would have to be pushed, and pushed hard. "We've got to have a crisis to bargain with," King's right-hand man Wyatt Tee Walker explained at the SCLC retreat. "To take a moderate approach hoping to get white help doesn't help. They nail you to the cross, and it saps the enthusiasm of the followers. You've got to have a crisis."

Birmingham appeared to answer King's diverse needs. The Reverend Fred Lee Shuttlesworth, the fearless head of the Alabama Christian Movement for Human Rights, an SCLC affiliate, had just invited King to conduct nonviolent demonstrations in Birmingham, the most segregated big city in America. No other undertaking would be more audacious. Absolute segregation was the rule—in schools, restaurants, rest rooms, drinking fountains, and department-store fitting rooms. Municipal officials closed down the city parks and playgrounds rather than desegregate them. Birmingham abandoned its professional baseball team rather than allow it to play desegregated clubs in the International League. It even banned a textbook because it had black and white rabbits in it. Although over 40 percent of the population was African-American, fewer than ten thousand of the 80,000 registered voters were black. White racism permeated the city; and it was reinforced daily, wrote a reporter in *The New York Times*, "by the whip, the razor, the gun, the bomb, the torch, the club, the knife, the mob, the police and many branches of the state's apparatus." To crack this solid racist wall would be a mighty achievement.

Birmingham was more than unyielding on segregation. It had the reputation of a dangerous city. Blacks dubbed it "Bombingham" for the eighteen racial bombings and more than fifty cross-burning

incidents that occurred between 1957 and 1963. Leading the vanguard of the brutal, last-ditch defenders of segregation was Eugene
T. "Bull" Connor, who vowed: "We're not going to have white
folks and nigras segregatin' together in this man's town." The jowly,
thickset police commissioner prided himself on being as vigilant as
he was cruel in "keeping the niggers in their place." The SCLC
could count on Connor to respond viciously to any effort to alter
the city's racial order; they believed this could create the crisis that
would force the President to act. "We presumed that Bull would
do something to help us," recalled Wyatt Walker. Connor's un-
witting assistance to them would thus enable SCLC to "turn Bull
into a steer." King decided to aid Shuttlesworth, but to avoid having
their nonviolent campaign used as a political football, they post-
poned the demonstrations until after the April 2 mayoralty runoff
election. In the meantime, King and his associates prepared a top-
secret plan which they called "Project C"—for Confrontation.

King and his task force arrived in Birmingham the day after the
election. They promptly issued a manifesto calling for an immediate
end to racist employment practices and Jim Crow public accommodations, and for the rapid formation of a biracial committee to
plan for further desegregation. "We're tired of waiting," Shuttlesworth told a packed church meeting that evening. "We've been
waiting for 340 years for our rights. We want action. We want it
now." As the congregation responded with spirited renditions of
"Woke Up This Mornin' with My Mind Stayed on Freedom" and
"Ain't Gonna Let Nobody Turn Me 'Round," King rose to vow
that he would lead an economic boycott and demonstrations against
the downtown merchants until "Pharaoh lets God's people go."

The first stage of Project C began the next morning. Small groups
of protesters staged sit-ins at the segregated downtown lunch
counters. The anticipated arrests followed. King continued this tactic for several days, patiently piquing the concern of the Kennedy
Administration and the interest of the national news media while
arousing the black community.

On April 6 the second stage of Project C began with a march of fifty African-Americans, led by Shuttlesworth, on City Hall. Connor arrested them all. The next day, Palm Sunday, Connor similarly intercepted and jailed a column of blacks marching on City Hall headed by Martin Luther King's brother, the Reverend A. D. King. Day after day the public marches and arrests continued, in the full glare of newspaper photographers and television cameras. King had counted on these incidents and the economic boycott accompanying them to activate larger numbers of Birmingham blacks, to focus national attention on the issue of civil rights, and to discomfort the city's economic elite. He had calculated right. On April 10, city officials secured an injunction barring racial demonstrations. They thought it would stop the SCLC campaign in its tracks, dampening the fervor of the black community. But King announced that he saw it as his duty to violate this immoral injunction and that he would do so on Good Friday, April 12. Accompanied by Abernathy and Al Hibbler, the popular blind blues singer, King led some fifty hymn-singing volunteers on yet another trek toward City Hall. Chanting "Freedom has come to Birmingham!" nearly a thousand blacks lined their route. An infuriated Connor, escorted by a squad of snarling, snapping police dogs, ordered their arrest.

While in jail, King composed an essay justifying the strategy of the black freedom struggle. Ostensibly written to the eight Birmingham clergymen who had condemned the SCLC campaign as "unwise and untimely," King addressed his reply to the many whites and blacks who apparently shared his goals but questioned his tactics, especially those who urged the movement to be patient, moderate, and law-abiding. Begun in the margins of newspapers and continued on bits of scrap paper smuggled to him by a prison trusty, King worked for four days on his nineteen-page "Letter from the Birmingham Jail." Soon after, several national periodicals published it in its entirety and reprints were distributed across the nation. Widely quoted, the epistle proved to be a potent weapon in the propaganda battle to legitimate the direct-action movement. By depicting the protesters, rather than the forces of "law and order," as the defenders of the Judeo-Christian heritage and the

Constitution, King quieted some influential critics of civil disobedience.

King's letter began with a refutation of the charge of "outside agitator," arguing that as a Christian and an American he had the duty to combat injustice wherever it existed. Then King explained how the white leadership of Birmingham left blacks no alternative but to demonstrate at this time. He detailed the broken promises and refusal to negotiate by the white elite, juxtaposing them against his portrayal of the dismal, brutal plight of black Birmingham. Something had to be done to break the crust of apathy and indifference that enabled white America to ignore such injustice; something had to be done to create a crisis so the city could no longer evade a solution. To those who asked blacks "to wait," King retorted that "wait" generally meant "never." He had never "yet engaged in a direct action movement that was 'well timed,' " King observed, "according to the timetable of those who have not suffered unduly from the disease of segregation."

> I guess it is easy for those who have never felt the stinging darts of segregation to say wait. But when you have seen vicious mobs lynch your mothers and fathers at will and drown your sisters and brothers at whim; when you have seen hate-filled policemen curse, kick, brutalize, and even kill your black brothers and sisters with impunity; when you see that vast majority of your twenty million Negro brothers smothering in an airtight cage of poverty in the midst of an affluent society; when you suddenly find your tongue twisted and your speech stammering as you seek to explain to your six-year-old daughter why she can't go to the public amusement park that has just been advertised on television, and see tears welling up in her little eyes when she is told that Funtown is closed to colored children, and see the depressing clouds of inferiority begin to form in her little mental sky, and see her begin to distort her little personality by unconsciously developing a bitterness toward white people; when you have to concoct an answer for

a five-year-old son asking in agonizing pathos: "Daddy, why do white people treat colored people so mean?"; when you take a cross-country drive and find it necessary to sleep night after night in the uncomfortable corners of your automobile because no motel will accept you; when you are humiliated day in and day out by nagging signs reading "white" men and "colored"; when your first name becomes "nigger" and your middle name becomes "boy" (however old you are) and your last name becomes "John," and when your wife and mother are never given the respected title "Mrs."; when you are harried by day and haunted by night by the fact that you are a Negro, living constantly at tiptoe stance never quite knowing what to expect next, and plagued with inner fears and outer resentments; when you are forever fighting a degenerating sense of "nobodiness"—then you will understand why we find it difficult to wait.

King next turned to a philosophical vindication of civil disobedience. Because segregation laws injured the soul and degraded the human personality, he defined them as unjust, and then contended that one has a moral responsibility to disobey unjust laws. He reminded his fellow ministers that the laws of Hitler had been "legal," and further emphasized the undemocratic nature of the segregation ordinances by indicating that blacks had been excluded from the political process which enacted these state and local laws. To those still unwilling to accept the justness of nonviolent civil disobedience, King underlined the alternative: "Millions of Negroes, out of frustration and despair, will seek solace and security in black nationalist ideologies, a development that will lead inevitably to a frightening racial nightmare." Disappointed with the moderates who cared more about law and order than about justice, King hoped they would someday recognize the nation's true heroes.

They will be the James Merediths, courageously and with a majestic sense of purpose, facing jeering and hostile mobs and the agonizing loneliness that characterizes the life of the pioneer. They will be old, oppressed, battered Negro women, symbolized in a seventy-two-year-old woman of Montgomery, Alabama, who rose up with a sense of dignity and with her people decided not to ride the segregated buses, and responded to one who inquired about her tiredness with ungrammatical profundity: 'My feets is tired, but my soul is rested.' They will be the young high school and college students, the young ministers of the gospel and a host of their elders, courageously and nonviolently sitting in at lunch counters and willingly going to jail for conscience's sake. One day the South will know that when these disinherited children of God sat down at lunch counters they were in reality standing up for the best in the American dream and the most sacred values in our Judeo-Christian heritage, and thus carrying our whole nation back to great wells of democracy which were dug deep by the founding fathers in the formulation of the Constitution and the Declaration of Independence.

That day had certainly not yet arrived in Birmingham. As the disinherited children of God continued to try to march to City Hall, Connor's police acted with less and less restraint. The movement responded to police violence with larger demonstrations. And Birmingham blacks reacted by tightening the economic boycott which pinched the merchants more and more. As the racial tension mounted, events outside of Birmingham heightened the sense of impending crisis.

On April 21, William L. Moore, a white Baltimore mail carrier and CORE member, set off from Chattanooga on his "freedom walk." Wearing a sandwich-board sign proclaiming "Equal Rights for All—Mississippi or Bust," Moore intended to hike to Jackson and personally deliver a letter to Mississippi Governor Ross Barnett protesting Southern segregation. On the afternoon of April 23, he walked through Gadsden, Alabama. That evening he was found murdered on a lonely road ten miles outside the city. Moore had been shot in the neck and head.

The killing of Moore embittered the movement. As officials throughout the nation bemoaned the outrageous crime, Diane Nash Bevel led a group of eight Birmingham blacks to Gadsden to complete Moore's pilgrimage. All were jailed. Then an interracial group of CORE and SNCC staffers left Chattanooga on May 1 to take up the freedom walk. Nearly a hundred cars filled with bottle- and rock-throwing whites followed them across the Alabama state line, shouting "Kill them!" "Throw them niggers in the river!" Alabama highway patrolmen immediately arrested the freedom walkers, repeatedly shocking them with electric cattle prods. The CORE–SNCC contingent refused to accept bail and spent a month in prison. Two weeks later, a third attempt to resume Moore's freedom walk, organized by CORE, resulted in the arrest of another six blacks and five whites. By this time King had been released from jail and had launched the third stage of his confrontation with Birmingham's establishment.

D Day, May 2, an astonished national audience, generated by the sit-ins, protest marches, police brutality, and the slaying of William Moore, watched over a thousand black children, some only six years old, march out of the Sixteenth Street Baptist Church to demonstrate and be arrested. Before the cameras, the young blacks sang freedom songs, chanted freedom slogans to the hundreds of cheering adult spectators, and knelt to pray as the police corralled them. They offered no resistance to Connor's stupefied forces, clapping, dancing, laughing, and skipping to the patrol wagons waiting to take them to jail. "Black and glad," determined yet not somber, the children stunned the nation.

Criticism of King for his "children's crusade" came from every quarter. Moderates anguished about the safety of the children. Conservatives denounced the tactic as cynical and exploitative. Radicals demeaned it as unmanly. "Real men," objected Malcolm X, "don't put their children on the firing line." King retorted that, by demonstrating, the children gained a "sense of their own stake in freedom and justice," as well as a heightened pride in their race and belief in their capacity to influence their future.

In fact, King had accepted Bevel's plan to use Birmingham's black children as demonstrators because most adults had been reluctant to march and the campaign would have soon fizzled out. Bevel had also asserted that the news photographs of young girls and boys being hauled off to jail would dramatically stir the nation's conscience. The needs of victory were all that mattered; and the rules of the game had changed. Another thousand black children of Birmingham packed the Sixteenth Street Baptist Church that evening to shout their approval of King and his promise: "Today was D Day. Tomorrow will be Double-D Day."

The *New York Times* account of the May 3 demonstrations began: "There was an ugly overtone to the events today that was not present yesterday." No one would accuse the reporter of overstatement. An enraged "Bull" Connor, watching a thousand more students gather in the church to receive their demonstration assignments, abandoned all restraint. He ordered his forces to bar the exits from the church, trapping inside about half the young protesters, and then had his men charge into those who escaped and had gathered in Kelly Ingram Park. The police, swinging nightsticks indiscriminately, beat demonstrators and onlookers. Attack dogs set loose sank their fangs into three fleeing children. Horrified at this mistreatment of their young, adults in the park hurled bricks and bottles at the policemen. "Let 'em have it," Connor commanded the firemen with the high-pressure hoses. With a sound like gunfire, streams of blistering water roared from the nozzles, blasting blacks against buildings and sweeping kids down slippery streets. The hundreds of pounds of pressure ripped the bark off trees; it also tore the clothes off young people's backs, cut through their skins, and jerked their limbs weightlessly. Those jailed that Friday brought the number of children arrested in two days to nearly thirteen hundred.

King had his confrontation, and more. On Saturday, an additional two hundred students were arrested, and several thousand adult blacks skirmished with the police, pelting them with rocks. Again, graphic illustrations of clubbings, police dogs, and fire hoses appeared on the front pages of newspapers and on television sets throughout the country. The appalling pictures of snarling dogs lunging viciously at youthful marchers, of bands of policemen ganging up to beat children and women, of high-pressure hoses knocking the very young and the very old off their feet, brought a surge of anger and determination across black America and aroused the conscience, or guilt, of millions of previously indifferent whites. King suddenly had massive support. Kennedy now had to act.

The pictures of violence in Birmingham made him "sick," the President admitted to a delegation from the Americans for Democratic Action that Saturday. Yet he doubted aloud that he had a constitutional mandate to act. He termed impossible the liberals' suggestion that he intervene immediately and forcefully in Birmingham, but acknowledged: "I am not asking for patience. I can well understand why the Negroes of Birmingham are tired of being asked to be patient." Privately, the President knew that the time had come to act. He had to resolve the conflict with the least possible political damage to himself. He shared the sense of national outrage at Southern white atrocities yet shrank from the prospect of using federal force to impose a new racial order. Kennedy simply wanted the quickest possible restoration of civil peace. Secretly he ordered Justice Department mediators to Birmingham to persuade the contending groups to negotiate a settlement. Concurrently, key Administration officials began an intensive campaign to pressure Birmingham's most influential businessmen, especially those connected with U.S. Steel, to accept a compromise agreement.

Until this moment in the crisis, the Senior Citizens' Committee, covertly organized by the Birmingham Chamber of Commerce to deal with desegregation problems, would not even talk with King and his associates. They were the so-called white moderates of the South—the gentlemen who said "nigra" rather than "nigger"— supposedly too busy making money to hate, yet for a month they had avoided even a hint of willingness to end the disorder and violence. Now, suddenly, they were ready to talk. They had felt the heat from Washington. They feared the city was on the verge of a major bloodletting. And they had reckoned the toll of the black boycott: sales in April had dropped more than a third in the downtown stores. So Birmingham's economic elite started to negotiate in earnest on May 4, even agreeing to hold all-night sessions. They talked and listened but would not accede. The SCLC would not back down. Deadlock. King ordered the demonstrations to continue.

The most massive black protest to date began early Monday, May 6, and police violence intensified accordingly. A flyer distributed near Negro schools urged all students: "Fight for freedom first, then go to school. Join the thousands in jail who are making their witness for freedom. Come to the Sixteenth Street Baptist Church now . . . and we'll soon be free. It's up to you to free our teachers, our parents, yourself and our country." In some schools, attendance dropped nearly 90 percent.

Dick Gregory, the well-known black comedian, led the first group of demonstrators out of the church. Police hurried them into the waiting paddy wagons as the students sang: "I ain't scared of your jail / cause I want my freedom / want my freedom / want my freedom now." Then another group left the church singing "I ain't scared of your dogs cause. . . ." They, too, were quickly herded off to jail. Out spilled another group singing "I ain't scared of your hoses cause . . ." and another singing "I ain't scared of no Bull . . ." and then another, and another. For an hour, wave after wave of twenty to fifty black students, chanting for freedom, defiantly offered themselves up for arrest. The huge crowd in the park roared their approval for each contingent leaving the church. Some sang a new ditty: "It isn't nice to go to jail / There are nicer ways to do it / But the nice ways always fail."

The audacity of the students, the contempt of the blacks, stirred Connor's fear and loathing. After more than a thousand demonstrators had been seized, he turned his police on the crowd in the park. Shoving and kicking, the men in blue vented their fury. As the television cameras rolled and the photographers focused their lenses, snapping police dogs once again leaped at the throats of taunting children, fire hoses bowled over rock-throwing blacks, and Connor's minions clubbed onlookers.

A shocked nation demanded federal action to end the conflict. Kennedy's mediators pressed King to yield on his demands for immediate desegregation and an end to discrimination in employment. They warned him of the folly of prolonging the crisis in the expectation of intervention by federal troops. Separately, the Justice Department officials urged the city's business establishment to make real concessions, not merely promises of future action. They threatened the white elite with the probable consequences of federal action and the economic effects of a bloodbath in Birmingham. Neither negotiating team would budge. The talks resumed, and so did the confrontation.

Tuesday, May 7, the conflict peaked. A larger number of students than ever before, and far less submissive, appeared on the streets. Rather than march from the church and court arrest, some two thousand young blacks suddenly converged on the downtown area at noon. Most staged sit-ins. Others picketed the major stores. Some held pray-ins on the sidewalks. Several thousand adult spectators then spontaneously joined a raucous black parade through the business section. Over and over they shouted "Freedom! Freedom! Freedom!" "We're marching for freedom!" Others chanted "The police can't stop us now. Even 'Bull' Connor can't stop us now."

Connor certainly tried. Adding an armored police tank to his arsenal, he ordered his men to drive the protesters back into the black ghetto. Brutally, they did so, penning nearly four thousand in Ingram Park. Connor commanded that the high-pressure hoses be turned on the trapped blacks. The water shot from the nozzles whacked the bark off trees. It tore bricks loose from the walls. The crowd screamed. Rocks flew. SCLC aides circulating in the crowd pleaded for nonviolence. Few could even hear them over the crashing of the huge hoses; and not many who could hear wanted to listen. Soon after Shuttlesworth entered the park to try to calm his

followers, a blast of water slammed the minister against the side
of a building. On hearing that an injured Shuttlesworth had just
been placed in an ambulance, Connor laughed. "I waited a week
to see Shuttlesworth get hit with a hose. I'm sorry I missed it. I
wish they'd carried him away in a hearse." Not until the crowd
had been thoroughly pacified and dispersed did the dogs cease biting, the clubs stop crashing bones, and the hoses end knocking
blacks down and washing them along the sidewalks. A reporter
who watched in despair mumbled "God bless America."

That afternoon, as the downtown demonstrations erupted, a secret emergency meeting of the Senior Citizens' Committee resolved
to end the disorder that had caused Birmingham to become an
international byword for unrestrained police brutality. With the din
of freedom chants in their ears, the business leaders directed their
negotiators to come to terms with the SCLC. A three-hour bargaining session brought the two sides close to agreement. Differences remained, but the premonition of unchecked violence affected
both negotiating teams. Following three more days of talk, they
reached agreement.

The SCLC had won its demands for the "desegregation of lunch
counters, rest rooms, fitting rooms and drinking fountains"; for the
"upgrading and hiring of Negroes on a nondiscriminatory basis
throughout the industrial community of Birmingham"; and for the
formation of a biracial committee. It accepted, however, a timetable
of planned stages, relenting on its insistence that these changes take
effect immediately. The SCLC, moreover, acceded to the release of
arrested demonstrators on bond, giving up its demand for the out-
right dismissal of all charges against them. Although this was a
compromise that pleased neither black nor white hardliners, King
claimed with pride "the most magnificent victory for justice we've
ever seen in the Deep South."

Before returning to Atlanta, King pleaded for reconciliation and
brotherhood in Birmingham, but too many in that steel town, black
and white, wanted neither. That Saturday, Connor and other leading local and state officials broadcast their denunciations of the

biracial accord. They assaulted the Senior Citizens' Committee and the Kennedy brothers as well as King and the SCLC. At nightfall, over a thousand robed Ku Klux Klansmen met to hear further diatribes against the agreement. Shortly after the rally ended, two dynamite bombs rocked the home of A. D. King, strewing glass and timber in every direction. Sullen neighbors milled about, vowing vengeance. The Police and Fire Department officials inspecting the rubble were jostled and threatened. As the crowd grew, so did calls for retribution.

Minutes later, another bomb exploded, blasting a gaping hole in the Gaston Motel, the SCLC's headquarters in Birmingham. Thirsting for vengeance, the black underclass of Alabama's steel town streamed out of the bars and pool halls in the ghetto. They pelted the arriving police and firemen with stones and bottles. They stabbed one officer and assaulted several others. When some of King's aides urged them to stop throwing rocks and go home, the mob responded, "Tell it to 'Bull' Connor. This is what nonviolence gets you."

As police reinforcements swarmed into the area, additional blacks joined the rampaging mob. Many were parents of arrested children who had just heard tales of brutality and mistreatment in the prison. Martin Luther King, Jr., to the contrary, they would not love their enemy. Others had been so ground down by racist oppression that they wanted only to kill "whitey." They had never accepted King's talk of nonviolence, and this night they felt emboldened to display their hatred. Pandemonium reigned for several hours. Sporadic battles between the mob and the police flared. A white cabdriver, lost in the ghetto, was attacked by blacks, his car overturned and set on fire. Two grocery stores owned by whites were put to the torch. Soon an entire block was ablaze. "Let the whole fucking city burn," Wyatt Tee Walker heard a young black scream. "I don't give a good goddamn—this'll show those white motherfuckers!" Some blacks, however, struggled throughout the night to prevent bloodshed. Their exertions managed to keep the surge of violence from becoming a flood. Still, over fifty had been injured and the Birmingham *News* estimated property damage at more than $40,000.

King hurried back from Atlanta the next day to calm black Birmingham and to see that the accord held. He and other SCLC officials made the rounds of black bars and pool halls, schools, and churches, preaching the necessity of avoiding any provocation that might jeopardize the agreement. King pleaded that blacks stay on the nonviolent road to freedom. "Don't stop," he urged. "Don't get weary. There is a great camp meeting coming." How long? He was asked; not long, he promised. "We sh.'l overcome." The familiar refrain reassured and comforted. The furor subsided. City officials and business leaders began to implement the desegregation pact on schedule. Order returned to Birmingham.

Further racial disorder, however, swept across much of the rest of the nation as a result of the impact of Birmingham on black America. The audacity of taking on "Bull" Connor's "Johannesburg" and vanquishing it, the unprecedented children's crusade and savage white response, the determination of all strata of black Birmingham to fight racial oppression by whatever means they chose, all combined to affect more African-Americans, more passionately, than any previous protest. The age of Negro submissiveness ended; the era of black struggle reached a new plateau.

Birmingham fully awakened blacks to a sense of their new power; it ignited a mighty confidence in the potency of mass social dislocation to overcome white intransigence. If such a bastion of segregation could be defeated then any other city or area could be brought to heel by an aroused black community. Birmingham also spurred self-pride, a spirit of black unity, a willingness to join the struggle. James Farmer termed this optimistic assertiveness "a spiritual emancipation" and journalists trumpeted the emergence of a "New Negro," dwelling endlessly on their loss of fear, their readiness to go to jail, and their urgent quest for Freedom Now! "The most important thing that happened," Wyatt Tee Walker later acknowledged, "was that people decided that they are not going to be afraid of white folks anymore. Dr. King's most lasting contribution is that he emancipated black people's psyche. We threw off the slave mentality. Going to jail had been the whip which kept black folks in line. Now going to jail was transformed into a badge of honor."

In part, the bravery of Birmingham's black children inspired this commitment. The image of the young, first seen on television and then seared in memory, volunteering to face down Connor's bullies and dogs and hoses, goaded thousands more to demonstrate. The same images also shamed blacks into the struggle. If children could court jail so that all blacks could be free, how could their elders do less. Simultaneously, the pictures of violence against women and kids engendered new depths of anger and widespread bitterness. The catalysts of hatred and retaliation in part dissolved black apathy and helped spark a brushfire of "little Birminghams" across the country in mid-1963.

More significant than the numbers, the nature of the struggle changed after Birmingham. Nearly a decade after *Brown*, African-American parents no longer would wait patiently for their children to attend desegregated schools. The militant "never" of hard-core segregationists would be matched by their own militancy. En masse, they forsook gradualism for immediacy. Tokenism and, for some, even nonviolence, no longer sufficed. *Freedom Now* meant, at a minimum, sweeping basic changes without either delay or dilution. "The package deal is the new demand," wrote Bayard Rustin. Instead of accepting further protracted, piecemeal alterations in the racial system, blacks clamored now for "fundamental, social, political and economic change." The price of racial peace, they insisted, must be decent jobs and housing for blacks as well as the franchise, an end to police brutality as well as immediate desegregation of all schools and public accommodations. To underscore their determination, moreover, blacks demonstrated for these concerns in an exceedingly relentless manner.

Birmingham also induced the previously torpid, very poorest blacks to participate in the racial struggle. Their entry into the movement both reflected and accelerated the radicalization of strategies and goals. The unemployed and working poor had little interest in the symbolic and status gains that the college students, professionals, and religious Southern middle-class blacks, who had constituted the bulk of the movement prior to Birmingham, had centered their energies on. They had even less sympathy for, or knowledge of, the spirit of *Satyagraha*. King's talk of love left them cold. His request that they nobly accept suffering and jailing made them snicker. As the black struggle became more massive and encompassing, impatience multiplied, disobedience became barely civil, and nonviolence, at best, a mere stratagem.

In addition, both deliberately and inadvertently, all the major civil-rights organizations further radicalized the movement. All responded to the changes wrought by Birmingham with an increasing militancy. "There go my people," King often quoted Gandhi at this time. "I must catch them, for I am their leader." And as King hurried to capitalize on the new spirit and participants in the struggle, so did James Forman of SNCC, James Farmer of CORE, Roy Wilkins of the NAACP, and even Whitney Young, the executive director of the National Urban League since 1961. Far more outspoken than his predecessors, Young in 1963 constantly harped on the themes that civil rights are not negotiable, that the time for compromise or delay had passed, and that the nation owed blacks a "domestic Marshall Plan." "The only fair and realistic way of closing the gap and correcting historic abuses," Young insisted, "calls for a transitional period of intensified special effort of corrective measures in education, in training and employment, in housing and in health and welfare." Although never a direct-action organization, the Urban League in 1963 publicly defended that strategy and urged blacks to demonstrate and protest.

So did the NAACP. Wilkins, who had chided black demonstrators in Jackson in 1961, returned to that city two years later to be arrested for picketing a Woolworth store that refused to desegregate. At the NAACP annual convention in July, Wilkins demanded that the association "accelerate, accelerate, accelerate" the civil-rights attack. For the first time, the national office provided support for its local branches engaging in direct action, especially in the

Carolinas, Mississippi, and Philadelphia, where Cecil Moore, the branch president, led blockades of the job sites of lily-white construction unions and boasted: "My basic strength is those 300,000 lower-class guys who are ready to mob, rob, steal and kill."

CORE, however, took the lead in the North in 1963. It organized rent strikes and school boycotts, demonstrated against job bias and for compensatory employment, and focused public attention on police brutality in the ghetto. And as CORE involved more urban blacks in the struggle, its stridency escalated. Militancy begat militancy, spurring ever more radical demands and tactics. At the same time, responding to pressure from local blacks, CORE put forth a greater effort in the South, mounting voter-registration campaigns and demonstrations against segregation. To the extent that it could, CORE tried to harness the uncompromising impatience of its many new adherents; but, in the main, events were in the saddle: the followers were leading, the leaders following.

Competition *among* the civil-rights organizations added to the militancy injected into the movement by those most recently mobilized. All the groups in the fight against racism sought the money necessary to battle successfully. Each tried to gain influence in Washington and standing in a local community, as well as the approval of the masses and the active support of true-believers. And each group, believing its solution best, sought power to affect the outcome of events. Competition among organizations in the civil-rights movement had always existed. Prior to 1963, however, it had been muted. Despite tactical differences, their goals had remained close, and their combined weakness relative to the opposition had placed a premium on cooperation or, at a minimum, absence of open opposition.

Birmingham changed the rules of the competition, and the stakes. There was a lot more to compete for, and more reason to win. The pool of prospective dues-paying members, of bodies to be utilized in demonstrations, and of committed activists willing to work full-time in the movement increased spectacularly after Birmingham. So did the potential of white backing. The door swung open to the possibilities of immense financial contributions, alliances with business and political leaders, and public endorsements and assistance from the nation's major white religious, civic, and labor groups.

Variances between the groups, in style and substance, once easily glossed over, now began to appear insurmountable. CORE, SNCC, SCLC, and the NAACP each hungered for the lion's share of the resources they believed would enable them to set the terms of future agreements and legislation. Each tried to outdo the others, to be more successful in its campaigns, to be more devoted to the struggle. The NAACP and CORE demonstrated that in their competing efforts in a score of cities in the North and in the Carolinas; the same was true of the rivalry of SNCC and SCLC in Danville, Virginia, and in Gadsden and Selma, Alabama; and the contest for primacy in the civil-rights struggle in Mississippi among the NAACP, SNCC, and CORE generated still further momentum and militancy within the movement.

Impatience and demands escalated, moreover, because the civil-rights leadership recognized that the new mood in black America would not be long sustained. They feared that delay could dissipate the intense involvement generated by Birmingham. Worrying that anything smacking of "business as usual" might precipitate individual blacks' hasty withdrawal into the private struggle for a better life, the leaders pressed for "all, now!" The civil-rights organizations concertedly demanded as much as they could as quickly as possible.

Blacks responded with a siege of direct action. A far greater number of blacks participated in many more demonstrations against a broader array of discrimination than ever before, and with unprecedented verve. Describing the change, King wrote that with Birmingham the African-American quiet "lament became a shout and then a roar and for months no American, white or Negro, was insulated or unaware." Nearly eight hundred boycotts, marches, and sit-ins in some two hundred cities and towns across the South occurred in the three months after the Birmingham accord. By the end of 1963, more than 20,000 protesters had been arrested, and at least ten had been killed. Over 80,000 disfranchised African-

Americans cast ballots in a Mississippi freedom election to protest their being denied the vote. And thousands of Northern blacks demonstrated their solidarity with their Southern brothers and sisters, staging walk-outs against de facto school segregation, picketing against discrimination in employment, and conducting rent strikes against racism in housing. Indeed, vivid daily accounts of blacks demonstrating and being brutally attacked by police and white mobs became the number-one feature of the news media in mid-1963.

This onslaught of disruptive militancy forced the white South to retreat. Many Southern white leaders suddenly began bargaining for peace, fearing the loss of business profits and/or an all-out race war. White officials acceded to the desegregation of public accommodations in some fifty Southern and border cities in the five months from May to the end of September. Scores of localities established biracial commissions and hired their first black policemen. And demagogues who had vowed "Never" registered African-Americans to vote and enrolled blacks in previously all-white schools. More racial change came in these few months than had occurred in three-quarters of a century. But it did not come everywhere in the South; and even in those areas that did start to alter their racial system, numerous whites remained unreconciled to any black advance.

From southwest Georgia across the Black Belt to the Louisiana delta, white supremacists mobilized for a last-ditch stand. They viewed themselves as the defenders of an isolated outpost—abandoned by the rest of white America, outnumbered by blacks, and under attack by an alliance of the federal government and civil-rights agitators. Embattled and endangered, they grew desperate, anxious to go down fighting and wound the hated black movement in whatever ways they could. First they tried all manner of harassment and intimidation, especially economic coercion. When that failed to stop the civil-rights troops, they called on sheriffs and deputies, who arrested thousands of demonstrators in the Deep South during the summer and fall of 1963. In each citadel of white racism, police brutally clubbed protesters, teargassed them, scarred their bodies with electric cattle prods, and turned biting dogs and high-powered hoses on the volunteers in the movement. Still, the demonstrations continued.

Fearful, frustrated, furious whites turned to terrorism and murder. Fiery crosses placed on the lawns of civil-rights spokesmen and carloads of whites night-riding ominously through the black part of town served as preludes to the burning and bombing of homes and businesses owned by integrationists, or the destruction of schools due to be desegregated. In Mississippi, the closed society, where cars owned by whites bore license-plate legends such as MOST LIED ABOUT STATE IN THE UNION, FEDERALLY OCCUPIED MISSISSIPPI, KENNEDY'S HUNGARY, whites put to the torch several NAACP leaders' homes and stores in Gulfport, demolished the cars of civil-rights workers in Biloxi, wounded five SNCC staffers by shotgun blasts in Canton, and shot and killed a young movement organizer in Tchula. In Greenwood, 1963 brought the destruction of the SNCC office, the gasoline bombing of at least a half dozen black businesses and homes, the shooting of as many voter-registration workers, and the machine-gunning of SNCC's Jimmy Travis. Not to be outdone, whites in Jackson burned a restaurant that agreed to hire blacks, ravaged the homes and churches of integrationists, and fired rifles at cars driven by civil-rights workers. Returning from a mass meeting to his home in the capital shortly after midnight on June 11, Medgar Evers, the NAACP field secretary in Mississippi, was murdered by a sniper lying in ambush. Evers had just vowed to fight to end "all forms of segregation in Jackson."

Three months later, after two dozen black youths in defiance of Governor George Wallace had desegregated several previously all-white schools in Birmingham, a bomb constructed from fifteen sticks of dynamite shattered the Sunday-morning peace of the Sixteenth Street Baptist Church, the staging center of the spring protests. Dozens of children attending a Bible class were injured by the explosion. Four black girls, two of them fourteen, one eleven, and one ten, who had been changing into choir robes in the basement, lay dead and buried under the debris. Later in the day, a sixteen-year-old black youth was shot in the back and killed by a policeman with a shotgun, and a black thirteen-year-old riding his bicycle was shot to death by some white boys.

The next day a visibly agitated white attorney, Chuck Morgan, addressed the all-white Young Men's Business Club. Responding to the question on their minds, *who* bombed the church, an angry Morgan exclaimed:

> The "who" is every little individual who talks about the "niggers" and spreads the seeds of his hate to his neighbor and his son. . . . The "who" is every governor who ever shouted for lawlessness and became a law violator. . . . Who is really guilty? Each of us. Each citizen who has not consciously attempted to bring about peaceful compliance . . . each citizen who has ever said, "They ought to kill that nigger." Every person in this community who has in any way contributed to the popularity of hatred is at least as guilty, or more so, as the demented fool who threw that bomb.

After Morgan finished, a member moved that the Business Club admit an African-American to membership. The motion died for lack of a second.

Revulsed by the South's racist violence, embarrassed by the proponents of white supremacy, white Northern opinion swung behind the call for a civil-rights law. Attracted by the religious and patriotic idealism of the movement, dozens of student associations, labor unions, and religious organizations provided financial and political backing. Hundreds of liberal groups went on record in resolutions of support for the movement. Polls and surveys in the summer of 1963 disclosed overwhelming majorities in favor of laws to guarantee blacks voting rights, job opportunities, good housing, and desegregated schools and public accommodations. For a season, at least, Birmingham had altered the minds and hearts of millions of white Americans.

Northern whites, like their Southern counterparts, responded from fright as much as from conscience. Birmingham revealed how easily black discontent could flare into rioting, and melees throughout the summer, especially in Cambridge, Maryland, in Jackson after the assassination of Evers, and in Birmingham again, highlighted the disposition of blacks to meet racist violence with retaliatory rampages. In the main, blacks in 1963 vented their accumulated hostility against whites with rhetoric, but the words were so brutally frank, so uncompromising, so filled with fury, that they constituted an act as foreboding to whites as an assault. What whites heard and read, mostly for the first time, chilled them.

The news media accentuated such fears, popularizing many of the most apocalyptic prophets of doom and destruction. They played up Robert F. Williams's 1962 tract, *Negroes with Guns*, which preached the necessity of armed force by blacks to gain their freedom. They stressed the growing impatience with nonviolence among the more aggressive CORE and SNCC field secretaries, and they sensationalized the terrorist fantasies of quasi-Maoist black revolutionaries.

Mostly, the media focused on the black threat vividly articulated by James Baldwin and Malcolm X. Baldwin's *The Fire Next Time* forced into the consciousness of whites a new sense of African-American rancor. Emphasizing that blacks would turn to violence if their nonviolent demands were ignored, Baldwin admonished white America of the destruction to come if it did not quickly and completely change its oppressive racial ways. He delineated the African-American past of

> rope, fire, torture, castration, infanticide, rape; death and humiliation; fear by day and night, fear as deep as the marrow of the bone; doubt that he was worthy of life, since everyone around him denied it; sorrow for his women, for his kinfolk, for his children, who needed his protection, and whom he could not protect; rage, hatred and murder, hatred for white men so

deep that it often turned against him and his own and made all love, all trust, all joy impossible.

He evoked the bleakness blacks presently faced. "For the horrors of the American Negro's life," he wrote, "there has been almost no language." Neither religion nor reason has persuaded whites to treat blacks decently, so, not surprisingly, the appeal of the Black Muslims keeps growing. "There is *no* reason that black men should be expected to be more patient, more forbearing, more farseeing than whites; indeed, quite the contrary." Whites must expect retaliation, unless they change and accept the unconditional freedom of blacks. The price of white security, Baldwin summed up, "is the liberation of the blacks—the total liberation, in the cities, in the towns, before the law, and in the mind." Anything less, he warned in the words of a Negro spiritual: *"God gave Noah the rainbow sign / No more water, the fire next time!"*

The popularity of the Black Muslims' incitement of violent enmity, described by Baldwin, had first been impressed on white America by CBS's inflammatory documentary in 1959, *The Hate That Hate Produced*. The Nation of Islam was depicted as an army of black fanatics planning for the inevitable race war. Little or nothing most whites read and heard informed them of Muslim success in rehabilitating blacks whom others considered beyond reclamation, or of the Muslim gospel that blacks had to conquer their own shame and poverty by adhering to such traditional American virtues as hard work, honesty, self-discipline, mutual help, and self-respect. Rather, the media spotlighted Malcolm X's most extremist visions of separatism and violence; and Malcolm quickly learned that the more shocking his comments, the more white attention the Black Muslims received. He played to the media, conjuring fantasies of jet fleets piloted by blacks bombing all-white neighborhoods, and publicly thanking *his* God for answering black prayers on the occasion of a plane crash in France which killed 120 white Atlantans. Malcolm X appeared on television more than any other black spokesman in 1963, and few whites remained unaware of his

expressions of contempt for all things white, his appeal to blacks
to fight racism "by any means necessary," and his insistence that
the "day of nonviolent resistance is over."

What often frightened whites instilled a fighting pride in blacks.
An apostle of defiance, Malcolm particularly gave voice to the anger
and pain of young blacks in the ghetto. His hostility toward all
whites—always referring to them as white devils—epitomized their
feelings. They cheered when he preached "an eye for an eye," when
he brought "whitey down front," and when he rejected the nonviolent civil-rights movement as no substitute for the revolution
needed by blacks: "Revolution is bloody, revolution is hostile, revolution knows no compromise. . . ." Such utterances expressed the
rarely publicized longings of many of the dispossessed, as did Malcolm's affirmations of black pride and unity, of black self-reliance
and separatism, of black self-assertion and self-defense. His pros-
elytizing for black nationalism—for blacks to control, by any means
necessary, their own lives and culture—struck yet deeper chords
among African-Americans demanding faster and more fundamental
changes in racial conditions and insisting on more forceful means
to achieve these ends. To them, of all black leaders, only Malcolm
seemed to understand the depth of the racial conflict; and only
Malcolm appeared to view the black struggle for equality as a power
struggle, not a moral one. To virtually all blacks, moreover, Malcolm X stood as an implacable symbol of resistance and a champion
of liberation.

Malcolm X remained a reproach to all white hypocrites and
compromising blacks. His extremism, together with the threats of
violence and revolution epitomized by Robert F. Williams, provided
a sharp cutting edge to the black struggle. They kept the pressure
on civil-rights leaders to be bolder, more militant. Simultaneously,
their radicalism made the movement's leadership and objectives
appear responsible and moderate. And they scared some white leaders into accepting the civil-rights demands as the only effective way
to avert potential disaster. The more Malcolm loomed as the alternative that whites would have to confront if CORE, SNCC, and

SCLC failed, the more white officials acceded to the stipulations posed by the established leadership of the campaign for racial equality.

The threat of black insurrection, and even of more Birminghams and the intensification of black economic boycotts, especially touched the national corporate community. Businessmen saw no profit in turbulence, and many concluded in mid-1963 that meeting the reasonable aims of the civil-rights movement was the best way to banish the specter of increasing racial disorder. Corporate leaders began to put pressure on local governments, where they had substantial plants and offices, to negotiate their differences with movement organizers. On June 19, 1963, nearly a hundred chairmen of corporations and foundations answered the call of the president of the Taconic Foundation to aid the civil-rights movement financially. Meeting at the Hotel Carlyle in Manhattan, they pledged over a million dollars to the five major civil-rights groups. These leaders of finance and industry perhaps assumed that by assisting the established black organizations to secure their goals they could prevent the emergence of radicalism. Whatever their intentions, these funds, and the sizable contributions from other whites and blacks, enabled the black struggle to expand, to reach more potential supporters, and to plan larger, more ambitious campaigns. The staffs of SCLC and SNCC nearly trebled; the number of CORE chapters jumped from sixty to over a hundred; and NAACP membership increased by a third, to more than half a million.

"The sound of the explosion in Birmingham," wrote King, "reached all the way to Washington." The profound consequences of the SCLC campaign forced the President's hand, altering his perception of what needed to be done and what could be done. In response to Birmingham and the rush of spring and summer events that followed, Kennedy traveled in fits and starts toward a commitment to civil rights, and an identification with the movement, that he had previously resisted. Although he never fully reached that destination, he moved nearer to it than any previous American President.

Kennedy began to act decisively on civil rights in the summer of 1963, in part because of his personal sense of morality, and in part because of his political calculations. He needed to satisfy the millions of Americans protesting federal inaction and calling for an end to disorder. The President also had to dampen the explosive potential of widespread racial violence and to maintain the confidence of the mass of blacks in government. Additionally, Kennedy considered it necessary to assist Farmer and King and Wilkins in securing their objectives lest the movement be taken over by extremists.

With the ebbing of Cold War tensions now allowing the President to focus on domestic issues, Kennedy demonstrated his resolve shortly after the Birmingham accord had been reached. On May 21, a federal district judge ordered the University of Alabama to admit two black students to its summer session. Governor George Wallace immediately threatened to defy the court order and to bar the entrance of any black who attempted to desegregate the university. Wallace had announced in his inaugural address: "I draw the line in the dust and toss down the gauntlet before the feet of tyranny, and I say, Segregation now! Segregation tomorrow! Segregation forever!" and he now promised his white constituents: "I will not let you down." The nation braced for a repeat of the confrontation at Ole Miss. But Kennedy was determined to keep Tuscaloosa from becoming another Oxford. Unlike his behavior in the events leading to the crisis at the University of Mississippi, Kennedy in 1963 acted promptly and forcefully, leaving Wallace no doubt as to the President's resolve. The governor capitulated.

Several hours after the first black students at the University of Alabama had registered, just a couple of hours before the assassination of Medgar Evers, Kennedy spoke to the nation on the race issue in a televised address that most of his advisors had counseled him against. He had decided to assert his leadership on what he called "a moral issue . . . as old as the Scriptures and . . . as clear as the American Constitution." It ought to be possible, Kennedy intoned, for American students of any color to attend any public institution without having to be backed up by troops. It ought to be possible for American consumers of any color to receive equal service in places of public accommodation, such as hotels and restaurants and theaters and retail stores, without being forced to resort to demonstrations in the street, and it ought to be possible for American citizens of any color to register and to vote in a free election without interference or fear of reprisal.

The President reviewed with intense emotion the plight of the American Negro, and asked:

If an American, because his skin is dark, cannot eat lunch in a restaurant open to the public; if he cannot send his children to the best public school available; if he cannot vote for the public officials who represent him; if, in short, he cannot enjoy the full and free life which all of us want, then who among us would be content to have the color of his skin changed and stand in his place?

Who among us would then be content with the counsels of patience and delay? One hundred years of delay have passed since President Lincoln freed the slaves, yet their heirs, their grandsons, are not fully free. They are not yet freed from the bonds of injustice; they are not yet freed from social and economic oppression. And this nation, for all its hopes and all its boasts, will not be fully free until all its citizens are free.

Then Kennedy warned that "events in Birmingham and elsewhere have so increased the cries for equality that no city or state or legislative body can prudently choose to ignore them. The fires of frustration and discord are burning in every city," and the moral crisis "cannot be met by repressive police action" or "quieted by token moves or talk. It is a time to act in the Congress, in your state and local legislative body, and, above all, in all our daily lives."

A week later, saying that the time had come for a national commitment "to the proposition that race has no place in American life or law," Kennedy asked Congress to pass a civil-rights law that included provisions for desegregating public accommodations; granting authority to the Attorney General to initiate school-desegregation suits; establishing a Community Relations Service to prevent racial conflicts; improving the economic status of blacks; and empowering the government to withhold funds from federally supported programs and facilities in which discrimination occurred. Mississippi's Senator James Eastland termed the bill a "complete blueprint for a totalitarian state," but congressional liberals moved quickly to strengthen it further, adding provisions for a permanent Fair Employment Practices Commission and for federal registrars to enroll black voters.

On August 28, over two hundred thousand Americans, black and white, and from almost every state in the union, converged on the Capitol, chanting: "Pass that bill! Pass that bill! Pass that bill!" Joyously, harmoniously, they marched to signify their belief in equal rights. Gathered in unity before the Lincoln Memorial, the vast, exalted throng cheered the nation's religious and civil-rights leaders' concerted declarations of support for black freedom. They accepted with delight the approval offered by the scores of government officials and dignitaries crowded on the platform behind the speaker's stand. Afterward, the President stated publicly that he had been "impressed with the deep fervor and the quiet dignity" of the marchers, and he lauded the demonstration as one of which "this nation can properly be proud." It appeared to be the apogee of the civil-rights movement. But it had not been so conceived, the unanimity was deceptive, and many of those who participated in and praised the march had opposed it when first announced by seventy-four-year-old A. Philip Randolph, the civil-rights movement's elder statesman.

The legendary head of the Brotherhood of Sleeping Car Porters, Randolph had long nurtured a hope for a march on Washington. He had previously broached the idea in 1941 to force President

Roosevelt to open defense jobs to blacks, and in 1948 to pressure President Truman to desegregate the armed services. In December 1962, he and Bayard Rustin began to plan a march for economic justice, centered on demands for a hike in the minimum wage and passage of fair-employment legislation. With little enthusiasm, CORE, SCLC, and SNCC approved Randolph's call for a mass pilgrimage to Washington to dramatize the black-unemployment crisis. The NAACP and NUL bowed out. The idea drifted until Birmingham. Then it picked up steam as Rustin oriented it toward civil rights, rather than economic legislation, and Randolph agreed to a renamed March on Washington for Jobs and Freedom.

The President met with the civil-rights leadership on June 22 to dissuade them from encouraging blacks to march on Washington. "We want success in Congress, not just a big show at the Capitol," he stressed. "Some of these people are looking for an excuse to be against us; and I don't want to give any of them a chance to say 'Yes, I'm for the bill, but I am damned if I will vote for it at the point of a gun.'" There had been talk of encampments on the White House lawn and mass sit-ins in the legislative galleries. Kennedy warned that their only effect would be "to create an atmosphere of intimidation—and this may give some members of Congress an out." The NAACP and NUL concurred, fearing that a mass demonstration might erupt into violence, discredit the movement, and harm congressional prospects for a civil-rights bill.

Randolph, King, and Farmer stood fast. "The Negroes are already in the streets," Randolph informed the President. "It is very likely impossible to get them off. If they are bound to be in the streets in any case, is it not better that they be led by organizations dedicated to civil rights and disciplined by struggle rather than to leave them to other leaders who care neither about civil rights nor about non-violence?" Sustaining the argument, King stated that it was not a choice of a demonstration or legislation. The march "could serve as a means through which people with legitimate discontents could channel their grievances under disciplined non-violent leadership. It could also serve as a means of dramatizing the issue and mobilizing support in parts of the country which don't know the problems at first hand." "We understand your political problem in getting the legislation through," Farmer added, "and we want to help in that as best we can." Then the head of CORE reinforced the contentions of King and Randolph. "We could be in a difficult if not untenable position if we called the street demonstrations off and then were defeated in the legislative battle. The result would be that frustration would grow into violence and would demand new leadership." The President seemed almost persuaded, but he held off approving the march until he felt secure in its content and logistics.

The march organizers turned their energies to alleviating the qualms of the President and the moderates in the civil-rights camp who still did not back the proposed demonstration in Washington. They blurred Randolph's original focus on economic demands, and shelved plans for a sit-in at the Capitol in favor of staging a mass rally to support Kennedy's legislation.

Instead of laying siege to Capitol Hill, they would parade peacefully from the Washington Monument to the Lincoln Memorial. By July, Rustin had the active cooperation of the NAACP, NUL, and nearly two hundred religious, labor, and civic organizations. Endorsements poured in. At his July 17 press conference, Kennedy characterized the coming demonstration as being "in the great tradition" of peaceful assembly "for a redress of grievances." His aides worked closely with the march leaders on arrangements. A month later, the President even worried that the march might not be massive enough, that the promised one hundred thousand people might not materialize.

The turnout exceeded all expectations. Nearly a quarter of a million attended the March on Washington to petition for black rights, including at least seventy-five thousand whites. They took heart in their numbers. The day became a celebration. The assemblage clasped hands as Joan Baez intoned "We shall overcome," sang along with Peter, Paul, and Mary when they asked "How many times must a man look up before he can see the sky?" and hushed to hear Bob Dylan sing a ballad about the death of Medgar Evers. They clapped and cried their accompaniment to Odetta's "If they ask you who you are, tell them you're a child of God" and Mahalia Jackson's renditions of "I been 'buked and I been scorned." Good-naturedly, they endured the heat and humidity and the seemingly endless introduction of notables and repetition of clichés by speaker after speaker. As the afternoon wore on, some grew listless, and chose to nap, to play with the many children brought by parents, and to wade in the Reflecting Pool between the Washington Monument and the Lincoln Memorial. It did not matter. They had made their point by their presence and demeanor. Then Randolph introduced Martin Luther King, Jr., who had been, as Wilkins put it, "assigned the rousements."

"Five score years ago," King began to the sound of a thunderous ovation, "a great American in whose symbolic shadow we stand, signed the Emancipation Proclamation." The crowd grew quiet as King surveyed the century that had passed since that day, declaiming over and over "One hundred years later . . ." and finding that not much had changed. "So we have come here today to dramatize an appalling condition." He termed the promises of the Declaration of Independence "a sacred obligation" which had proved to be, for blacks, a bad check—"a check which has come back marked 'insufficient funds.' " But, King continued, as tens of thousands roared their agreement, "we refuse to believe that the bank of justice is bankrupt. We refuse to believe that there are insufficient funds in the great vaults of opportunity of this nation."

King's rich baritone melodiously praised the "veterans of creative suffering" and urged them to continue the struggle. "*Now* is the time to make real the promises of Democracy. *Now* is the time to rise from the dark and desolate valley of segregation to the sunlit path of racial justice. *Now* is the time to open the doors of opportunity to all of God's children. *Now* is the time to lift our nation from the quicksands of racial injustice to the solid rock of brotherhood." He reminded the nation that there "will be neither rest nor tranquility in America until the Negro is granted his citizenship rights," and in rising tones answered those who asked, "When will you be satisfied?"

> We can never be satisfied as long as our bodies, heavy with the fatigue of travel, cannot gain lodging in the motels of the highways and the hotels of the cities. We cannot be satisfied as long as the Negro's basic mobility is from a smaller ghetto to a larger one. We can never be satisfied as long as our children are stripped of their selfhood and robbed of their dignity by signs stating: "For Whites Only." We cannot be satisfied as long as the Negro in Mississippi cannot vote and the Negro in New York believes he has nothing for which to vote. No, no, we are not satisfied and we will not be satisfied until justice rolls down like the waters and righteousness like a mighty stream.

He appealed to the multitude: "Go back to Mississippi, go back to Alabama, go back to South Carolina, go back to Georgia, go back to Louisiana, go back to the slums and ghettos of our modern cities, knowing that somehow this situation can and will be changed."

"I still have a dream," King added extemporaneously. "It is a dream deeply rooted in the American dream," a dream of racial justice and social harmony. Rhythmically blending Amos, Isaiah, and "My Country 'Tis of Thee," King's dream rolled over the crowd, becoming more utopian and yet believable as the audience's antiphonal response rose tumultuously.

> I have a dream that one day on the red hills of Georgia the sons of former slaves and the sons of former slaveowners will be able to sit down together at the table of brotherhood.
>
> I have a dream that one day even the State of Mississippi, a state sweltering with the heat of injustice, sweltering with the heat of oppression, will be transformed into an oasis of freedom and justice. I have a dream that my four little children will one day live in a nation where they will not be judged by

the color of their skin but by the content of their character. I have a dream today.

I have a dream that one day down in Alabama with its vicious racists, with its Governor having his lips dripping with the words of interposition and nullification—one day right there in Alabama, little black boys and black girls will be able to join hands with little white boys and white girls as sisters and brothers.

I have a dream today.

Spines tingled and eyes teared as King ended:

When we let freedom ring, when we let it ring from every village and every hamlet, from every state and every city, we will be able to speed up that day when all God's children, black men and white men, Jews and Gentiles, Protestants and Catholics, will be able to join hands and sing in the words of that old Negro spiritual, "Free at last! Free at last! Thank God almighty, we are free at last!"

In less than fifteen minutes, King had transformed an amiable effort at lobbying Congress into the high-water mark of the black freedom struggle. "That day," James Baldwin wrote, "for a moment, it almost seemed that we stood on a height, and could see our inheritance; perhaps we could make the kingdom real, perhaps the beloved community would not forever remain that dream one dreamed in agony." King's dream had buoyed the spirit of African-Americans and touched the hearts of whites. Not all, to be sure. It changed neither votes in Congress nor the minds of those most opposed or indifferent to racial equality. Billboards in the South proclaimed: "Kennedy for King—Goldwater for President." But, for many, King's eloquence and vision offset the ugly images of black violence that the demonstrations had started to evoke, replacing them with an inspiring picture of the movement at its benevolent best. To the extent that any single public utterance could,

this speech made the black revolt acceptable to white America.
King's dream capped the wave of direct action starting in Birmingham which in 1964 resulted in the passage of the civil-rights act.

Some blacks, however, felt betrayed by King and those responsible for the March on Washington. As most in the crowd cried and cheered when King perorated, one young black shouted furiously: "Fuck that dream, Martin. Now goddamit, NOW!" Others mocked "De Lawd." Malcolm X called the demonstration the "Farce on Washington." Ridiculing the March as "a circus, nothing but a picnic," Malcolm wondered: "Who ever heard of angry revolutionists swinging their bare feet together with their oppressor in lily-pad park pools, with gospels and guitars and 'I Have a Dream' speeches?" James Farmer spent the day in a Louisiana jail, refusing bail. Annoyed at the moderating influence of Kennedy and King, he stayed in his cell to make the point that he did not consider the March on Washington sufficiently militant. SNCC staffers were livid that John Lewis, their chairman, had been forced to soften his words in deference to the demand of some of the white speakers. Lewis had prepared a speech describing the civil-rights bill as too little, too late, denouncing both Republicans and Democrats as hypocrites, threatening the South with a Sherman-like "scorched earth" march through the heart of Dixie, and demanding of Kennedy: "I want to know—which side is the federal government on?" The civil-rights establishment forced Lewis to launder such remarks from his address, turning the demonstration for jobs and freedom into, according to James Forman, "a victory celebration for the Kennedy Administration." But the angry reactions to the March on Washington and King's leadership, largely hidden from view that serene August afternoon, forecast the divisions and differences that would one day wreck the movement.

Nevertheless, throughout 1963, the black struggle remained outwardly united. An end to segregation appeared at hand, although Congress dawdled. In November the sudden crack of a rifle in Dallas precipitated the overdue legislation. The assassination of the President immediately stirred sympathy for the attainment of the goals

Kennedy sought and an abhorrence of violent fringe politics, like those associated with the Klan and other extreme white supremacists. Many considered passage of the civil-rights bill the most fitting memorial to their slain leader.

The House of Representatives acted quickly after the 1964 session began. It considered the measure for eleven days and passed it overwhelmingly. The Senate took nearly three months to debate before voting 73 to 27 for the bill. On July 2, President Lyndon Johnson signed the act which prohibited discrimination in most places of public accommodation, authorized the government to withhold federal funds to public programs practicing discrimination, banned discrimination by employers and unions, created an Equal Employment Opportunity Commission, established a Community Relations Service, and provided technical and financial aid to communities desegregating their schools. The movement barely had time to celebrate. It was in the midst of the Mississippi Freedom Summer and a mighty effort to secure the franchise for blacks, the final item on the established civil-rights agenda.

# SIX

# How Many Roads

Until then I'd never heard of no mass meeting and I didn't know that a Negro could register and vote. Bob Moses, Reggie Robinson, Jim Bevel and James Forman were some of the SNCC workers who ran that meeting. When they asked for those to raise their hands who'd go down to the courthouse the next day, I raised mine. Had it up as high as I could get it. I guess if I'd had any sense I'd a-been a little scared, but what was the point of being scared. The only thing they could do to me was to kill me and it seemed like they'd been trying to do that a little bit at a time ever since I could remember.

FANNIE LOU HAMER

The struggle for black equality reached its crest and rapidly began to recede in the two years following the March on Washington. It swept aside the last vestiges of legal discrimination and segregation and ended black disenfranchisement. But, in the process, all the fissures in the movement became major cleavages. In part a victim of its own success, the movement created aspirations it could not fulfill and developed a new sense of racial pride that verged on being black racism. Many in the struggle for racial justice became disenchanted with American society, disinclined to compromise, and disdainful of white support, as white racist violence did not abate. "The paths of Negro–white unity that had been converging," Martin Luther King, Jr., would later write, "crossed at Selma and like a giant X began to diverge." The split, however, started in Mississippi, not Alabama. And SNCC, not SCLC, charted the course.

CORE and SNCC field secretaries returning to the South after the March on Washington plunged into the tasks of voter registration. Believing Jim Crow an anachronism soon to be abolished, the young staffers, like Bob Moses of SNCC, now considered the ballot box the key to empowering the dispossessed. They sought to organize the political strength of the black masses as a weapon against both racism and poverty. Time and again they cited the statistics proving the stark nexus between disenfranchisement and indigence. In Mississippi, where only one out of twenty adult blacks could register to vote, the median black-family income was a paltry $1,444, barely a third that of Mississippi whites. As Lawrence Guyot, a SNCC field worker, explained: "There is a relationship between your not being able to feed your children and your not registering to vote." African-Americans in Dallas County, Alabama, where one percent were registered to vote, had a median income of $28 a week; in neighboring Lowndes and Wilcox counties, where African-Americans constituted nearly 80 percent of the population and eked out a median income of $20 a week, not a single black had been registered to vote. To assist the poorest black sharecroppers and tenants, still largely untouched by the civil-rights movement, CORE concentrated its voter registration effort in Florida, Louisiana, and South Carolina; SNCC operated in Alabama and, especially, Mississippi.

The poorest, most backward and illiterate state in the nation, as well as the stoutest bastion of discrimination and segregation, Mississippi remained impervious to the black struggle for equality. "Every datum of economics and every fact and twist of history," stated the Southern Regional Council, "have conspired to keep its white people deeply and ofttimes harshly resistant to change and its Negro people ill-equipped for it." To Moses, the clear and compelling necessity for reform, both economic and racial, was matched by the potential for black political power, for Mississippi's 916,000 blacks totaled 42 percent of the state population and a majority in more than a third of its counties. Accordingly, Moses sought both to force the national government to enforce the voting rights of African-Americans and to encourage the emergence of indigenous black community leaders to continue the struggle after SNCC had left.

The very enormity of the challenge appealed to Moses. No other battle on the civil-rights front posed greater risks than voter registration in Mississippi. No other campaign required such commitment and courage.

Following the withdrawal of the VEP from Mississippi in the fall of 1963, Moses had redoubled his efforts to make voter registration in the Magnolia State the focus of the movement. He revitalized the Council of Federated Organizations, a statewide composite of racial-advancement groups which had been established in 1961 to secure the release of jailed Freedom Riders, and became its program director; he chose David Dennis of CORE as his assistant; and he persuaded Aaron Henry, the respected Clarksville druggist and head of the state NAACP, to serve as its president. COFO and SNCC became indistinguishable; the NAACP and SCLC participated only nominally and CORE confined its energies to one of the state's five congressional districts. The preponderance of workers for COFO came from SNCC. Shortly before the regular November elections in 1963, Moses conducted a Freedom Election to prove that blacks wanted to vote. On the same day that Mississippi whites went to the polls, nearly eighty thousand disenfranchised blacks cast freedom ballots for Henry for governor and for the Reverend Edwin King, the white chaplain of Tougaloo College, for lieutenant governor.

Moses considered the Freedom Vote Campaign of 1963 a stunning success. It disproved the white assertion that Mississippi blacks did not vote because of apathy. It also provided the psychological reinforcement that Moses thought necessary for organizing blacks politically. Black morale had been boosted as a result of actually participating in a political process, even one not legally recognized. He looked forward to additional black political involvement that would inspire black self-confidence. Moses had also rethought his initial opposition to the use of white student volunteers from outside the state. Recognizing that the presence of young whites might provide protection against blatant acts of racist violence, he accepted the suggestion of Allard Lowenstein, a white liberal activist, to have some sixty students, largely from Stanford and Yale, assist in the mock election. This had brought national attention to the Freedom Election, as well as some more security for African-American registration workers. Moses's thoughts raced ahead to a full-scale summer project to register Mississippi blacks, aided by thousands of white students.

A week after the Freedom Election, COFO met in Greenville to consider the question: "Where do we go from here?" In Moses's absence, Dennis presented the idea for a Freedom Summer in 1964. The forty SNCC and five CORE representatives present immediately began considering the role of whites in the movement. Charles Cobb of SNCC stated that the invitation to whites to join in massive numbers indicated an admission of weakness by blacks, a concession that blacks could not deal with the situation. Others seconded his contention, still resenting Allard Lowenstein's abrasive attempt to control the 1963 campaign, to force SNCC to take a firm no-Communist stand, and to tie the voter-registration effort to the white liberal wing of the Democratic Party. Some remained peeved that white volunteers had elbowed aside African-Americans less skilled in typing, writing press releases, and handling budgets, thus undermining the self-confidence of black activists, perpetuating the stereotype of black inferiority, and reinforcing the concept of white paternalism. Still others joined Hollis Watkins in asserting that a large influx of whites would squash the "initiative that the people in Mississippi had just begun to take," stifling SNCC's resolve to build self-confident indigenous black leadership. And some condemned the white students for hogging the publicity, and then going home, leaving the African-Americans of Mississippi to face reprisals alone. Decisively, the COFO staff voted down the proposal.

Moses returned the next day. He understood the staff's feelings; but he also knew that the Mississippi blacks they had been working with wanted the assistance of white volunteers, and that the success of the project necessitated recruiting students from the North. "Look, I'm not gonna be a part of anything all-black," he told the staff. Integration was the heart of SNCC's ideal of the beloved community; furthermore, Moses hinted, the presence of white volunteers would guarantee the summer project federal protection and national publicity. "That's cold," Dennis later acknowledged, "but that was also in another sense speaking the language of this country. What we were trying to do was get a message over to the country, so we spoke their language. . . . We made sure that we had the children . . . of some very powerful people in this country over there. . . . We didn't plan any of this violence. But we just wanted the country to respond to what was going on." Significant federal intervention would come only after the blood of whites had been spilled.

Gradually, the COFO staffers reached a consensus. Officially they reaffirmed their color-blindness, accepting the perspectives of Bob Moses (that it is not a matter of "Negro fighting white, it's a question of rational people against irrational people") and Fannie Lou Hamer ("If we're trying to break down segregation, we can't segregate ourselves"). Although not everyone was reconciled to the idea of white volunteers, the COFO assemblage approved Moses's plan for a Mississippi Freedom Summer.

While COFO went to work on the logistics of the summer project, Mississippi whites prepared for what the Jackson *Daily News* called an "invasion." "This is it," said Jackson mayor Allen Thompson. "They're not bluffing, and we're not bluffing. We're going to be ready for them. . . . They won't have a chance." He expanded the city's police force from two hundred to more than three hundred officers and set up the fairgrounds as a makeshift prison. The state legislature more than doubled the number of highway patrolmen on duty, and made it a crime either to distribute flyers calling for a boycott or to operate a freedom school without a government permit. For the first time in the modern era, a Mississippi KKK was organized; and FBI chief J. Edgar Hoover made it clear that he did not intend to use his agency to "wet-nurse" student volunteers in Mississippi. As summer approached, white violence rose throughout Mississippi. Bombs exploded outside the headquarters of COFO, CORE, and SNCC. Fire destroyed at least a half a dozen black churches connected with the project. Unprovoked killings of blacks and unpunished crimes against blacks multiplied. And not a single summer volunteer had entered the state.

On June 15, the first third of the nearly nine hundred volunteers for the Mississippi Summer Project assembled at the Western College for Women in Oxford, Ohio. One-third women, average age twenty-one, most of the volunteers hailed from the Northeast, especially New York State. Primarily from prestigious universities, the highly idealistic and liberal young whites quickly learned some new freedom songs and then gathered around Bob Moses. "When Mrs. Hamer sang," he began quietly, " 'If you miss me from the freedom fight, You can't find me nowhere, Come on over to the graveyard, I'll be buried over there . . .' that's true." He dwelled on the dangers they faced. "Our goals are limited. If we can go and come back alive, then that is something." Almost whispering, Moses concluded: "Mississippi has been called 'The Closed Society.' It is closed, locked. We think the key is in the vote. Any change, any possibility for dissidence and opposition, depends first on a political breakthrough." Six days of intensive instruction on the intricacies of voter registration followed. The volunteers learned how to instill political awareness while teaching the 3 Rs, and how to protect themselves nonviolently while being beaten. They headed for Mississippi singing:

> They say that freedom is a constant struggle.
> They say that freedom is a constant struggle.

*They say that freedom is a constant struggle,*
*Oh, Lord, we've struggled so long,*
*We must be free, we must be free.*

As Moses began his opening talk to the next group of several hundred volunteers, a SNCC field secretary interrupted him, whispering. Moses turned to the white students: "Yesterday morning, three of our people left Meridian, Mississippi, to investigate a church-burning in Neshoba County. They haven't come back, and we haven't had any word from them." As best they could, COFO workers carried on the week-long classes to prepare the college students for the Mississippi Summer Project. But everybody's mind was on the three missing freedom fighters. Suddenly they learned that the car the three had been driving in had been found badly burned just outside Philadelphia, Mississippi. Fear enveloped the group. Moses said: "The kids are dead." Officially, the three were missing, but no one disputed Moses. Only a handful of students went home. Expecting the worst, the rest left for Mississippi.

By then, President Johnson had ordered a massive search for the three civil-rights workers and an FBI investigation of their disappearance. Six weeks later, federal agents uncovered their bodies in a newly constructed earthen dam five miles southwest of Philadelphia. Goodman and Schwerner had each been killed by a single bullet. Chaney, the sole African-American, had been beaten with a chain and shot three times. In December, acting on a tip from an informant reportedly paid $30,000, the FBI arrested twenty-one men, including the sheriff and deputy sheriff of Neshoba County. Then the nation learned the details of the murders plotted by the KKK, whose leader, Robert Shelton, claimed: "The Bible proves the Nigger is inferior to us white Anglo-Saxons. The Jew is inferior, too. God is a segregationist."

Michael Schwerner and his wife, Rita, deeply affected by the Birmingham demonstrations, had joined CORE in June 1963 and left New York City in January 1964 to run COFO's community center in Meridian. There the young white couple worked closely with a local high-school dropout and black CORE fieldworker, twenty-one-year-old James Chaney. For five months Rita taught reading, sewing, and citizenship to Meridian blacks, while Chaney and her social-worker husband canvassed the surrounding rural areas to prepare for a voter-registration campaign. In mid-June the three went to Oxford, Ohio, to serve as instructors in the training school for volunteers. When Michael was informed that a black church in Neshoba County, planned for use as a Freedom School, had been burned to the ground and that several of their supporters had been beaten, he decided to return to Mississippi to investigate and bolster the morale of Neshoba's blacks. Chaney insisted on accompanying him, and they asked twenty-one-year-old Andrew Goodman, assigned to work in Neshoba County, if he cared to join them. Goodman, a Summer Project volunteer and a junior at Queens College in New York, readily agreed. All three thought the long drive from Oxford to Meridian would give them ample opportunity to discuss the details of the summer activities.

Early Saturday, June 20, they said goodbye to Rita and headed south. They paused in Meridian on Sunday morning just long enough for Chaney to inspect carefully the CORE station wagon and for Schwerner to remind a volunteer working in the COFO office: "There's an immutable rule here—no one is to remain in Neshoba after 4 p.m. If for any reason we aren't back by 4 p.m., you should alert Jackson and begin checking every city jail, county jail, sheriff's office, police station, and hospital between Meridian and Neshoba. O.K.?"

The three civil-rights workers made the fifty-mile drive to the Mt. Zion Methodist Church, passed through the county seat, Philadelphia, did what they could to check the destroyed building and to reassure the local blacks that the Summer Project would continue, and then started their return trip to Meridian. The Philadelphia Klan was ready for them. Just outside town, Deputy Sheriff Cecil Price apprehended Chaney, Goodman, and Schwerner on a fictitious charge of speeding and jailed them in Philadelphia. The KKK waited until dark. Then the deputy took the three young men to a deserted road where three cars filled with Klansmen awaited them. According to William Bradford Huie, an investigative reporter who learned the details of the murders from a paid informant, later confirmed by testimony at the federal court trials of the killers, the Klan jeered at the three as they were pulled out of their car. "Several of the murderers chanted in unison, as though they had practiced it:

"Ashes to ashes, Dust to dust, if you'd stayed where you belonged, You wouldn't be here with us."

Another said: "So you wanted to come to Mississippi? Well, now we're gonna let you stay here. We're not even gonna run you out. We're gonna let you stay here with us."

When Schwerner was pulled from the car and stood up to be shot, I was told that the man with the pistol asked him: "You still think a nigger's as good as I am?" No time was allowed for a reply. He was shot straight through the heart and fell to the ground.

The Klansmen killed Goodman the same way, and then savagely beat Chaney before shooting him, burned the car of the civil-rights workers, and buried the three bodies with a bulldozer. The next day, as concern for the missing men mounted, Sheriff Lawrence Rainey told reporters he saw no cause for alarm: "If they're missing, they just hid somewhere, trying to get a lot of publicity."

The COFO staff and volunteers never believed Rainey and they labored throughout the summer under a pall of fear and suspicion that widened every cleavage between whites and blacks in the movement. No one would dispute the truth of Rita Schwerner's statement: "We all know that this search with hundreds of sailors is because Andrew Goodman and my husband are white. If only Chaney was involved, nothing would've been done." It intensified the guilt of most white volunteers. It traumatized COFO blacks, making overt all the tendencies previously latent: lack of faith in nonviolence as a tactic, much less as a way of life or moral principle; distrust of all government institutions; and antagonism toward white liberals.

Although President Johnson made much of the vastly increased FBI presence in Mississippi, its failure to apprehend the killers during the summer or even to offer much protection to the Mississippi Summer Project workers deeply angered the movement. While the President talked of extending the federal authority in the state, white terrorists bombed another thirty homes, burned thirty-five more churches, assaulted at least eighty COFO partisans, and shot at some thirty civil-rights workers. "I wake up in the morning sighing with relief that I was not bombed, because I know that 'they' know where I live. And I think, well, I got through that night, now I have to get through this day, and it goes on and on," wrote one volunteer. On the flimsiest of pretexts, local law-enforcement officers made hundreds of arrests to hinder the movement; and J. Edgar Hoover, decrying the "overemphasis" on civil rights in the media, declared that the FBI "most certainly" would *not* give special protection to the movement volunteers in Mississippi.

By the middle of the summer, many SNCC field secretaries in Mississippi carried a gun. All the despair, frustration, and rage that had been slowly building because they had been victimized too often, too brutally, with too little to show for it, burst when the FBI uncovered the bodies of Chaney, Schwerner, and Goodman. SNCC and CORE would be sacrificial lambs no longer. "I'm sick and tired of going to the funerals of black men who have been murdered by white men," David Dennis cried out for them as he delivered a eulogy at Chaney's funeral. "I'm not going to stand here and ask anyone not to be angry, not to be bitter tonight. We've defended our country. To do what? To live like slaves?" His voice rose: "I've got vengeance in my heart tonight." Sobbing and shouting, Dennis continued: "Don't just look at me and go back and tell folks you've been to a nice service. Your work is just beginning. And I'm going to tell you deep down in my heart what I feel right now. If you go back home and sit down and take what these white men in Mississippi are doing to us . . . if you take it and don't do something about it . . . then God damn your souls!" He stopped suddenly. Never again would Dennis speak of nonviolence. Nor would most COFO staffers. At the end of the year, SNCC would be officially defending the right of its field secretaries to wield weapons and CORE in Louisiana would openly accept the armed protection of the black vigilante Deacons for Defense and Justice.

The shock of the murders accentuated the bitterness corroding relations between blacks and whites in the movement. The concerns that had come up at the Greenville meeting regarding white volunteers flared into the open as many of the battle-weary activists cracked under the strain. Resentful that the whites could, and would, return to affluent suburban homes and private colleges, while African-Americans would have to struggle on alone, some in COFO ridiculed the white students as "fly-by-night freedom fighters" and relished assigning them the most menial of tasks. Angered that the nation paid attention only when whites were killed, or jailed, or beaten, some African-Americans even blamed the white volunteers for unleashing the terror in Mississippi.

Aggrieved and bewildered, few white volunteers could understand the rage of SNCC activists, as did Sally Belfrage: "They were automatically suspicious of us, the white volunteers; throughout the summer they put us to the test, and few, if any, could pass. Implicit in all the songs, tears, speeches, work, laughter, was the knowledge secure in both them and us that ultimately we could return to a white refuge." Yearning for recognition, if not appreciation, many white volunteers judged SNCC workers harshly, or not at all, romanticizing and patronizing them. Some recoiled from the heavy use of alcohol or marijuana by African-American activists seeking refuge from the strain of struggling amidst pervasive hatred. They could not fathom the depths of anxiety and fear experienced by SNCC staffers nor comprehend the different lifestyles of African-Americans. They resented black men in SNCC having sex with white women volunteers, viewing such liaisons as simply black lust for "forbidden fruit" and the naked coercion of whites to prove their lack of prejudice. Concurrently, black women in the movement grew furious at the willingness of white women to sleep with African-Americans, believing that the whites desired black males only because of guilt or their belief in the stereotype of black men as exotic, supersexual studs. The rapidly developing belief in black racial pride among SNCC staffers augmented the complexity of resentments. "SNCC is not populated with Toms who would wish to be white," wrote Belfrage. "They accept their color and are engaged in working out its destiny. To bend to us was to corrupt the purity of their goal."

Despite the misunderstandings and anger, the Mississippi Summer Project persisted. It succeeded in establishing and operating nearly fifty Freedom Schools throughout the state and about the same number of community centers. The volunteers taught blacks to articulate their needs and discontents, and aided in the creation of future bases of political power. They encouraged the emergence of new young leaders, like Johnny Johnston, who would become the mayor of Whitehall, and helped African-Americans in Mississippi to understand both their society and the mechanisms of change. Their dedication inspired others, generating a long-lasting activism. And the deaths of Chaney, Schwerner, and Goodman spurred the resolve of Mississippi blacks to fight for themselves. "There was no real civil-rights movement in the Negro community in Mississippi before the 1964 Summer Project," recalled Fannie Lou Hamer. "There were people that wanted change, but they hadn't dared to come out and try to do something." But, after the summer, "Negro people in the Delta began moving. People who had never before tried, though they had always been anxious to do something, began moving."

The Summer Project also riveted national attention on the extent of racial oppression in Mississippi. The nine hundred white volunteers, many of them sons and daughters of prominent politicians, doctors, and lawyers, brought the Mississippi Freedom Summer front-page coverage. Assisted by the flagrant brutality of white racists, the project helped foster a national consensus that the intolerable racial situation in Mississippi had to be overhauled. For all its exertions, however, COFO managed to add only sixteen hundred African-Americans to the registration lists. The reluctance to register, one volunteer wrote home, was "a highly rational emotion, the economic fear of losing your job, the physical fear of being shot at. Domestic servants know that they will be fired if they register to vote; so will factory workers, so will Negroes who live on plantations. In Mississippi, registration is no private affair. . . ."

Unable to register blacks, and kept by the regular Mississippi Democratic Party from participating in the precinct, county, and state conventions, COFO set up a new party open to all. It enrolled nearly eighty thousand disenfranchised blacks in the Mississippi Freedom Democratic Party. Following the rules prescribed by the Democratic National Committee, the MFDP selected sixty-eight delegates and alternates, including four whites, to attend the national convention in Atlantic City. Pointedly, the MFDP pledged itself to support the Democratic Party's nominees and platform, which the lily-white regulars refused to do. The insurgents planned to contest the seats traditionally held by white Mississippians, on the grounds that the MFDP representatives belonged to the only freely chosen party in the state, blacks being systematically denied access to the delegate-selection process of the Mississippi Democratic Party.

COFO had initially conceived the challenge to the white Mississippi delegation only as means of dramatizing the illegal exclusion of African-Americans from the political process. It had not expected to be seated at the convention. The widespread sympathetic response from white liberals took COFO strategists by surprise, and they soon began believing that the Freedom Democrats would indeed be seated. The MFDP would be represented by Joseph Rauh, a noted white liberal attorney, and those testifying in its behalf would include Rita Schwerner, James Farmer, Martin Luther King, and Roy Wilkins.

Of all those addressing the nationally televised hearings of the Credentials Committee, none had greater impact than the heroic, unlettered Fannie Lou Hamer. The youngest of twenty children of sharecropper parents, she had been working in the cotton fields since the age of six, when some forty years later she attended a SNCC meeting in a church in Ruleville, Mississippi, and learned for the first time that she had the right to vote. Her account of the "woesome times" that followed her effort to register to vote in the home county of Senator James Eastland stunned the listening delegates and nation. In simple rhythmic words evoking all the pain of the blues, Hamer described how her attempt to exercise the most elementary right of citizenship caused her to be thrown off the plantation she had labored on for eighteen years, to be shot at, and to be brutally beaten by Mississippi law-enforcement officials until her skin turned blue and she could no longer walk. "Is this America, the land of the free and the home of the brave?" Hamer thundered. "Where we have to sleep with our telephones off the hook, because our lives be threatened daily?"

Hamer's words haunted the delegates, but Lyndon Baines Johnson's authority compelled them. The President wanted nothing to interfere with "his" convention in Atlantic City or *his* plans for a stunning triumph in November. There would be no divisive floor fight over the MFDP. Johnson insisted on a compromise solution acceptable to a majority of white Southern delegates. In just six months he had given blacks and liberals a civil-rights act, an urban mass-transit and a food-stamp program, new education and health legislation, and an Office of Economic Opportunity to wage war on poverty. Now the President demanded that the blacks and liberals show their gratitude. Moreover, Johnson mused: Where else could they go? Certainly not to the GOP, which had nominated Barry Goldwater in a blatant turn to the far right. Johnson believed he had the blacks and "conscience liberals" securely in his corner. It made sense now to solidify his support among Southern white and working-class Democrats.

Five Southern delegations had already stipulated that they would walk out if the convention seated the Freedom Democrats. The President feared being blamed as the one responsible for forcing white Southerners out of the party. He believed he needed the cooperation of the powerful Southern committee chairmen in Congress to enact the social and economic reform bills of his Great Society. Johnson, moreover, feared not just a Southern defection. George Wallace had proved the potency of the "white backlash" in the spring, garnering 34 percent of the Democratic primary vote in Wisconsin, 30 percent in Indiana, and 43 percent in Maryland. The President did not want to lose working-class Democrats to Goldwater, and that necessitated that he not appear to capitulate to black militancy.

Johnson got his way. He called in Hubert Humphrey, dangled the Vice-Presidential nomination before him, and co-opted the leading advocate of civil rights in the Senate to dispatch the MFDP. Northern liberals, very much wanting Humphrey as the number-two man on the ticket and fearful of Goldwater's "backlash" appeal, fell quickly in line. And they applied intense pressure on the established civil-rights leadership to accept a compromise proffered by Johnson.

For three days the strategists of CORE, NAACP, SCLC, and SNCC wrestled with the conflict of expediency and principles. Gradually, most of the civil-rights leaders relented. They believed they had no other choice, since they now wanted to move from protest to politics—to make, said Bayard Rustin, "real gains and not only bear witness to injustice." What they desired for black advancement had to come from the federal government, and they risked losing all they had struggled for if they now rejected an alliance with a powerful President and a majority coalition. Nor could they easily spurn the white liberal, labor, and religious groups, which provided the bulk of funds for the movement, who now demanded a compromise. Virtually every ally insisted that the blacks accept Johnson's offer: "It's not what any of us wanted, but it's the best we could get." To do anything else would be futile and result not in the seating of the MFDP but in the isolation of the movement and the strengthening of its opposition. Forsaking morality for political effectiveness, Farmer and King reluctantly agreed with Rustin and Wilkins to lobby for a resolution providing for the seating of two of the Freedom Party leaders as delegates at large with full right to vote, the seating of *only* those Mississippi regular delegates that pledged allegiance to the Democratic ticket, and the unseating of *all* delegations from states which disfranchised African-Americans at all future Democratic conventions.

But it was not enough to satisfy the young militants of SNCC. Although some of the older MFDP delegates accepted the compromise agreement as a symbolic victory legitimating the MFDP's basic claims, and as the start of the real inclusion of blacks in the nominating process, the young black veterans of COFO derisively labeled the compromise a "back-of-the-bus" agreement. Fiercely idealistic, they argued that the MFDP must never place politics over principles and that to compromise now meant conciliating the forces responsible for the murder of their colleagues. Responding to Rustin's argument that while protest is based on morality, politics requires compromise, Bob Moses proclaimed that the MFDP had come to put morality into politics. Angry at the betrayal of their supposed friends and allies, SNCC lashed out that "this token offer of recognition was too much like the usual bone thrown to Negroes who showed signs of revolt." Mrs. Hamer agreed, describing the proposal as "a token of rights on the back row that we get in Mississippi. We didn't come all this way for that mess again."

The MFDP voted down the compromise decisively. The Freedom Democrats bitterly resented the brazen paternalism of the Credentials Committee choosing who the MFDP at-large delegates would be. Even more, the "sell-out" by their "false friends" disillusioned the COFO veterans. It proved to SNCC and CORE's field secretaries that white liberals could not be counted on, that they would compromise black needs whenever it suited them, and that real change would come only when blacks possessed the independent power to "remain a threat to the power structure."

The President's manipulative attempt to force the MFDP to endorse the compromise, moreover, completed SNCC's alienation from the mainstream of the movement and its estrangement from the federal government and the Democratic Party. Bitterness over the defeat of the convention challenge worsened all the ill feelings that had festered during the summer's interactions between SNCC field secretaries and white volunteers in Mississippi. The treatment of the Freedom Democrats snapped the frayed ties that bound SNCC to interracialism and nonviolence, and to seeking solutions through the political process. SNCC seethed at its betrayal by Roy Wilkins, Bayard Rustin, and, especially, Martin Luther King; and, determined to seek fundamental social change rather than just civil-rights legislation, it recognized that establishment liberals had interests quite different from those of SNCC, and that they could not be trusted. "I will have nothing to do with the political system any longer," Moses announced to TV reporters.

The time had come to forge new tactics of struggle. SNCC's field secretaries were done with redemptive suffering and the use of soul force. The American dilemma had become irreconcilable, they believed, and the American dream a nightmare. Charles Sherrod announced after the convention that SNCC now was "demanding power," and that the only options left were whether African-Americans would share power in "reconciliation" or seize it in "rioting and blood." "Things could never be the same," added Cleveland Sellers, voicing the sentiment of most of SNCC's battered and bloodied troops. "Never again were we lulled into believing that our task was exposing injustices so that the 'good' people of America could eliminate them. We left Atlantic City with the knowledge that the movement had turned into something else. After Atlantic City, our struggle was not for civil rights, but for liberation."

But the allure of liberation did not easily become a blueprint for its realization, and SNCC sank into despondency. Most whites considered it inexplicably extremist, as both unamenable to reasonable compromise and ungrateful for real concessions; and the majority of African-Americans in the South, who believed the movement was making progress, did not share its disillusionment. Embarrassed by its antics at the Democratic convention, most African-American leaders distanced themselves from SNCC and/or explained its behavior as a consequence of battle fatigue. Exhausted from overwork and tension, filled with pain and disappointment, the young radicals expressed their rage rather than the needs of most African-Americans. Rather than concerning themselves with a realistic political program to improve daily existence in African America, they vented their own fury. Rustin noted: "They had nothing but death and destruction and fear all around them and to come up to Atlantic City and take any other position I think was psychologically impossible." But still wrong, Rustin insisted: the time had come for the movement to think politically.

The election results in November buoyed the spirit of all those who thought with Rustin that the success of the civil-rights struggle depended on the political success of the same coalition that had orchestrated the March on Washington: "Negroes, trade unionists, liberals, and religious groups." The six million African-Americans who had voted in 1964, two million more than in 1960, went 94 percent for L.B.J., who won an astounding 61 percent of the popular vote and carried every state but Goldwater's Arizona and the five Deep South states of Alabama, Georgia, Louisiana, Mississippi, and South Carolina, where fewer than 45 percent of the eligible blacks could vote. Where Southern blacks did freely participate in the election, their ballots gave Johnson the margin of victory. Without the black vote, the Democrats would have lost Arkansas, Florida, Tennessee, and Virginia. Blacks hoped the message was clear: voter registration in the Deep South would benefit the Democrats. And the Democrats could now do something about it, for the 1964 election shattered the Republican–Dixiecrat coalition in Congress.

"Hurry, boys, hurry," the President implored his aides to draft the Great Society bills he wanted enacted. "Get that legislation up to the Hill and out. Eighteen months from now, Ol' Landslide Lyndon will be Lame-Duck Lyndon." But voting rights was not on Johnson's agenda. He feared the growth of the "white backlash" would diminish votes for his Great Society legislation; and he remained piqued at the civil-rights movement for the MFDP antics at the convention. Particularly jealous of Martin Luther King's stature as Time's 1964 Man of the Year and as the winner of the Nobel

Peace Prize, Johnson wanted to do nothing that would enhance ✲
King's reputation. In fact, Johnson did nothing to stop an FBI
vendetta against King; and he remained silent when Hoover denounced King as "the most notorious liar in the country" and
charged that SCLC was "spearheaded by Communists and moral
degenerates." Hoover made much of King's reliance on Bayard
Rustin, who had been a Communist in the 1930s, had gone to jail
as a conscientious objector during the Second World War, and had
been arrested on a morals charge for homosexuality, and on Stanley
Levinson, who the FBI claimed was a secret member of the Communist hierarchy. Determined to destroy King's reputation and influence, Hoover also privately circulated copies of the tapes made
by the FBI which recorded King's dalliances with various women
in bugged hotel rooms. President Johnson, who relished playing the
tapes of King's amorous acts and words, made no move to halt the
Bureau's efforts to blackmail King into inaction or, as Hoover
stated, to "completely discredit the effectiveness of Martin Luther
King, Jr., as a Negro leader."

Contrary to Johnson's wishes, SCLC in late 1964 plotted a strategy to force the federal government to protect African-American
voting rights. It had changed and learned much on the long road
from Montgomery to Albany to Birmingham to St. Augustine. Unlike the CORE and SNCC cadres who no longer even paid lip-
service to nonviolence, the years of anguish and chagrin transformed
SCLC's commitment to nonviolence from *satyagraha*, peaceful persuasion to change the hearts and minds of their oppressors, to
*duragraha*, tactical nonviolence as an effective means to coerce a
demanded end. Once an ethic, nonviolence was now a tactic. Birmingham had convinced SCLC that white savagery against unre-
sisting civil-rights protesters could provoke the national response
necessary to move the Administration and Congress. King outlined
the desired scenario for Project Alabama: (1) "nonviolent demonstrators go into the streets to exercise their constitutional rights";
(2) "racists resist by unleashing violence against them"; (3) "Americans of conscience in the name of decency demand federal inter-

vention and legislation"; and (4) "the Administration, under mass pressure, initiates measures of immediate intervention and remedial legislation." Success required Southern racists to act their brutal worst to arouse national indignation, so King and his aides carefully chose Selma as the focal point of their campaign to have the federal government end all barriers to black voting.

Birthplace of the Alabama Citizens' Council and of "Bull" Connor, Selma, an antebellum slave market, epitomized the difficulty of African-American voting in the Deep South. Although a majority of Selma's inhabitants, African-Americans comprised just three percent of those on the voting rolls. As King wrote in *The New York Times*: "Selma has succeeded in limiting Negro registration to the snail's pace of about 145 persons a year. At this rate, it would take 103 years to register the 15,000 eligible Negro voters of Dallas County." Selma, moreover, was already infamous within the movement for the vicious and violent treatment of civil-rights workers by its county sheriff, James G. Clark. His behavior toward SNCC's voter-registration efforts in Selma, begun in February 1962 by Bernard Lafayette and his wife Colia, had convinced Diane Nash and her husband, James Bevel, now working for the SCLC, that King should go to Selma, because his adversary would be another "Bull" Connor. They were sure that Clark's inability to rein in his rage would produce the notoriety and martyrdom necessary for the national attention and support that would result in voting-rights legislation. SCLC staffers arriving in Selma were neither surprised nor disappointed when they encountered Sheriff Jim Clark wearing a huge button on his shirt containing one word: "Never!"

"We will dramatize the situation to arouse the federal government by marching by the thousands to the places of registration," King announced in Selma on January 2, 1965, just weeks after accepting the Nobel Peace Prize in Oslo. "We are not asking," he warned, "we are demanding the ballot." As in Birmingham, SCLC started slowly. In daily marches to the Dallas County Courthouse, King led dozens, then scores, and finally hundreds of blacks to attempt to get their names on the voter lists. By the end of the month, over

two thousand blacks had been arrested, and Selma became national
news. But Sheriff Clark, largely kept in check by public safety director Wilson Baker, denied the SCLC the confrontation it sought,
forestalling any sense of national outrage.

Eager to exploit Clark's violent tendencies, King led a giant demonstration on February 1, getting himself arrested along with 770
other protesters, many of them schoolchildren. The following day,
Clark imprisoned some 520 blacks for parading without a permit,
and on February 3 he arrested another 300 students. Throughout
the month, marches and demonstrations persisted. As the number
of the arrested grew, Clark became more high-handed and brutal;
yet he contained himself enough to frustrate SCLC's calculated
strategy of confrontation. SCLC failed to arouse the national indignation it needed to pressure the federal government, despite the
murder of Jimmie Lee Jackson by an Alabama state trooper during
a civil-rights march in nearby Marion. Even Malcolm X's public
threat that if the demonstrations in Selma did not result in change,
"other ways" would be employed, failed to prod Washington into
action.

Checkmated, some SNCC activists and the SCLC staff decided
that a fitting response to Jackson's death would be a mass march
from Selma to the state capitol in Montgomery to present a petition
of grievances to the governor. "I can't promise you that it won't
get you beaten," King intoned at Selma's Brown Chapel. "I can't
promise you that it won't get your house bombed. I can't promise
you won't get scarred up a bit. But we must stand up for what is
right." Governor Wallace responded: "Such a march cannot and
will not be tolerated," and he issued an order proscribing the demonstration. Receiving warnings of a threat on his life, King left for
Atlanta, claiming the need to attend to his congregation. Not wishing to antagonize President Johnson, moreover, King hoped to postpone the march until a federal judge had voided Wallace's ban. But
the next day SCLC's Hosea Williams agreed with SNCC militants
that the march not be delayed. On Sunday morning, March 7,
Williams and John Lewis led some five hundred chanting protesters

gathered outside Brown Chapel toward U.S. Highway 80, the route
to Montgomery.

As the TV cameras whirred and scores of news reporters took
notes, the long column of freedom-singing African-Americans carrying their sleeping bags approached the Edmund Pettus Bridge, the
gateway out of Selma. About a hundred of Sheriff Clark's deputized
possemen lined both sides of the bridge, and another hundred state
troopers, commanded by Major John Cloud, barred the opposite
end. Twice Hosea Williams sought to speak to Cloud. "There is
no word to be had," the major responded. "You have two minutes
to turn around and go back to your church." Williams began to
confer with his aides and Cloud suddenly ordered: "Troopers forward!" As the state forces rushed forward in a flying wedge, Clark's
mounted posse attacked from the sides, voicing a rebel yell and
swinging bullwhips and rubber tubing wrapped in barbed wire. The
marchers, kneeling in prayer, panicked, fleeing the tear gas, the
charging horsemen, the flailing chains and electric cattle prods. The
savage attack left fifty African-Americans hospitalized and at least
that many injured, though less severely.

The nation saw it all, and now understood the reign of terror by
which Southern bigots kept African-Americans from voting. ABC
interrupted its Sunday movie to broadcast film of the carnage, and
the other network news programs stunned viewers with repeated
images of billowing tear gas, stomping horses, and law officers
venting their fury on limping, bleeding African-American marchers
and bystanders. The pictures on television of irrational police violence stimulated an uproar of indignation and a broad consensus
in favor of action by Washington. The White House was besieged
with demands for federal intervention. Some four hundred rabbis,
pastors, and nuns rushed to Selma, and at least ten times that
number of clergymen converged on Washington to press Congress
for voting-rights legislation and to denounce the President for his
"unbelievable lack of action" in the crisis. Fourteen students insisting that the President send troops to Selma staged a seven-hour
sit-in at the White House, while another three hundred students

sat-in in the snow to support their call. Tens of thousands, white and black, showed their solidarity with the disenfranchised Alabamians by joining Selma sympathy marches in cities across the country.

Overwhelmed by the response, King promised in Atlanta to lead a second march on Tuesday, March 9, and to seek a federal injunction to prevent Governor Wallace and Alabama police authorities from interfering with the march. Monday morning, Judge Frank M. Johnson, Jr., heard the SCLC and Justice Department attorneys' request for an order to guarantee the safety of the marches and to void the governor's ban. Pending further hearings, however, Judge Johnson enjoined the SCLC from undertaking the march. King had never before defied a federal court order, but returning to Selma that evening, he told a rally: "We've gone too far to turn back now. We must let them know that nothing can stop us—not even death itself."

Once again King found himself painfully torn between conflicting needs and constituencies. For two months he had been nurturing the militancy of Selma's blacks and now, embittered by the Sunday violence, they insisted on marching across the bridge, and continuing on to Montgomery. The youth, many of whom had been jailed in the previous demonstrations, proclaimed that they would march regardless of what the adult leaders decided. Their ranks swelled by hundreds of movement supporters who had journeyed to Selma for the second march, SNCC organizers clamored for a rematch. "We were angry," wrote Cleveland Sellers. "And we wanted to show Governor Wallace, the Alabama State Highway Patrol, Sheriff Clark, Selma's whites, the federal government and poor Southern blacks in other Selmas that we didn't intend to take any more shit. We would ram the march down the throat of anyone who tried to stop us." In addition, such civil-rights leaders as James Farmer, Jim Forman, and Fred Shuttlesworth had hurried to Selma to resume the march. To postpone the confrontation until the injunction was lifted, King understood, meant risking the split of the Selma movement. He would surely be accused of being a toady of L.B.J. and a coward, and by default, leadership of the black struggle would fall into the hands of those wanting him to fail.

Yet, in no uncertain terms, President Johnson demanded that the illegal march not take place. Administration officials and congressional leaders pressed King to avoid a repetition of "Bloody Sunday." The SCLC leader knew he could not forfeit their support by defying the federal courts, which had been a major ally of the civil-rights movement since the *Brown* decision of 1954. His goal remained effective voting-rights legislation and enforcement, and it would not come to pass without the cooperation of the White House. When Leroy Collins, head of the federal government's new Community Relations Service, arrived in Selma Tuesday morning with a face-saving plan to avert a clash, King accepted the arrangement. In return for an agreement by Alabama authorities not to molest the marchers, King would lead his followers across the Pettus Bridge, stop when halted by the troopers, pray briefly, and then order the marchers to turn back. None of the marchers or other civil-rights leaders knew of King's compromise when he entered the Brown Chapel shortly after noon to lead the assemblage to Montgomery. "We have the right to walk the highways," King began:

> I have no alternative but to lead a march from this spot to carry our grievances to the seat of government. I have made my choice. I have got to march. I do not know what lies ahead of us. There may be beatings, jailings, tear gas. But I would rather die on the highways of Alabama than make a butchery of my conscience by compromising with evil.

Nearly a thousand blacks and half as many white sympathizers from the North proudly filed out of the church after King. Singing stanza after stanza of "Ain't Gonna Let Nobody Turn Me 'Round," the column crossed the bridge and stopped fifty feet from Major Cloud's line of state troops. "This march will not continue," Cloud commanded. The major granted King's request to pray; then, departing from the agreed-upon scenario, to embarrass King further,

Cloud ordered his men to break ranks and move to the sides of the highway. The road to Montgomery lay open. King hesitated, then turned to his astonished followers and instructed them to return to the Brown Chapel. "All of a sudden I realized that the people in front were turning around and coming back," remembered a white minister from Boston, "and I was aghast. What is going on? Are we not going through with this confrontation? What's happening?" At the church King tried to gloss over his decision, pretending that the demonstrators had made their point, rather than explaining why he had acted as he did. Few could accept the hollow rhetoric, and King stirred no excitement when he promised that there would yet be a march on Montgomery. The SNCC was long angered by the repeated pattern of SNCC activists doing the dangerous ground-work and then seeing SCLC sweeping into town to grab all the glory. SNCC's distrust of SCLC was driven to a higher level by the "turnaround" than had ever been reached before; and the Selma movement came close to expiring.

One more time, however, white racist violence revived the struggle for equality. While militant blacks voiced their disillusionment with King, a gang of white hoodlums attacked three white Unitarian ministers who had come to Selma to participate in the march. Beaten unconscious with a club, the Reverend James J. Reeb of Boston died two days later of multiple fractures of the skull, provoking a national outcry and renewed demonstrations across the country. Reeb's death aroused white demands for federal action. Hundreds of clergymen, union officials, schoolteachers, and college students began their pilgrimage to Selma. Tens of thousands of letters and telegrams poured into Washington petitioning for voting-rights leg-islation, a plea echoed by most of the nation's press.

On Monday evening, March 15, President Johnson delivered a televised address to a joint session of the Congress to request the passage of a voting-rights bill. He compared the struggle at Selma to that at Lexington and Concord, and told the legislators that the "real hero of this struggle is the American Negro. His actions and protests, his courage to risk safety, and even to risk his life, have awakened the conscience of this nation. His demonstrations have been designed to call attention to injustice, designed to provoke change, designed to stir reform. He has called upon us to make good the promise of America. And who among us can say that we would have made the same progress were it not for his persistent bravery and his faith in American democracy?"

Because local officials had deviously denied suffrage to blacks, Johnson went on, he would submit a bill to "establish a simple uniform standard which cannot be used, however ingenious the effort, to flout the Constitution. . . . What happened in Selma is part of a far larger movement which reaches into every section and state of America. It is the effort of American Negroes to secure for themselves the full blessings of American life." Eloquently he pleaded: "This cause must be our cause too. It is not just Negroes, but all of us, who must overcome the crippling legacy of bigotry and injustice. And," the President concluded emphatically, "we *shall* overcome." Johnson expressed what most in the movement had hoped for. Although SNCC's James Forman angrily denounced it as empty symbolism, John Lewis termed it "historic, eloquent, and more than inspiring" and a member of SCLC's executive staff claimed: "It was a victory like none other. It was an affirmation of the movement." Just a decade earlier, another President of the United States would not even state his agreement with the Supreme Court's school-desegregation ruling.

President Johnson also acted. He prevailed upon Judge Johnson to issue a ruling to permit the march and he called in Governor Wallace and laid down the law: the marchers would be protected and he would brook no interference with their demonstration.

Six days after Johnson's address to Congress, King spoke to the more than three thousand black and white marchers gathered in front of Brown Chapel: "You will be the people that will write a new chapter in the history books of our nation. Those of us who are Negroes don't have much. . . . Because of the system, we don't have much education. . . . But thank God we have our bodies, our feet and our souls. Walk together, children," King preached, "don't you get weary, and it will lead us to the Promised Land." The joyous throng surged forward, singing and laughing, barely noticing the white hecklers lining the route with crude placards reading "Bye, Bye, Blackbird" and "Martin Luther Coon." Protected by the federalized Alabama National Guard, the marchers tramped uneventfully through fifty miles of Alabama countryside, singing "Oh, Wallace! Segregation's got to fall . . . you never can jail us all." Four days later, on the outskirts of Montgomery, nearly thirty thousand more blacks and whites joined them for the final three miles to the grounds of the Alabama capitol, yet another step in the long, black-led trek toward racial equality. "I was glad I had on dark glasses," Price Cobbs, an African-American psychiatrist, recalled, because "tears were streaming down my cheeks. I just wasn't prepared for the overwhelming feeling of love. I didn't realize that people of every color, every background could really feel together."

As at the March on Washington, the huge interracial crowd in Montgomery, representing grassroots movements from across the South, waited for King, while one civil-rights leader after another spoke. Then the nation on its television sets, and Governor Wallace through the slats of his venetian blinds, watched King stride to the podium and heard the assemblage's amens begin to rise. "We have walked on meandering highways and rested our bodies on rocky byways," he began, calling for more marches, everywhere—on segregated schools, on poverty, and on "ballot boxes until race baiters disappear from the political arena. Let us march on ballot boxes," King reiterated, "until the Wallaces of our nation tremble away in silence."

"I know some of you are asking today, 'How long will it take?' I come to say to you this afternoon," King concluded triumphantly, "however difficult the moment, however frustrating the hour, it will not be long because truth pressed to earth will rise again. How long? Not long, because no lie can live forever. How long? Not long, because you will reap what you sow. How long? Not long, because the arm of the moral universe is long but it bends toward justice. How long? Not long. Because mine eyes have seen the glory of the coming of the Lord."

Demented white violence had made this moment possible, and it struck again that evening, ending all doubt that Congress would speedily enact an uncompromising voting-rights bill. Viola Liuzzo, the white wife of a Detroit labor-union official and mother of five children, had come to Alabama, she had told her husband, because "it was everybody's business—she had to go." Following King's speech, she volunteered to transport marchers back to Selma in her car. As she was returning to Montgomery later in the night to pick up a second group of marchers, a car with four Klansmen pulled even with Liuzzo's car. Rifle bullets shattered Liuzzo's head, killing her instantly. Sixteen hours later, an angry Lyndon Johnson appeared on television to deplore the murder and demand quick passage of his suffrage legislation.

As in the preceding years, the brutal outrages committed by white supremacists and by Southern law-enforcement officers forced policymakers to take actions that they would have preferred avoiding or postponing. On August 3, 1965, the House of Representatives passed the voting-rights bill by better than a four-to-one margin. The Senate followed suit the next day. Signing the act which authorized federal examiners to register qualified voters and suspended discriminatory devices like literacy tests, Johnson proclaimed: "Today is a triumph for freedom as huge as any victory that has ever been won on any battlefield." The lock on the ballot box for blacks had been broken. Following the arrival of a federal examiner in Selma, the percentage of voting-age African-Americans registered rose in just two months from less than 10 percent to more than 60 percent. The fewer than 22 percent of Alabama blacks registered in 1964 became 57 percent in 1968. In Mississippi, the percentage of black registrants leaped from 7 percent in 1964 to 59 percent in 1968. In those four years, the number of Southern African-American voters tripled.

The movement for black equality could indeed be proud. The awesome power of nonviolent direct action to dramatize racism to the nation had again been demonstrated. More than ever before, the fear of African-Americans in the South had been vanquished. The movement had changed the nation, and buoyed the dreams of equality of people of every color around the world. But the favorable political environment in the United States—a relatively high level of general liberalism, a prosperous, booming economy, and a White House and Congress controlled by the Democrats—would soon change, and the struggle to assure African-Americans the ballot, the most elementary right of citizenship, had left indelible scars and open sores. The movement would march together no more.

·····················

# SEVEN

# HEIRS OF MALCOLM X

A race of people is like an individual man; until it uses its own talent, takes pride in its own history, expresses its own culture, affirms its own selfhood, it can never fulfill itself.

MALCOLM X

Black and white, few paid much attention to the rumblings of discontent within the movement and within the black ghettos as the nation celebrated Independence Day in 1965. Most accepted the civil-rights gains of the first half of the decade as necessary and just; many saw them as a prelude to further progress. Addressing the graduating class of Howard University in June, President Lyndon Johnson promised bold, new efforts in housing, employment, welfare, and education to assist the blacks' struggle to move beyond the goal of equality of opportunity to racial equality as a reality. Early in August, in a grandiose ceremony televised from the Capitol rotunda, the President signed the voting-rights bill into law and vowed swift and vigorous enforcement. Even as he spoke, federal voting registrars hurried into action. The movement had never seemed more accepted, or more assisted by religious, student, and liberal organizations; and the Leadership Conference on Civil Rights had never seemed more potent in influencing the three branches of the federal government. At this relatively peaceful and prosperous moment, public support for King's dream appeared unprecedented.

On August 11, however, just five days after Johnson signed the voting-rights act, the most destructive race riot in more than two decades began in Watts, a Los Angeles ghetto of a quarter of a million African-Americans, brutally patrolled by a force of two hundred white and five black police officers. That explosion of bitterness over unfulfilled African-American hopes for dignity and equality sparked a succession of "long, hot summers." The violent upheavals hopelessly splintered the civil-rights coalition, hastened the decline of CORE and SNCC, and virtually ended significant white support, both financial and political, for the movement. Just as the struggle had hit its stride, the riots cut the legs off the team of runners best equipped to stay the course successfully. The era of nonviolence ended. The age of Malcolm X's angry heirs began. Strategies of social change gave way to expressions of rage. "Black Power" drowned out "Black and White Together." "Burn, Baby, Burn" supplanted "Freedom Now." By the end of 1968, 250 African-Americans had died, over eight thousand had been wounded, and some fifty thousand had been arrested in the nearly three hundred race riots and disturbances since 1965. An estimated half million blacks had participated in the burning and looting. An equal number of Americans served in Vietnam in 1968. The war in Asia had among its many unintended consequences the destruction of the consensus for racial reform. As the United States disgorged its firepower into Vietnam and the ghettos burst into flames, the hopes of the blacks went up in smoke and King's dream turned to ash.

A confrontation between white police and young blacks ignited the tinder in Watts, as it would in most of the subsequent racial disorders of the 1960s. Shortly before 8 on a sultry Wednesday evening, an ordinary arrest for drunken driving brought a typical crowd of onlookers. Such incidents were everyday occurrences in the ghetto. On this particular night, however, the arrested youth's mother scuffled with the patrolmen, and blacks observing the tussle responded with menacing jeers, causing the arresting policemen to brandish rifles and to radio for reinforcements. The black spectators refused to be cowed by a show of superior force; they pelted the newly arrived law officers with rocks and bottles. By 10 p.m. the angry crowd had become a rampaging mob, overturning the cars of passing white motorists and smashing shop windows. Looting began at midnight, and for several hours a few thousand blacks openly vented the anger they had so long repressed and concealed. Calm returned at dawn. The police confidently announced that the riot was over.

But the mob reassembled the next evening. Many carried arms. In the shabby, littered streets of the ghetto, the hostility toward all whites became palpable. Black violence raged. This time it did not cease with the light of day. Indeed, the more than five thousand rioters roaming Watts on Friday morning, crying "Long live Malcolm X" and shouting "Burn, baby, burn," the hip slogan of a local disc jockey, the Magnificent Montague, protested against both the brutality of the Los Angeles Police Department and the indignities of segregated, substandard housing, inadequate transportation, and an unemployment rate of 30 percent for adult males. Most looted and trashed. Some firebombed white-owned businesses and attacked whites wandering in the ghetto. A few returned police fire, sniped at them from rooftops, and ambushed firemen responding to the increasing number of alarms. Law-enforcement officials called for help, and National Guard troops rushed to Watts on Friday afternoon to restore order. They could not. The number of rioters multiplied. The damage soared. By late Saturday, over fourteen thousand Guardsmen augmented the fifteen hundred law officers struggling to contain the insurrection of an estimated fifty thousand African-Americans. Traditional restraints on black anger had evanesced and for three more days and nights the burning, looting, and sniping continued. When the six-day melee ended, thirty-four had been killed, some nine hundred injured, nearly four thousand arrested, and about $30 million of property had been devastated.

While a shocked nation viewed the Watts conflagration on its TV sets, the outrage of Chicago blacks erupted after a fire truck accidentally struck and killed an African-American woman on August 12. For two days and nights, the West Side of Chicago resembled the Watts battlefield. Thousands of blacks rushed to the ghetto streets to battle police and National Guardsmen, and to loot and burn the stores owned by whites. Then the arrest of eighteen blacks outside a nightclub in Springfield, Massachusetts, on August 14, ignited another outbreak of collective violence. Once again, blacks looted and burned and returned the fire of the police and National Guard.

In retrospect, the racial tumult of 1965 was merely a prelude to the acts of destruction and desperation to come. The summer of 1966 brought more than a score of race riots and an even larger number of serious racial disturbances. Across the nation, ghetto blacks went on a rampage, violently declaring their fury over unmet demands for meaningful work, for housing without rats and police protection without brutality or contempt, for a decent measure of control over their own destiny. Hardly a day seemed to pass without the evening news showing film of surging African-American mobs breaking windows, smashing cars, ransacking stores, putting the torch to white businesses, and hurling bricks and bottles at embattled police and firemen. To quell the turbulence in 1966, National Guard troops patrolled the streets of Chicago, Cleveland, Dayton, Milwaukee, and San Francisco. At least seven blacks died in the racial disorders, more than four hundred were injured, and another three thousand arrested.

The most intense and destructive wave of racial violence the nation had ever witnessed came in 1967. Violence convulsed Boston, Buffalo, Cincinnati, New Haven, Providence, Wilmington, Cambridge, Maryland, and a hundred other cities. North and South, from coast to coast, authorities reported unprecedented numbers of blacks throwing Molotov cocktails, looting and burning stores, and firing upon police.

No riot was more expected than Newark's; none was more bloody. With the nation's highest rates of black joblessness, condemned housing, crime, new cases of tuberculosis, and maternal mortality, Newark verged on the brink of a race war between its despairing majority black population and a callous, corrupt, almost all-white city administration. The arrest of a black taxidriver and rumors that he had been beaten to death triggered the bloodbath on July 12. Looting began immediately. Then the arsonists took over. On the second night, the police began using live ammunition. They killed five African-Americans. Although the rioting seemed on the wane the third day, the Governor of New Jersey described the situation as "a city in open rebellion" and ordered in the National Guard. Over the weekend, the Guardsmen and police fired over thirteen thousand rounds of ammunition, killing twenty more blacks and wounding some twelve hundred. Over thirteen hundred blacks had been arrested and property losses were put at $10 million.

More unexpectedly, yet just as bloodily, Detroit erupted the next Sunday. In death and destruction it was the worst race riot in half a century. Unlike Newark, the Motor City had a progressive mayor who, backed by African-American voters, attended to ghetto problems. Many of the city's officeholders were black, and Washington had lavished millions of dollars on Detroit's anti-poverty and urban-renewal programs. The auto industry, the economic mainstay of Detroit blacks, was booming. Unemployment was low and wages high. As opposed to the large-scale black poverty of Newark, nearly two-thirds of the black families in Detroit owned cars and almost half owned their homes. Yet relations between the police and the Detroit ghetto duplicated those in Newark and Watts and scores of other Northern cities. Recurring instances of unwarranted police brutality had caused massive black resentment toward law-enforcement officers and a constant, unrelenting low level of warfare between black citizens and white cops.

On July 23 the mass arrest of African-Americans at a nightclub selling liquor after the legal closing time detonated six days and nights of epidemic arson and vandalism, six days and nights of black defiance of a system of law and order which seemed so terribly biased against them. Nearly four thousand fires destroyed thirteen hundred buildings. The devastation left five thousand blacks homeless and an equal number jobless. Observing the smoking ruins from a helicopter, the Governor of Michigan remarked that Detroit looked like "a city that had been bombed." Added to the damage caused by burning, looting by tens of thousands of blacks brought the total of lost property to a quarter of a billion dollars. Worse, frightened and untrained National Guardsmen, firing without discipline, accounted for most of the riot's forty-three dead and over a thousand wounded. All told, the 1967 summer riots resulted in at least ninety deaths, more than four thousand casualties, and nearly seventeen thousand arrests.

Self-serving politicians and pundits of every ideological shade offered explanations to a bewildered nation. Leftist black radicals described the riots as calculated revolutionary violence to overthrow a reactionary society. They compared them to the colonial rebellions in Africa and Asia, and predicted that the urban guerilla warfare and sabotage by the oppressed masses would not cease until the ultimate destruction of white capitalist rule. Sharing much of this fantasy, white reactionaries also saw the specter of revolution in the riots. However, they blamed the efforts of the mass of blacks to bring down the United States on foreign agitators and black Communists rather than on social conditions. To meet fire with fire, the far right demanded a government vendetta against radical black groups, and the incarceration of all black extremists. They urged patriotic whites to arm themselves to defend the nation against an African-American insurrection.

Eschewing economic nostrums, black nationalists depicted the riots as a repudiation of the "Uncle Toms" and "handkerchief-head niggers" in the NAACP and SCLC and a rejection of their goal of an integrated society. "The Negro was really in exile in America," they repeatedly quoted Malcolm X, insisting that only separatism could end the violence. Some nationalists stipulated that the government finance the black repatriation to Africa as compensation for slavery. Others clamored for the United States to deed blacks a separate homeland on the continent so that the two races could live apart. Most settled for urging ghetto autonomy and complete black control over African-American institutions. All agreed that the alternative to separatism would be significantly more black retaliatory violence.

Liberals, both African-American and white, explained the riots as a response to deprivation, as a consequence of the inequalities and inequities in the ghetto, as a cry from the forgotten people of the Negro Revolution; and they advocated programs targeted to African-Americans for better housing, quality integrated education, improved job opportunities, and more generous welfare benefits. Responding to the disorders in Watts, Lyndon Johnson exclaimed: "It is not enough simply to decry disorder. We must also strike at the unjust conditions from which disorder largely flows." As the number of riots mounted, the President confided to an aide: "As I see it, I have moved the Negro from D+ to C−. He's still nowhere. He knows it. And that's why he's out in the streets. Hell, I'd be there too." The National Advisory Commission on Civil Disorders, appointed by Johnson in 1967, blamed the riots on the "explosive mixture" of poverty, unemployment, slum housing, and segregated education caused by white racism. Focusing on the African-American ghetto, the commission charged that "white institutions created it, white institutions maintain it, and white society condones it." To allay black discontent, the commission recommended the creation of two million new jobs in the ghetto, an attack on de facto segregation, the construction of six million new units of public housing, and the institution of a national system of income supplementation. Although liberals squabbled among themselves over how much should be spent on particular items, and about what could be done to end police brutality and white racism, they unanimously advocated massive federal expenditures to improve the material conditions of the ghetto as the surest way to end the rioting. But, while many local governments and private firms initially responded to the riots with programs for jobs, slum clearance, recreational facilities, and improved relations between residents and the police, the rapidly rising costs of the escalating war in Vietnam sealed the doom for massive domestic spending, and L.B.J. never endorsed the recommendations of the commission he appointed.

At the same time, conservatives considered the proposals of the National Advisory Commission on Civil Disorders tantamount to rewarding criminal behavior. Poverty and squalor did not cause the riots, they argued: young hoodlums were responsible; agitators preying on the idle were to blame; the cause was the dominant ethos of liberal permissiveness, which encouraged African-American avarice and aggressiveness. Accordingly, conservatives preached the gospel of "law and order." Rather than shackle the police with civilian review boards, they wanted to strengthen law-enforcement agencies with additional manpower and riot control weapons, and to encourage the police to get yet tougher with the lawless, even "to shoot to kill" looters. Instead of letting the media disseminate the advocacy of violence by black demagogues, they urged the government to repress radical black organizations. In place of ameliorating the horrors of ghetto life, conservatives exhorted the government to punish rioters.

Most of these commonly accepted interpretations of the racial turbulence had little basis in fact. Although no single set of generalizations can encompass all the unique and varying conditions in some two hundred cities and towns, in different years, or the individual motivations and behavior of hundreds of thousands of participants in the riots, certain inferences can be drawn from the vast data collected during and immediately after the riots. Outside agitators played no significant role in the disturbances. Most upheavals showed little or no evidence of planning. Yet, for all their apparent randomness, the vast majority of African-American rioters acted purposefully. They looted and destroyed tenements and businesses owned by whites, especially those reputed to exploit African-Americans, and spared those of blacks who scrawled "soul brother" on their windows. They sought to avoid damaging the institutions that served them, such as churches, libraries, and schools. In some instances, nearly half the adult population of the ghetto joined the riot. In almost all others, those who participated constituted a cross section of the black community. Neither criminals nor teenagers predominated. Only a minority came from the ranks of the unemployed or most deprived. Men and women of the black working class in the main, the majority supported the goals of the civil-rights movement and accepted the leadership of Martin Luther King, Jr. Most sought neither to separate from nor to destroy American society.

Ghetto blacks rioted to enter the mainstream of that society. They rioted to protest the pervasiveness and depth of white racism in the supposedly racially egalitarian North. They rioted to draw attention to the squalor of the slums and the savagely oppressive behavior of the police in the ghetto. They rioted to make the needs of the ghetto visible, to smash the narrow view of the race problem as just a Southern phenomenon, to force whites to pay heed to the plight of urban African-Americans. They rioted to assert their unrequited plea for all the decencies and dignities possessed by other Americans. They rioted to raise the economic questions which the civil-rights movement had ignored; and, nationwide, a huge preponderance of blacks who had never burned or looted expressed approval for the protest articulated by those who had.

Urban blacks chose to protest by rioting in the second half of the sixties because they had no other viable strategy of change and because the struggle for equality in the South had changed the psychology of the Northern ghetto. The battle for civil rights gave the blacks of Watts in 1965, of Cleveland in 1966, of Detroit in 1967, a far different sense of themselves than they had had in 1950. The movement shook the ghettos out of their lethargy. It proved that protest could succeed and it raised black consciousness. It stimulated expectations for a better life. For the better part of a decade, Northern blacks watched their brethren in the South gain concessions by creating disorder. They would have to do no less. Ghetto blacks saw the movement reform Dixie, and they grew hopeful and impatient. Surely, if the massive edifice of Southern racism could be toppled, then a solution to the urban problems of race could be expected.

Television's transmission of the civil-rights story especially encouraged anticipations of speedy success. Each evening's news program brought accounts of protest and progress; and, increasingly, they were accompanied by dramatic exhortations for yet greater militancy. Television also whetted the resentments of the deprived by constantly depicting an affluent lifestyle among whites that contrasted vividly with their own. And the repeated scenes of white violence against African-American protesters shown on television helped transform Northern black grievances into deep loathing and bitterness. The vivid depiction of white brutality in Alabama, Georgia, and Mississippi, observed by blacks throughout the nation, generated an obsessive hatred of the white police in the ghetto, who seemed to behave no differently from "Bull" Connor or Jim Clark.

The success of the struggle for racial equality in the South accelerated aspirations but did nothing to improve the day-to-day lot of ghetto blacks. The panoply of court decisions, congressional acts, and executive orders failed to affect the subordinate status of blacks in the North. None of the marches, pickets, rallies, or other forms of peaceful protest abolished filthy dope-ridden streets or inferior segregated schools. No lawful strategy of social change dented the hostility of police departments or the discrimination of labor unions. All the tactics that had worked in the South miscarried against greedy slumlords and their intransigent political allies. And even when many African-Americans did see improvement in the material aspects of their lives, their expectations outpaced their progress and they observed whites experiencing even more rapid rates of advancement. The result was increasing frustration and anger, a broadly, deeply, intensely felt bitterness, and its accompanying aggression. By the mid-1960s, moreover, the very immensity of the ghetto and the dominance of liberal attitudes in the nation made it safer for African-Americans to direct their aggression against its real causes.

Simultaneously, the closer African-Americans came to attaining their aspirations—the only truly effective means of diminishing dissatisfaction and frustration, and thus of aggression—the more apprehensive and resentful Northern whites became. Many of the same whites who praised the actions of the civil-rights movement in Birmingham and Selma exhibited anti-black prejudice comparable to the worst in the South when they felt their neighborhood school or lily-white union threatened by the presence of blacks. The white backlash grew harsh. Resistance to open housing flared in every Northern city, as did opposition to funding the War on Poverty, to ending de facto school segregation, and to establishing civilian review boards for the police. The adamant refusal of whites to correct the abuses that had been legally and peaceably protested forced blacks ultimately to desperate and destructive acts.

Within the movement, the emergence of Black Power paralleled the rage expressed by Northern blacks in the urban riots. The reaction against nonviolence as a tactic and integration as a goal similarly grew out of frustration over the limited pace and scope of racial change and out of bitterness toward unceasing brutal white opposition to the most minimal black advances. Black Power, like the riots, brought important psychological gains for blacks at the cost of further polarizing the races, sanctioning the cult of violence, and fueling the white backlash.

On June 5, 1966, James Meredith, who had integrated the University of Mississippi in 1962, set out to march the 225 miles from Memphis to Jackson. He believed that by demonstrating his bravery he could bolster the courage of African-Americans in Mississippi to assert their right to vote. When Meredith was barely ten miles inside his native state, a Klansman jumped out of the bushes beside Highway 51 and emptied the birdshot in his shotgun into the black veteran, wounding Meredith in the legs, back, and neck. The major civil-rights organizations, which had initially derided Meredith's march, rushed their leaders to Memphis to confer on how best to capitalize on the shooting. In addition to Martin Luther King, Jr., Roy Wilkins, and Whitney Young, two newcomers joined the circle: Floyd McKissick of CORE and SNCC's Stokely Carmichael. Both symbolized the major transformations occurring within their organizations, and the new paths their groups would tread.

After the Selma campaign, the leading organizations of the movement had floundered in their search for new programs. Everyone agreed on the need to move beyond the traditional civil-rights agenda. But none developed a viable strategy for solving the complex problems of inadequate housing, dead-end jobs, and inferior schooling. A sense of irrelevancy particularly rankled the dedicated activists in CORE and SNCC. They considered themselves the cutting edge of the movement, yet they now stood still. They yearned to lead the struggle to improve the living conditions of poor rural and ghetto blacks, but did not know how. They had paid too high a price in suffering and bloodshed to confess futility, so their impotence festered and turned bitter.

In the midst of this malaise, the young militants altered their former beliefs and ideals. Continued school and residential segregation convinced the disenchanted blacks that King's goal of an integrated society was an impossible dream. Embittered, SNCC and CORE began to transform the struggle for desegregation into a battle for self-determination. They would engage in grass-roots organizing that built the power of black communities and enabled African-Americans to control their own destinies. Whites could not help in this endeavor. The new liberation struggle required a restricted and subordinate role for whites, if not their total exclusion.

The movement radicals also adopted McKissick's description of nonviolence as "a dying philosophy" that had "outlived its usefulness." They had turned the other cheek too often, with too little to show for it. Traumatized by years of pain and fear, by too many vicious beatings and jailings at the hands of the Klan and sadistic sheriffs, by too many funerals for close friends killed by white racists, the militants in CORE and SNCC eagerly trumpeted their new inalienable right of self-defense. After the Watts riot, that concept rapidly metamorphosed into the doctrine of retaliatory violence. Ultimately, it would blossom into the advocacy of violence as a legitimate tactic wherever feasible.

In charting this new course, the young militants borrowed much from the New Left and even more from Malcolm X. The rhetoric of CORE and SNCC often seemed indistinguishable from that of the Students for a Democratic Society in its condemnation of the Vietnam War, criticism of capitalism, rejection of bourgeois values, and attack on liberalism as the problem rather than the answer. Mostly, SNCC and CORE's new thrust resembled that of Malcolm X, who had left the Nation of Islam in 1964 to promote greater black awareness of and identification with Africa, and to espouse black control of African-American communities. On February 21, 1965, as he approached the lectern in Harlem's Audubon Ballroom to address his Organization for Afro-American Unity, three men affiliated with Elijah Muhammed's Black Muslims suddenly rose from their seats in the first row and, like a firing squad, felled Malcolm X with their shotgun and revolvers. Several months later, his autobiography appeared. An extraordinary account of his life and exposition of his beliefs, *The Autobiography of Malcolm X* swept African America and particularly influenced young blacks. In death, Malcolm X achieved a far greater eminence and a larger following than he had in life.

Malcolm's rejection of Gandhian nonviolence and condemnation of integrationist ideals fit the mood of African-Americans whose hopes had been dashed. "The Negro was really in exile in America," he had repeatedly insisted. "No, I'm not an American. I'm one of the 22 million black people who are the victims of Americanism," he had lashed his critics. "And I see America through the eyes of the victim. I don't see any American dream; I see an American nightmare." Malcolm's black nationalism crystallized the feelings of those whose expectations had been frustrated, and of those whose lives the civil-rights movement had hardly touched. Especially insightful in depicting the cultural and psychological legacies of African-American oppression, Malcolm instilled a positive sense of black identity among his followers. His ideas of racial pride, pan-Africanism, and African-American control of black community institutions both expressed and shaped the changing consciousness of young black activists.

SNCC and CORE eagerly noted the extent to which the rioters in Watts, and ghetto youths throughout the nation, acknowledged the slain prince of black nationalism as their standard-bearer. It meshed with their own transformation, and the two movement groups acted accordingly. They took up his plea for black pride. They acted on his exhortation to raise racial consciousness rather than eradicate it. They embraced his identification of the African-American struggle with the worldwide struggle of the Third World for national liberation.

By the time of Meredith's shooting, SNCC and CORE had abandoned their initial emphases upon integration, interracialism, and nonviolence in the hope of remaining vital, viable forces for social change. "The light that shines is the light of love / Lights the darkness from above / It shines on me and it shines on you / And shows what the power of love can do" was superseded by "Too much love / Too much love / Nothing kills a nigger like / Too much love." In a series of votes during the year following the march from Selma to Montgomery, CORE and SNCC gradually, agonizingly, and often acrimoniously rejected their traditional goals and adopted new tactics. The Beloved Community had become irrelevant.

Reacting to the interplay of the urban race riots and the escalation of the war in Vietnam, the assassinations of Malcolm X and Sammy Younge (a SNCC organizer killed for attempting to use a "whites only" bathroom at a service station near Tuskegee Institute in January 1966), and the need to develop an organizing strategy for Northern cities, SNCC elected Stokely Carmichael over John Lewis as its new head and CORE selected Floyd McKissick to replace James Farmer as national director. The two organizations which had done so much to impress the noblest ideals of the movement on the nation now had new leaders eager to popularize their new ideas. The Meredith March gave them their chance.

All the leaders of the five major civil-rights groups wanted to resume the Memphis-to-Jackson March, and each had their own agenda. The Urban League and NAACP wanted an interracial trek to support new civil-rights legislation. CORE and SNCC wanted an all-black march, to "put Johnson on the spot" and to highlight the urgency of empowering African-Americans independent of the Democratic Party; and they wanted it to be protected by the Deacons for Defense, an African-American group from Louisiana whose members carried guns. Seeking to hold the civil-rights coalition together, King persuaded Carmichael and McKissick to accept his plan for a nonviolent, interracial march in return for his assent to a manifesto that indicted the government for failing to protect black rights and that called on Washington to enact A. Philip Randolph's proposed anti-poverty budget of $185 billion.

King's effort to be a moderating influence failed. Wilkins and Young wanted no part of the march and quickly left Memphis; SNCC and CORE, despite King's wishes, dominated the processions. On June 9, the first day of the Meredith March Against Fear, Carmichael shouted to a rally: "The Negro is going to take what he deserves from the white man." Thereafter, the rhetoric of the militants grew ever more bellicose and incendiary. When King preached nonviolence, the young African-Americans shouted: "White blood will flow." If King spoke of Christian love, the militants clamored: "Seize power." Each attempt of King's followers to sing "We Shall Overcome" was drowned out by the new SNCC version, "We Shall Overrun." Along the march route, Mississippi blacks, taking their cue from Carmichael, chanted: "Hey! Hey! Whattaya know? White folks must go—must go!" And each evening, as the marchers pitched their camps, Carmichael's aides proclaimed loudly to the amazed Mississippians looking on: "If anybody touches one of our workers, we're going to tear this place up!"

Following the arrest of Carmichael in Greenwood for erecting a sleeping tent on the grounds of a black high school contrary to the orders of state troopers, the CORE–SNCC contingent of the Meredith March Against Fear scheduled a special protest rally. Word of Carmichael's jailing brought out a large and angry crowd, as well as numerous correspondents of the national news media. The fiery young head of SNCC grabbed his chance for the limelight. Straight from the jail, he leaped on a flatbed truck to stir the Greenwood rally with a raised-arm and clenched-fist salute. "This is the twenty-seventh time I have been arrested—and I ain't going to jail no more!" he hurled defiance. "The only way we gonna stop them white men from whippin' us is to take over. We been saying freedom for six years and we ain't got nothin'. What we gonna start saying now is Black Power!" Mesmerizing his audience, Carmichael repeated rhythmically: "We . . . want . . . Black . . . Power!" Soon the crowd roared back in unison. "That's right," Carmichael shouted, "that's what we want. Now, from now on, when they ask you what you want, you know what to tell them. What do you want?" "Black Power!" "What do you want?" "BLACK POWER!" "What do you want? Say it again!" "BLACK POWER! BLACK POWER! BLACK POWER!"

"The phrase had been used before by Richard Wright and others but never until that night had it been used as a slogan in the civil-rights movement," Martin Luther King would write. "For people who had been crushed so long by white power and who had been taught that black was degrading, it had a ready appeal." Conceding the psychological value of Black Power as an assertion of black manhood, King, nevertheless, condemned it as a "nihilistic philosophy born out of the conviction that the Negro can't win. It is, at bottom, the view that American society is so hopelessly corrupt and enmeshed in evil that there is no possibility of salvation from within." King believed that the African-American minority could not achieve effective political and economic power in isolation from the white majority that controlled its sources, and that black violence would bring more harm to African-Americans than to whites. Fearing that the term Black Power would isolate the Negro community and leave "the impression that we are talking about black domination rather than black equality," King tried to mute the implied threat of the slogan.

But Carmichael relished feeding rhetorical red meat to the media and countered King's efforts to dilute the impact of the electrifying phrase. Every time SCLC representatives chanted "Freedom Now!" Carmichael bellowed "Black Power!" With intensifying bravado, he challenged African-Americans to "stop begging and take power—black power," and insisted: "Power is the only thing respected in this world, and we must get it at any cost." In response to King's pleas for nonviolence, Carmichael kept exhorting: "It's time we stand up and take over. Take over. Move on over, or we'll move on over you." When the fifteen thousand marchers reached the Mississippi capital on June 26, they heard Carmichael urge African-Americans to "build a power base . . . so strong that we will bring whites to their knees every time they mess with us." By then, most were shouting, with neither coaxing nor coaching, "Black Power! Black Power! Black Power!" Few of the many who had once followed King stood behind him in Jackson as McKissick declared: "1966 shall be remembered as the year we left our imposed status as Negroes and became *Black Men* . . . 1966 is the year of the concept of Black Power."

"I had no idea that Black Power was going to take off the way it did," admitted Cleveland Sellers, the militant new SNCC program chairman, and neither he nor any of his comrades had a cohesive strategy to accompany the slogan. Indeed, Black Power would remain more a mood, a mystique, than a systematic plan or program. Carmichael kept altering its meaning, defining and redefining it to suit the needs of different audiences. Although a few civil-rights leaders completely repudiated the expression (Wilkins castigated Black Power as "the father of hatred and the mother of violence"), most black spokesmen sought to hitch the popularity of the phrase with blacks to their own wagon. Each gave it a congenial connotation. Each elaborated on it in line with its own ideology. Revolutionaries used it to preach guerilla warfare, liberals to demand reform, and conservatives to emphasize self-help. Both separatists and integrationists employed it, as did proponents of love and of confrontation, of violence and of nonviolence. Politicians saw it as an instrument to win black votes, businessmen as a means to preserve and expand black markets, and artists as a basis for developing a black aesthetic. Black capitalists claimed it, and so did black socialists and publicists for black cooperatives. To some, it meant coalition politics; to others, alternative, independent politics and self-determination. Assertions of cultural autonomy vied with strategies for economic advancements; emphases on black identity competed with calls to "pick up the gun." Black Power became a goal and a means, something permanent and a temporary stage, a legal tool and a lawless one, a tactic and an end in itself.

Despite the confusion, Black Power generated valuable changes. It galvanized many whom the movement had never touched to mobilize for concerted action. It spawned an array of new associations, caucuses, and community organizations. It spurred self-reliance and a phalanx of assertive local leaders demanding "community control" over ghetto schools, police forces, and social agencies. Unlike the civil-rights movement, which had largely focused on the aspirations of the burgeoning black middle class, Black Power drew attention to the needs of the lower classes, and to the root of their plight: powerlessness. It called attention to the exigency of restructuring the nation's economic and political institutions. It pinpointed the urgency of transforming the culture's value structure. In the words of SNCC's Julius Lester:

> The social, political, cultural and economic institutions of white America are designed to tell whites that they are superior and to tell blacks that they are inferior. Either those institutions (and the attitudes which created them) must be changed or blacks must remove themselves from them and create their own social, political, cultural and economic institutions which will give them the opportunity to live their lives feeling that they are, indeed, "somebody."

Accordingly, the major thrust of Black Power was to make blacks proud to be blacks, a psychological precondition for equality. It fostered a new sense of racial pride and self-confidence that helped revolutionize the black perspective, confining to the dustbin of the African-American past the belief born out of centuries of oppression that what was white was good and what was black was inferior. Supplementing Northern black nationalist stirrings and the transformative successes of the Southern freedom struggle, which had heightened many an African-American's sense of efficacy and self-respect, the Black Power ethos equated "black" and "beautiful." Throwing away skin bleaches and hair straighteners, African-Americans emphasized their racial characteristics and joyously affirmed their skin color and life-styles, music and food, dialect and culture. "Say it loud—I'm black and I'm proud," sang James Brown, and a generation of blacks agreed. Wearing Afros and dashikis, self-assured blacks awakened interest in the neglected heritage of Africa and stimulated the writing and study of black history. They made "soul" the rage, preached a black theology, took Arabic surnames, celebrated Kwanzaa rather than Christmas, established black studies programs at universities, and wore their color, in Langston Hughes's words, "like a banner for the proud." In whatever form it took, pride in being black proved invaluable in aiding blacks to discard the disabling self-hatred inculcated by white culture.

But, as Carmichael observed, "to most whites, Black Power seems to mean that the Mau Mau are coming to the suburbs at night." His leadership did much to make that seem inevitable. Arguing that SNCC's Southern mentality caused it to fail in the North, and that it was too reformist, lacking an ideology, Carmichael prodded SNCC to become progressively more anti-capitalism and pro-black nationalism. Under his leadership, SNCC abandoned all pretense of working within the civil-rights movement. Recognizing the contradictions of using white field secretaries to inspire African-Americans to win their own freedom, to be proud of themselves, and to develop their inherent leadership potential, SNCC decided that the few whites remaining in the organization should henceforth work only within white communities. By 1967, without white support and financial backing, SNCC was bankrupt and reduced to some twoscore hardcore militants. Anathema to mainstream liberal and African-American politicians, Carmichael grew yet more shrill, now talking about blacks becoming "the executioners of our executioners," about "offing the pigs" and "killing the honkies." "When you talk of Black Power," he announced, "you talk of building a movement that will smash everything Western civilization has created." In his last act as SNCC's chairman, Carmichael toured the black colleges of the South in the spring of 1967 to urge students to "fight for liberation by any means necessary" and to stand up "to say 'To hell with the laws of the United States.' " Rioting followed his speeches at Fisk and Texas Southern Universities, and at Jackson State and Tougaloo College. Then Carmichael left to tour Cuba and North Vietnam.

His successor as head of SNCC, twenty-three-year-old H. Rap Brown of Louisiana, told reporters after his election: "The white man won't get off our backs, so we're going to knock him off. . . . America won't come around, so we're going to burn America down." He delighted in calling President Johnson a "mad wild dog" and a "hunky cracker," and in exclaiming: "If you give me a gun I might just shoot Lady Bird." "Violence is as American as cherry pie" became Brown's catchphrase. Just a month after taking office, he addressed an African-American rally in Cambridge, Maryland, during the week that the Detroit riot raged. Brown urged his audience to "get you some guns."

You'd better get you some guns. The man's moving to kill you. The only thing the honky respects is force. . . . I mean, don't be trying to love that honky to death. Shoot him to death. Shoot him to death, brother, cause that's what he's out to do to you. Like I said in the beginning, if this town don't come around, this town should be burned down. It should be burned down, brother.

"Don't you see what your brothers in Detroit are doing?" Brown implored. "It's time for Cambridge to explode." It did. Several hours after Brown's speech, flames destroyed the center of the black ghetto. Two days later, Brown was arrested for incitement to riot, beginning a series of jailings and bailings which did nothing to dampen the incendiary preachments of the head of SNCC.

The media's fascination with the Black Panthers in 1967–68 accentuated the violent image of black militancy. Founded by Huey Newton and Bobby Seale in Oakland, California, in October 1966, to combat police brutality in the ghetto, the Black Panther Party for Self-Defense publicly advocated armed revolt and flamboyantly displayed its firearms. Initially formed to monitor the behavior of the Oakland police ("the military arm of our oppressors") toward African-Americans, the Black Panthers were soon advocating full employment and self-determination for blacks, exemption from military service for African-American males, and freedom for all blacks held in prisons and jails. The glowering Panther, dressed in black trousers, black leather jacket, and black beret, became a media staple, and the revolutionary ranting of Eldridge Cleaver, a newly paroled inmate who became the party's chief publicist, achieved best-sellerdom. Although the Black Panthers also initiated free breakfast programs for schoolchildren and free health clinics, most whites, dependent on what the media reported, only heard their revolutionary bravado and only saw their bloody shootouts with the Oakland police. In February 1968, whites learned that SNCC and the Panthers would merge and that Stokely Carmichael had become "prime minister" of the party.

The prominence of CORE and SNCC, and especially King, in the anti-war movement further eroded the legitimacy of the black struggle in the eyes of most whites. At a time when an overwhelming majority of Americans considered opposition to the government's Vietnam policy to be disloyal, King demanded in 1965: "The long night of war must be stopped." His call for a negotiated Indochina settlement infuriated President Johnson and lost SCLC the support of influential and wealthy white liberals. Moderates in the movement stipulated to King that civil rights remain divorced from foreign policy, and the minister backed down, assured by the White House of the war's imminent end. But the promised peace did not come.

Early in 1966, Johnson admitted: "Because of Vietnam, we cannot do all that we should, or all that we would like to do." Drastic cuts in the domestic budget followed. Funds for the war on poverty amounted to less than 2 percent of the money spent on the military, and the government's efforts to achieve racial equality ground to a halt. CORE angrily insisted that the United States withdraw its forces from Indochina. Declaring its sympathy with "the men in this country who are unwilling to respond to a military draft," SNCC officially resolved: "Vietnamese are being murdered because the United States is pursuing an aggressive policy in violation of international law." Six SNCC staffers in Atlanta then invaded an induction center, provoking parallel anti-war maneuvers by militant, educated young blacks throughout the country, who chanted: "Hell, no! We won't go!" A hero of black youth, Muhammad Ali, capsulated their alienation in his adamant refusal to serve in a "white man's war." Nikki Giovanni delineated their anger in her poetry: "We kill in Vietnam / for them / We kill for UN & NATO & SEATO & US / And everywhere for all alphabet but BLACK."

King broke his silence. He knew it would be neither popular nor politic. But to say nothing about the heinous killing and destruction in Vietnam made a mockery of his life's work to teach love and nonviolence. King also believed his leadership could channel constructively the inchoate anti-war protests of young militants. The SCLC head deemed the war and racial injustice "inextricably bound together." Blacks could no longer concern themselves with just civil rights. "It is very nice to drink milk at an unsegregated lunch counter—but not when there is strontium 90 in it." As King sought to forge an interracial alliance of the poor and oppressed, moreover, he increasingly considered the unjust, immoral war ten thousand miles away to be robbing the nation of the resources necessary to create new jobs and to eradicate the slums. "The bombs in Vietnam

explode at home," the black minister preached. "They destroy the
hopes and possibilities of a decent America." Despite great pressure
from the White House, King kept reiterating that the United States
spent $500,000 to kill each enemy soldier but only $35 a year to
assist each American in poverty. "The promises of the Great Society," he intoned, "have been shot down on the battlefield of
Vietnam."

Shrugging off the suggestions of his closest advisors and the established African-American political leadership, King made opposition to the war his top priority in 1967. Speaking his conscience—"I knew that I could never again raise my voice against
the violence of the oppressed in the ghettos without having first
spoken clearly to the greatest purveyor of violence in the world
today—my own government"—he burned his bridges to the Johnson Administration, to the Congress, and to most of his erstwhile
allies. Rustin, Wilkins, and Young criticized him for speaking out
on foreign policy, and Senator Edward Brooke, Ralph Bunche, and
Jackie Robinson openly lambasted King for urging Americans to
become conscientious objectors. The media repeatedly described
King's criticism of the war as destructive to his people and his cause,
and Lyndon Johnson did all he could covertly to destroy the minister's influence. Deserted by the liberals for going too far in his
remonstrance, derided by the more vitriolic radicals for not going
far enough, King lost power and status. The intensification of black
violence and white backlash in 1967 underlined his ineffectuality.
Coming on top of his disappointing Chicago Freedom Movement
of 1966, an enervated King sank into despondency. The SCLC
leader had learned painfully that trying to negotiate desegregation
with the wily Mayor Richard Daley was a far cry from the moral
simplicity of confronting a "Bull" Connor, and that asking the
middle class to pay the cost of dealing with urban poverty demanded
something far more tangible from them than giving African-
Americans a seat on a bus or at a lunch counter.

Dispirited, yet frightened that the urban warfare that had

wracked Detroit and Newark in 1967 would worsen unless he lessened the despair in the ghettos, a weary King issued a call for a "Poor People's Campaign" to force the nation to confront the problem of poverty and end the suffering stunted lives caused by inadequate food and health care, poor schooling, and decrepit housing. To bring enormous pressure to bear on both the government and private business, King envisaged an interracial coalition of the dispossessed living in shanties in the capital and engaging in far more disruptive demonstrations than in any of his previous demonstrations against racial injustice. "Timid supplication for justice will not solve the problem," King announced. "We have got to confront the power structure massively. We can't live with another summer like the last. This is a desperate plea. I want to give the nation the opportunity to respond."

In March 1968, King interrupted his efforts to organize the Poor People's Campaign to accede to the request from his old friend, Memphis pastor James Lawson, that King support a newly begun strike for union recognition and decent wages by that city's mostly African-American sanitation workers. When the protest march he led degenerated into violent turmoil—as a black youth gang went on a burning and looting rampage and the police responded with tear gas and bullets—a shaken King, seeking to prove the viability of nonviolent protest, vowed to return to lead a peaceful and successful march to the Memphis City Hall.

On April 3, King addressed his last church rally. He rambled softly about the progress that had been made since 1955, and of the gains yet to be made. Quietly he told of recent threats on his life. "But it doesn't matter with me now. Because I've been to the mountaintop." He turned to face his aides on the platform behind him. "I don't mind. Like anybody, I would like to live a long life. Longevity has its place. But I'm not concerned about that now." His voice began to rise. "I just want to do God's will. And He's allowed me to go up to the mountain!" He faced the hushed audience. Some wept openly. "And I've looked over and I've seen the promised land!" King shouted emotionally: "I may not get there with you, but I want you to know tonight"—he paused—"that we as a people will get to the promised land."

The next evening, while the thirty-nine-year-old minister conversed with his friends on the balcony at the Lorraine Motel, a rifle shot rang out and Martin Luther King, Jr., fell, murdered by a paid white assassin, James Earl Ray.

Within hours after the announcement of King's death, African-American uprisings flared in the ghettos of more than a hundred cities, including Baltimore, Boston, Philadelphia, Pittsburgh, and San Francisco. Twenty blocks of the Chicago West Side went up in flames before Mayor Daley ordered the police to "shoot to wound" any looter and to "shoot to kill" any arsonist. In Washington, D.C., over seven hundred fires lit up the night as army units in full combat gear took up battle positions around the Capitol and on the grounds of the White House. By the end of the week, twenty-one thousand federal troops and thirty-four thousand National Guardsmen had been called out to quell the upheavals that had left forty-six dead, more than three thousand injured, some twenty-seven thousand arrested, and $45 million of property lost.

More incalculable, the loss of Martin Luther King, Jr., robbed the nation of its last best hope for fundamental change, without violence, without hatred. Ever since the beginning of the Montgomery bus boycott he had come to epitomize the struggle for black equality by nonviolent means, to symbolize African-American aspirations for unqualified integration into American society. Alone among the leaders of his era, King had been able to inspire African-Americans to struggle against racism *and* to encourage whites to acknowledge their responsibility for the plight of blacks without turning them against the movement. He was hardly perfect. At times, he compromised too much, too quickly. At times, florid rhetoric masked the lack of a clear strategy. As revelations of his plagiarism and marital infidelities made clear, he was more human than saintly. And despite good intentions, he had little success in desegregating the North, alleviating the misery of the impoverished, or promoting world peace. But he kept trying, despite the erosion of his stature and effectiveness after the Selma campaign, trying "to redeem the soul of America." In the last of King's thirty-nine years, that meant American withdrawal from the war in Vietnam and a radical redistribution of economic and political power to meet the needs of the destitute of all races. "The black revolution is much more than the struggle for the rights of Negroes," insisted King.

It is forcing America to face all its interrelated flaws—racism, poverty, militarism, and materialism. It is exposing evils that are rooted deeply in the whole structure of our society. It reveals systemic rather than superficial flaws and suggests that radical reconstruction of society itself is the real issue to be faced.

A week after King's assassination, Memphis authorities recognized the sanitation workers' collective-bargaining rights and raised their wages. But no other African-American leader could keep hope alive, could galvanize the struggle, could inspire dreams. The movement was moribund. The Second Reconstruction was over. With King, it had ended with a bang. And it also ended with a whimper, with many of the established African-American organizations and leaders valiantly struggling on, with diminishing funds and decreasing support.

The abject failure of the Poor People's Campaign crystallized the demise of the movement. The nation barely took notice of the passing mule train or the shantytown erected just off the Mall near the Lincoln Memorial. Bereft of vision and strategic savvy, Resurrection City rapidly sank in the muck of a deluge of rain and the mire of its own blatantly delinquent behavior and ethnic divisiveness. The arrest of the SCLC leaders and the brutal dispersement of the poor encamped in Washington aroused no major outcry. It appeared as if the successes of the Second Reconstruction, like that of the First Reconstruction, could, and would, be reversed.

# EIGHT

# THE DREAM DEFERRED . . .

## THE STRUGGLE

## CONTINUES

In so many ways, *so many ways*, have we been bred into insecurity. Du Bois, you know, talked about the burden of double consciousness of being black in America. You belong and yet you don't. You free but yet you're not. It's your place but yet you kept separated from it. You there but yet you ain't. Though it's more difficult trying to make it under that double role and double burden, once you survive it you have double muscles. But it's like we have almost to be superior just to be equal.

JESSE JACKSON

The movement had secured basic civil rights for African-Americans, yet much remained to be done. As the sixties ended, however, white backlash ruled the roost. The fiery riots had rationalized expressions of hostility toward blacks. The prominence of movement leaders in anti-war activities, associated by many with the counterculture and student rebellions, had reinforced old prejudices and justified new antagonisms. The anti-white connotations of Black Power had cooled the ardor of white liberals for the struggle. And the movement's work in the North had fired the anxiety of the white working class that racial equality would come at the expense of the safety of its neighborhoods and schools, the security of its jobs and homes. Northern politicians adapted to the white urge to end racial reform with alacrity. In California, Ronald Reagan, a former actor and Barry Goldwater enthusiast, came to power in 1966 on the strength of his opposition to the 1964 Civil Rights Act and his tough stance toward the rioters in Watts. In Boston, the adamant refusal of Louise Day Hicks to allow busing to correct the racial imbalance in that city's schools made her the most potent political force in the once abolitionist stronghold. Harbingers of American politics to come, "law and order" and "get tough with rioters" candidates triumphed throughout the nation.

For the first time in a decade, Congress rejected a proposed civil-rights bill in 1966, and that November the Republicans displaced forty-seven liberal Democratic incumbents in the House and three in the Senate. A voting majority pledged to preserve social order had superseded the coalition to promote social change. The reconstituted House of Representatives in 1967 refused to seat Harlem Congressman Adam Clayton Powell, Jr., for illegal payroll practices that whites in Congress went unpunished for, and defeated a minor appropriation for the control of rats in the slums, laughingly deriding it as a "civil-rats bill." Following King's assassination in 1968, Congress did enact civil-rights legislation—a fair-housing bill seen by many as an act of atonement for his murder. It sought to quiet the cries of angry blacks by outlawing racial discrimination in the sale and rental of housing. But the measure had impossibly weak enforcement provisions, and placed the burden of combating racial discrimination on individual litigants. In addition, the law appeased, even pleased, the white majority by making incitement to riot a serious federal offense. Still other manifestations of the backlash included the landslide defeats of referenda for civilian boards to review police actions, the deluge of support for teachers' strikes against black community control of schools, and the emergence of huge white mobs jeering, "Nigger, nigger, nigger!" and stoning black protesters in the North.

The Presidential election of 1968 further substantiated the shift in momentum to the opponents of racial equality. Appealing to those weary of protest, Richard Nixon rode the backlash into the White House. He campaigned against open housing and busing for racial balance. He promised to slow federal efforts at school integration and to appoint only conservative justices to the federal courts. Nixon particularly solicited the support of traditional Democratic voters disgruntled with the excesses of the black struggle. Many responded to the appeal. The Democratic nominee, Hubert Humphrey, long associated in the public mind with the civil-rights movement, won just one out of every three white votes. The ethnic working class that deserted Humphrey largely rallied to the banner of George Wallace, whose American Independent Party made the fear and resentment of blacks the central thrust of its campaign. "On November 5," Wallace had predicted, "they're going to find out there are a lot of rednecks in this country." He was right. Despite all the difficulties of mounting an independent run for the Presidency, Wallace amassed 9.9 million votes, just under 14 percent of the turnout. The anti-black crusader polled almost as many votes in the North as he did in the South in this best showing of a third-party candidate since 1924.

Immediately after entering the White House, President Nixon began wooing the Wallace constituency to insure his reelection in 1972. He deliberately pursued a "Southern strategy," conceding the votes of blacks and those committed to liberalism and going after those of white Southerners, suburbanites, and ethnic workers troubled by the specter of racial equality. Rather than follow the course counseled by his domestic advisor, the sociologist Daniel Patrick Moynihan, to behave with "benign neglect" on the race issue, the President intentionally focused public attention on the matter, and in a manner hardly benign to blacks.

The Nixon Administration took every opportunity to exploit the emotions of race. It urged Congress to impose a moratorium on court-ordered school busing, nominated conservative "strict constructionists" to the Supreme Court, and pleaded before the high tribunal for a postponement in the desegregation of Mississippi's schools. It lobbied in Congress to defeat the fair-housing enforcement program and the extension of the Voting Rights Act of 1965. While Vice-President Spiro Agnew played on the racial anxieties of Americans with his rhetoric, Nixon emasculated the Offices for Civil Rights in the Justice and Health, Education and Welfare Departments. To outflank Wallace, the President vetoed bills and impounded funds designed to assist blacks, and he fired government officials who sought to implement integration guidelines. In dismay, the chairmen of the Equal Employment Opportunity Commission and the United States Commission on Civil Rights resigned in protest, as did the head of the Small Business Administration's program for minorities. The president of the NAACP lamented: "For the first time since Woodrow Wilson we have a national administration that can rightly be characterized as anti-Negro." But Nixon had accurately gauged the national mood. In a resounding victory, the President swept every state save Massachusetts and the largely black District of Columbia in his 1972 reelection, winning the votes of almost all the whites who had backed Wallace in 1968.

The continued deterioration of the public perception of the black struggle contributed immeasurably in President Nixon's success. During his years in office the media highlighted the activities of only the most vengeful blacks. The residue of flickering TV images of armed black students seizing college buildings, of Black Panther shoot-outs with police and the FBI, of the Revolutionary Action Movement conspiring to murder Roy Wilkins and Whitney Young, and of bank robberies and kidnappings by the Symbionese Liberation Army diminished the already nearly exhausted sympathy for the movement. With SNCC no longer in existence, CORE reduced to one of many impotent black nationalist sects, SCLC ripped apart by dissension among King's associates, and the NAACP confining itself once again almost exclusively to the courtroom struggle, Angela Davis and Eldridge Cleaver dominated the airwaves with their exaltation of violent revolution. Disgusted by the mayhem and invective, the vast majority of whites fully approved of Nixon's racial policies.

After Watergate, Gerald Ford appealed to the same backlash emotions as had his predecessor. With less rancor, President Ford maintained Nixon's budgetary freezes and rigorous opposition to school busing. He did nothing to implement the legislative agenda, "Priorities for the Future," submitted by the congressional black caucus, and welcomed the Democratic denunciation of him as "the most veto-prone Republican President in the twentieth century." Ford shelved virtually every bill Congress passed that would have assisted the black poor. The President, in addition, earned the rebuke of the U.S. Civil Rights Commission for accelerating the trend toward resegregation by his resistance to open housing and school desegregation.

Given the surge of Republicanism in Dixie, Ford had looked to the South to help him win election in his own right in 1976; but the Democrats foiled him by nominating Jimmy Carter of Georgia, whose image as an "outsider" appealed to an electorate weary of Washington politicians. Speaking in the rhythm and idiom of African-American Christianity, and stressing his endorsement by Dr. King's family and closest associates, Carter successfully reached out to the newly enfranchised African-Americans in the South. Garnering 92 percent of their ballots, he eked out a slim victory over Ford. "The hands that picked the cotton," stated SCLC's Andrew Young, "finally picked the President." A grateful Carter promised to alleviate the plight of blacks; and during his four years in office the number of African-American Presidential appointees included thirty federal judges, two Cabinet and more than fifty sub-Cabinet officials, fifteen ambassadors, over a hundred members of advisory boards and commissions, and twenty-five aides on the White House staff. As never before, African-Americans had access to the levers of power in Washington. Unlike Nixon and Ford, moreover, Carter did not seek to inflame racial antagonisms.

But, like his immediate predecessors, Carter also never sought to make the perpetuation of racial inequality a central concern of Americans; and he proved as ready to beef up defense spending and balance the budget at the expense of school-lunch programs, financial assistance to black students, and health care for the poor as the Republicans had been. Carter would not expend his moral or political capital in the national debates raging over affirmative action and busing; and he selected as head of the Civil Rights Division of the Justice Department a man who hoped publicly that in the fight against segregation "the courts would not overreach." Blacks, moreover, became the chief victims of Carter's unsuccessful battles against inflation and recession. His economic failures resulted in the highest black jobless rate in over a decade, a deterioration of life for the black poor, and a weakening of the tenuous hold on middle-class status that a slim majority of blacks had recently achieved. "It is easy to see why many have concluded," Julian Bond commented, that "we voted for a man who knew the words to our hymns, but not the numbers on our paychecks."

Blacks faced a sorry choice in the 1980 Presidential election. Jimmy Carter asked for their support on the basis of his many black federal appointments, but avoided committing his Administration to alleviating the economic plight of depressed blacks or to pressing for an end to residential or school segregation. The Independent candidacy of John Anderson barely acknowledged the afflictions of African-Americans. And the Republican nominee, Ronald Reagan, made clear his continued opposition to busing to achieve racial integration in the schools, to affirmative action, and to the varied government programs designed to aid the poor and the unemployed. The vast majority of blacks voted Democratic, although in fewer numbers and with less unanimity than in 1976. But more than two out of every three white voters opted for the GOP alternative. In addition, the electorate ousted numerous staunch supporters of civil rights in Congress and gave Republicans control of the Senate. Although the number of African-American officeholders at state and local levels increased to some five thousand, blacks faced a Republican Administration ensconced in Washington hostile to the needs of the impoverished and a threat to the hopes of millions of working-class African-Americans to enter the American mainstream.

Nor could blacks look confidently to the Supreme Court any longer. The Court had boldly declared in 1969 that every school district was obligated to end dual school systems "at once" and "now and hereafter" to operate only unitary desegregated schools. It followed that with a decision in 1971 which granted broad authority to the district courts to order the desegregation of school systems by busing if necessary. But then the Nixon appointees to the high court signaled a halt, abandoning the familiar yellow school bus as a vehicle of racial reform. Because the suburbs had not themselves caused Detroit's segregation, the Court stated in 1974 that they need not be part of the solution. A five-to-four majority held that the equal-protection clause required racial busing only within school districts and not interdistrict busing. The Supreme Court then further restricted busing in cases involving Pasadena in 1976, Dayton in 1977, and Atlanta in 1980. Despite the near universality of racial apartheid in the housing patterns of metropolitan America, with the consequence that more than a majority of black students in the nation's cities attended schools at least 90 percent black, the Supreme Court rejected busing as the means for integrating the schools and offered no alternative procedure for achieving desegregation, further depressing the hopes that *Brown* had initially raised.

Another crushing blow to African-American expectations came from the Supreme Court's 1978 *Bakke* decision. The medical school of the University of California, Davis, had set aside sixteen spaces for minority students, and Alan Bakke, a rejected white applicant who had grades and test scores higher than some of the minority candidates admitted, sued to overturn the procedure on the grounds that racial quotas violated the equal protection clause of the Fourteenth Amendment and the 1964 Civil Rights Act's ban on discrimination in federally assisted institutions. Reflecting the intense and widespread emotions aroused by quotas, by preferential or compensatory treatment, and by affirmative action, the case attracted sixty *amicus curiae* briefs, more than had ever before been submitted in the history of the Supreme Court. *Bakke* polarized the

Court, as well as the nation, and resulted in a muddle of six different opinions, totaling 154 pages. Four justices upheld affirmative action and the denial of admission to Bakke; four ruled to admit Bakke and against preferential treatment; and one, to achieve some kind of judicial consensus, upheld Bakke's claim of unfair discrimination and ordered his matriculation into the medical school while also upholding affirmative action on the right of universities to seek diversity. Chastened by the explicit rejection of racial quotas as a means of overcoming the accumulated handicaps that past racism had imposed on African-Americans, civil-rights organizations did win court rulings in 1979 and 1980 that approved "narrowly tailored" remedial programs to assist minorities. Overall, however, the furor over *Bakke* reinforced the resurgent white opposition to "reverse discrimination" and weakened the commitment of private and public agencies to assist blacks in achieving equality by considering race in their policies. In 1965 President Johnson had stated: "You do not wipe away the scars of centuries by saying, now you are free to go where you want, do as you desire and choose the leaders you please. You do not take a person who, for years, has been hobbled by chains and liberate him, bring him up to the starting line of a race and then say, 'You are free to compete with all the others,' and still justly believe that you have been completely fair." Yet that is all that most whites would permit. They still wished to avoid the responsibility defined by Johnson: "It is not enough just to open the gates of opportunity. All our citizens must have the ability to walk through those gates."

Indeed, rather than helping those in need through the gates, the Reagan Administration began to close the gates of opportunity. The President appointed fewer than one-third the number of African-Americans to top-level positions than had Carter, and those he chose shared his desire to limit, if not eliminate, civil-rights programs. They followed his lead in weakening enforcement of fair-housing laws and in exempting nearly 75 percent of federal contractors from affirmative-action guidelines. Packing the Civil Rights Commission and the Equal Employment Opportunity Commission with like-minded conservatives, Reagan transformed them into forums opposed to court-ordered busing and to the preferential treatment of minorities. He refrained from criticizing South African apartheid and fought against the imposition of sanctions designed to compel reforms by the white supremacist regime. President Reagan even sought to restore federal tax exemptions to private schools that practiced racial discrimination (but was blocked by the Supreme Court in 1983), and lobbied against renewal of the Voting Rights Act (until severe criticism by Senate Republicans forced him to desist). Most vitally, to perpetuate his views through future Supreme Court decisions, Reagan elevated the ultra-conservative William Rehnquist to Chief Justice and replaced three retiring liberal-to-moderate justice with conservatives. Significantly, the President's efforts to turn back the clock on racial matters did little or nothing to deter his overwhelming reelection in 1984 or to lessen his enormous popularity throughout the decade.

Nor did racism impair Reagan's Vice-President, George Bush, in his own race for the White House in 1988. Despite denying any racist intent, Bush made the centerpiece of his campaign against Massachusetts Governor Michael Dukakis a strident TV advertisement focusing on Willie Horton, a black inmate serving a life sentence for rape and assault, who, while on a weekend furlough from his Massachusetts prison, had raped another white woman. "If I can make Willie Horton a household name," said Bush's campaign manager, "we'll win the election." And they did, carrying forty states and nearly 54 percent of the popular vote.

Although claiming to be "haunted by the lives lived by the children of our inner cities," President Bush did nothing in his first term to improve conditions for the disinherited. The black underclass grew both absolutely and as a percentage of all African-Americans, and as the number of decent paying jobs in or near the inner city continued to decline, the number of working-class blacks slipping below the poverty line increased. Rejecting anything that smacks of "big government," Bush claimed that the poor would best be helped by indirect measures such as a capital-gains tax cut and more foreign trade, and he vetoed a civil-rights bill in 1990, terming it a "quota bill." The level of racial hostility rose. Ignoring several large outbursts of racial rioting and violence in the Overtown and Liberty City sections of Miami in the 1980s, few heeded or even remembered the 1968 warnings of the National Advisory Commission on Civil Disorders of "ominous consequences" as the United States drifted "toward two societies, one black, one white —separate and unequal."

Then Los Angeles exploded in rage, loudly ringing yet again the "firebell in the night"—as Thomas Jefferson had called the problem of race in America. Despite evidence on videotape of excessive force by the Los Angeles police in the beating of an African-American, Rodney King, a jury that included no blacks acquitted the indicted white police officers in April 1992. The verdict ignited the anger and frustration of Los Angeles blacks, and they erupted in an orgy of arson, looting, beatings, and killings that left at least fifty-five dead, nearly two thousand wounded, and more than six thousand arrested. The rioting and the response to it exposed both the depth of African-American grievances and alienation and the widespread white fear and loathing of black criminality. They revealed a frightening tear in the social fabric and a vast racial chasm in the nation. They confirmed each race's worst phobias and misgivings about the other.

The racial furies unloosed in Los Angeles resulted in a flurry of pronouncements that the Second Reconstruction, like the First Reconstruction a century earlier, had been overthrown by complacency, neglect, and resurgent racism. Much pointed to that conclusion, and an era of hopeful promise appeared again to be superseded by an age of conservative "redemption." The *Brown* decision, the March on Washington, and the civil-rights acts of the 1960s seemed like relics of a bygone era. A quarter of a century later the United States remained a racially divided and unequal society. The African-American struggle had indeed made a difference. It had brought significant changes and achieved substantial advancements. Yet the full promises of the movement had not been realized. Prejudice and discrimination, both subtle and blatant, continued to poison race relations. Neither the franchise nor the demolition of de jure segregation had yet resulted in de facto equality or justice. The black ghettos had changed little, except in their enormous growth. More than ever before, these socially ravaged enclaves were ticking time bombs, and their anomic inhabitants combustible tinder. Whatever the movement had accomplished, the hardest and most paramount tasks still lay ahead, and retrogression in the status of African-Americans in the 1990s appeared more likely than progress.

"Anyone looking for the civil-rights movement in the streets is fooling himself. Politics is the civil-rights movement of the 1970s," beamed Maynard Jackson, who in 1973 became Atlanta's first African-American mayor. "Politics is our first hurrah. It's where things are today." The right to vote and the opportunity to hold political office had changed strikingly since *Brown*. Fewer than one in four adult African-Americans in the South could register to vote in 1954; over two-thirds were on the voting lists in 1970; and nationally, by 1990, blacks comprised 11.2 percent of the registered voters, just about their proportion of the population. In addition, their turnout at the polls trailed that of whites by only 4 percent. The magnitude of these changes transformed the face of American politics. Overt race-baiting rhetoric, in the main, went out of style. The onetime militant segregationist, George Wallace of Alabama, appointed blacks to high state offices, crowned an African-American homecoming queen at the very university he had once sworn to deny to black students, publicly applauded the inaugural remarks of Birmingham's first African-American mayor in 1979, and, following the twentieth anniversary commemoration of the Selma-to-Montgomery March, invited Jesse Jackson to the governor's mansion for tea and cakes and a discussion on civil rights. At the 1983 swearing-in for Wallace's final term as governor, a black minister pronounced the benediction, an African-American led the assemblage in the Pledge of Allegiance, and a black justice of the Alabama Supreme Court administered the oath of office. And just as the older generation of race-mongering politicians saw the light, a new generation of racially moderate, even liberal, politicians emerged, echoing Georgia Governor George Busbee's claim: "The politics of race has gone with the wind."

The consequences of African-American suffrage were also reflected in black officeholders. From fewer than a hundred in 1965 when Congress passed the Voting Rights Act, the number of African-Americans holding elective office in the South jumped from about 500 in 1970 to nearly 2,500 in 1980; and the national tally rose from 300 in 1965 to 3,000 in 1975, 5,000 in 1980, and more than 7,000 in 1992. The number of towns and cities with black mayors leaped from none in 1965 to eighty in 1970, 120 in 1980, and some 300 in 1992, including both black-majority cities such as New Orleans and Detroit and those with a minority of African-Americans such as Seattle and New York City. Black political influence, if not power, at the local and state levels brought incremental benefits, especially for better-educated African-Americans.

Yet enfranchisement has not proved a panacea. Despite impressive gains, African-Americans held fewer than 2 percent of the nation's elective offices in 1992, and fewer than 4 percent of them in the South, where they constituted 20 percent of the population. Nearly half the hundred counties in the South with majority black populations still have no elected African-American officials. The mobilization of black voters had spurred white opposition, leading to an array of gerrymandering schemes and local government reorganizations that sapped black political strength. Most important, local electoral clout could do little to counter the national and international economic trends worsening the plight of the poor and their segregated, poverty enclaves. Political power proved a frustrating form of empowerment in areas starved of the resources needed to offer their people minimal decencies. Nearly a quarter-century of African-American rule in Lowndes County, Alabama, where Stokely Carmichael first organized an all-black political party under the symbol of a snarling black panther, had not altered the fact that Lowndes was still among the nation's ten poorest counties, that nearly half its residents still lived below the poverty line. Despite African-American mayors and a legion of black officials, the burgeoning black slums of Atlanta and Newark, Detroit and New Orleans, remained among the most despair-ridden concentrations of the truly disadvantaged in the United States.

At the national level, the congressional black caucus numbered twenty-five in 1992. African-Americans had held no seats in Congress between 1901 and 1928, only one in the following fifteen years, and just two at the time of *Brown*. Their presence was augmented by scores of high-ranking black civil-service officials and political appointees. Yet they too could do little to diminish the lingering inequalities between white and black in an era of conservatism, of fashionable pessimism about government's ability to meliorate social conditions, of tax-cutting and budget-slashing. With the Republicans obeisant to the concerns of the white and wealthy, and the national Democratic Party obsessed with winning back the white middle-class "swing" voters who moved to suburbia and turned against it, the Reverend Jesse Jackson launched a bid for the Democratic Presidential nomination in 1984.

Jackson hoped to stem the rightward shift of both parties by empowering the discouraged who no longer even bothered to vote. "Our time has come!" the charismatic black minister would shout. "From the slave ship to the championship, from welfare to our share, from the outhouse to the courthouse to the statehouse to the White House, our time has come!" His appeal—"Keep hope alive"—stimulated many African-Americans to vote for the first time, and convinced many more that politics could indeed be the engine for social change. Winning 3.5 million primary votes, Jackson finished third in a field of eight candidates. Although aiming to fashion a "Rainbow Coalition" of Hispanics, college students, women's rights supporters, environmentalists, and struggling white working-class families, Jackson mustered just 5 percent of the white vote in the Democratic primaries, and had only a slight impact on the party platform and fall campaign. Four years later, a less strident and more experienced Jackson, stressing the theme of economic opportunity for all citizens, doubled his vote total ("More than any other second-place finisher in history," he beamed), and did nearly three times as well with white Democrats, winning fourteen primaries and caucuses and coming in second in thirty-six others. His candidacy again proved inspirational to African-Americans, and demonstrated greater acceptance of blacks in American politics. Yet the centrist Democratic nominee in 1988, Michael Dukakis, eager to appeal to middle-of-the-road whites, avoided identifying himself with Jackson or the concerns of most African-Americans.

Jesse Jackson had gained fame in the 1970s by exhorting black children to stay in school, and important changes did come in the educational levels of African-Americans. In 1954, about 75 percent of blacks aged five to nineteen were enrolled in school. In 1990, about 80 percent of African-American students completed high school, compared to 85 percent for whites. Two decades earlier, only some 40 percent of young African-Americans finished high school. Similarly, 20 percent of blacks aged eighteen to twenty-four enrolled in college in 1980, compared to 26 percent for whites. About one-third of all African-American high-school graduates were going to college, approximately the same proportion as among white high-school graduates. The number of African-Americans in institutions of higher education rose from 75,000 in 1954 to a quarter-million in 1964 to over a million in 1977, roughly 10 percent of the total college population. The growth of financial assistance available to black students and of the African-American middle class, greater access to predominantly white universities, and emphatic affirmative-action efforts made this increase possible. Then recessions and a stagnant economy, declining federal aid to education, and the deemphasis on affirmative action led to a slight lowering of the proportion of black high-school students both entering and graduating from college. By 1988, 12.7 percent of African-Americans aged twenty-five to thirty-five had received college degrees; a far cry from the 2.8 percent in 1950 or 7.3 percent in 1970, the rate for blacks, nevertheless, remained half that for whites. African-Americans in higher education, moreover, still were concentrated in community colleges providing vocational programs in fields that narrowed occupational options and opportunities.

Below the college level, most African-Americans faced resegregation and inadequate, inferior education. After the combination of passage of the Civil Rights Act of 1964 and strict implementation of desegregation guidelines by the federal courts brought the percentage of African-Americans in the South going to schools with whites from 2 percent in 1964 to 20 percent in 1968, and to nearly 60 percent in 1971, the government reversed course. That year, President Nixon warned federal officials to cease pressing desegregation or to find other jobs. In 1973, the Supreme Court began its retreat by barring the busing of Virginia schoolchildren across city-suburban lines. Resegregation surged. White flight to the suburbs, tracking, segregated private academies and church schools, and growing residential segregation caused the proportion of Southern blacks in desegregated schools to drop below 50 percent by 1980 and to continue to decline in the eighties. Resegregation particularly marked the urban South, which soon seemed little different from its Northern counterparts. There, in 1990, some three-quarters of African-Americans attended schools at least 90 percent black. As the nineties began, the combination of massive white opposition to busing for racial balance and increasing residential segregation had quieted even talk of integrated education. It no longer seemed an attainable, however distant, goal. Instead, most African-Americans sought a quality education that would prepare them for middle-class, post-industrial occupations. But the negative impact of cutbacks in compensatory programs, unqualified or uncaring teachers, schools plagued by drugs, violence, and low expectations, the absence of significant others encouraging study and excellence, and the typically inadequate resources of schools in less affluent neighborhoods perpetuates an interlocking cycle of poor education leading to poor or no jobs, which leads to living in poor areas, which means an inferior education for one's children.

This self-replicating, intertwined cycle now affects virtually every index of African-American well-being, further separating, spatially and socially, both black from white and those still in the ghetto from those who have worked themselves out of it. In varying degrees, matters of race, of race-based class, and of class independent of race determine black status in America. Despite class, for example, the majority of whites in 1992 lived in the suburbs while an even larger majority of African-Americans lived in the inner cities of the nation's largest metropolitan areas. The index of residential segregation in nearly every American city has risen since 1960, despite court rulings and legislation outlawing racial discrimination and segregation in housing.

And within the increasingly black cities are unequal African-American societies. In 1990 dollars, 30 percent of black families earned more than $35,000 annually, compared to 23.8 percent in 1970. They are the African-Americans who gained the most from equal-employment opportunity efforts and from affirmative action, from improved educational credentials and the greater willingness of many employers to treat blacks equitably, and from the combined earnings of two breadwinners. Still, in every occupation and region of the country, and at every educational level, the median African-American income is lower than for whites. In 1990, the median income of households of black college graduates was $37,958 and that of similar whites was $48,862; and the gap in their net worths (what they owned minus what they owed) was far greater. Despite the image of Clair and Cliff Huxtable on the *Bill Cosby Show*, the proportion of African-Americans in the legal profession rose from 1.3 percent in 1970 to just 3.2 percent in 1990, and in the medical field from 2.2 percent in 1970 to 3.0 percent in 1990. Among college professors, the increase was from 3.5 to 4.5 percent, and only *one* solitary African-American chief executive officer appeared in *Business Week*'s 1992 list of the heads of America's one thousand largest corporations.

Approximately another third of the black population is lower-middle class, earning between $13,000 and $35,000. Many lacked the skills or credentials to acquire better-paying and more secure white-collar positions, did not have the earnings of a spouse, and toiled at largely lower-paying, non-unionized jobs, in nursing homes and as domestics, in fast-food eateries and as sanitation workers, in hair salons and as bank tellers. They are the African-Americans who have been most adversely affected by the competition from Third World immigrants to the United States and by the export of American jobs to Third World countries offering manufacturers cheap labor, inexpensive energy, and low taxes. Living on the margin, often just an illness or accident or recession away from poverty, they are falling behind in the effort to keep pace.

The dramatic loss of manufacturing jobs, historically the entry-level positions for low-income Americans, has also worsened the outlook for the third of African-Americans, and half of all black children, living below the poverty level (defined in 1990 as $12,675 for an urban family of four, and $9,736 for a family of three). With a poverty rate already three times greater than for whites, this black poverty caste is growing both in absolute terms and as a percentage of all African-Americans. And nearly half the black poor have lived below the poverty line for at least ten years or have incomes below 50 percent of the poverty level. The poorest of the poor, the persistently poor, they are the underclass which is chronically jobless, barely educated, and trapped in isolated rural areas or, more often, in the densest census tracts of decaying neighborhoods where mainstream norms have been overwhelmed by decades of enforced second-class status, the despair of welfare dependency, and family deterioration; and where their very lives are unremittingly threatened by an epidemic of gang warfare, drug addiction, and AIDS. The inhabitants of South-Central Los Angeles, North Philadelphia, South Dallas, and the ghettos in between have been left dangerously alienated by the callous indifference to their plight of most whites and their political representatives. They have been angered by the massive loss of low-skill jobs caused by the deindustrialization of the inner cities and by the increased competition for dwindling employment opportunities from the more than 20 million new immigrants who legally entered the United States between 1970 and 1990. And they have been frustrated by the perverse incentives of a welfare system which rewards fatherless children and child mothers rather than a working couple.

Concomitantly, the percentage of African-American families headed by a female jumped from 20 in 1950 to 56.2 in 1990 (compared to 17.2 percent of white families). These are predominantly poor families, transmitting their poverty to the next generation. The proportion of children born to unmarried black girls and women leaped from 16.8 percent in 1950 to 40.3 percent in 1980, and to 66 percent in 1990 (compared to 16 percent for whites). Nearly 40 percent of all black mothers had no prenatal care in the first trimester of pregnancy in 1990, making them twice as likely as whites to have babies with low birth weights, often the cause of permanent impairment or infant death. In fact, the African-American infant mortality rate of 18.6 per thousand births (twice that of whites) was higher than that for Bulgaria or Costa Rica. Poor health, yet another part of the legacy of economic deprivation and racial oppression, makes African-American death rates higher than those for whites in all but two of the fifteen leading causes of death in the United States. After narrowing for several decades, the gap between black and white life expectancy increased in the mid-1980s from 5.6 to 6.2 years and is still widening.

The government's willingness to rescue Kuwait and bail out the Chrysler Corporation but not to salvage African-American ghetto youngsters is also linked to the whites' greatest dread of blacks—crime, particularly violent crime. Having little or no stake in society, or reason to emulate middle-class values, perhaps a majority of young black ghetto males turn to crime to get by or to pass hopeless time. Overall, about 12 percent of the population, African-Americans are 43.2 percent of those arrested for rape, 54.7 percent for murder, and 69.3 percent for robbery; and they are six times more likely to be the victims of those crimes than are whites. Homicide is now the leading cause of death for African-American men between the ages of eighteen and thirty-four. About 22 percent of the prison population in 1930, blacks are over 45 percent of that group in 1990. A study of Washington, D.C., that year revealed

that 42 percent of black males aged eighteen to thirty were prisoners, on parole, or sought by the police. Nationwide, one in four
young black males—more than are enrolled in college—are in jail
or on parole or probation (four times the rate of whites). As long
as black violence remained in the black ghetto, few whites cared
that a generation of African-Americans without hope were shooting
themselves up with drugs and shooting one another with guns. But
the reality behind the statistics is that a rapidly increasing number
of African-Americans face an ever-bleaker future with yet fewer
options and less likelihood of earning a lawful living, making more
black violence against whites more probable. Accordingly, as white
fears of black violence multiply, many demand more prisons and
longer jail sentences; many see race rather than the residue of deprivation and discrimination as the source of lawlessness; many shun
association with African-Americans and particularly resist all efforts
at residential desegregation; and many, insisting that blacks are
responsible for their own misery and that their problems cannot be
cured by government action, blame "bleeding-heart liberalism" and
"do-goodism" for encouraging the violent criminality of ghetto
dwellers.

No American, black or white, can be sanguine about the plight
of the underclass or worsening relations between the races, and
about their implications for the future welfare and tranquillity of
the country. More than a century and a half ago, a French visitor
to the United States, Alexis de Tocqueville, predicted that when
blacks realize that "they cannot become the equals of whites, they
will speedily show themselves as enemies." Shortly after, a Scottish
visitor, William Chambers, commented that continuing inequality
after emancipation would cause African-Americans to "grow up a
powerful alien people within the commonwealth, dangerous in their
numbers, but doubly dangerous in their consciousness of wrongs,
and in the passions which may incite them to acts of vengeance."
This is the crisis facing Americans. We know too well that deep
grievances left unattended eventually explode. That is what happened in Miami in May 1980. The days of racial violence and rioting

that followed an all-white jury's acquittal of several policemen who had beaten to death a black insurance executive left eighteen people killed and more than $100 million in damage. And that is what happened in Los Angeles and several other cities in 1992 after a similar acquittal of white Los Angeles policemen accused of using excessive force and brutality against a black man. Yet the afflictions deepen and the gulf of empathy, even of understanding, widens.

The searing, remorseless TV images—of Los Angeles policemen savagely beating a writhing African-American twisting on the ground; and of a hapless white driver being dragged from his truck by black youths and repeatedly bashed and kicked, while hordes of others loot stores and set the city aflame—will not quickly fade from consciousness. They confirm instinctive fears and spread the distrust blacks and whites have for one another. Anxious not to be consumed by the Fire Next Time, white Americans purchased guns in record numbers in the month after the riots. They demanded little from their political representatives that might substantively better either relations between the races or the deteriorating plight of the black underclass. Stereotypes of blacks as lazy, irresponsible, self-destructive, and prone to violence and criminality gained new life. And African-Americans, outraged at the injustices that sparked the mayhem, pessimistic that the United States will ever move beyond two societies, black and white, separate and unequal, found reinforcement for the suspicion—or conviction—that "in America black life is meaningless and black rights do not exist." The events in Los Angeles augmented both white perceptions of blacks, of black young men in particular, as a threat, as a danger whites needed police protection from, and African-American beliefs that equal justice is a myth and that blacks are victims and whites victimizers.

Much as they had a hundred years ago, many African-Americans faced a new century with little hope. An air of despondency, a feeling of impotence, a sense of losing ground permeated black America. From African-American hip-hop rappers to the Congressional Black Caucus, from those in the boardroom to those on welfare, from the old established civil-rights leadership to young civic activists in the ghetto came grim assessments of the current crisis and apprehension about the future. Nationwide public opinion polls indicated that more than half the African-Americans queried thought that the quality of life for blacks had gotten worse during the past decade and that prejudice and discrimination against blacks had become more prevalent in recent years. An increasing minority of African-Americans believed that whites "want to see us dead," and that the mushrooming growth of lethal weapons, AIDS, and crack cocaine in the black inner-city were part of a racist plot, "the plan" of the establishment. "This is genocide 1990s style," said an African-American Methodist minister in San Francisco. "There is a conspiracy to anesthetize and ultimately do away with as many blacks in American society as possible." Many more African-Americans assumed that the intertwined problems of black poverty, widespread unemployment, crime, failing schools, and family deterioration were the result of deliberate white disregard, of racist neglect; that if whites had been plagued by the same ills, the society would have acted decisively to cure the malady.

Whatever the cause—structural impediments or racial prejudice, intentional or not—most African-Americans expected little improvement, or further retrogression, in the conditions of black life. None of the presidential contenders in 1992 offered real promise. Congress was disinclined to lead. A conservative majority of Reagan-Bush appointees dominated the Supreme Court. The voting power of the suburbs dwarfed that of the cities, and the resources of already overburdened urban governments continued to dwindle while their social-welfare costs multiplied. Unlike in the 1960s, moreover, the economy remained sluggish, with no employment boom in sight. While major American corporations exported jobs and invested abroad, middle-class whites sought to preserve what they had by curtailing assistance to others. Few supported lowering their entitlements or raising their taxes to enhance African-American prospects. Some took solace in their "whiteness," and were comforted by the cushion of a subordinate black caste. Many more believed that "blacks have gone far enough" than that an "unfinished agenda" needed to be completed. Most now paid lip service to the right of equal opportunity but rejected compensation to African-Americans for past discrimination and denounced racial quotas or preferential programs that mandated equal results or a proportional distribution of benefits. From virtually every quarter came the refrain of disenchantment with government's ability to improve social conditions, of disillusionment with liberal reform, echoing Ronald Reagan's gibe: "We fought a war on poverty, and poverty won."

Adding to their pessimism, African-Americans now saw themselves as standing alone, as isolated. Despite their frequent commonality of interest, competition and contention, rather than cooperation, most often marked relations between blacks and the twenty million Asians and Latin Americans who had migrated to the United States since 1970. The Rainbow Coalition had not coalesced. And the rapid progress of some recent nonwhite immigrants, such as those from Jamaica and Korea, became yet another reproach to African-Americans: if these racial minorities can pull themselves up by their own bootstraps, why can't you. The white allies of the black struggle in the 1960s, particularly disheartened, had ceased supplying the funds and votes that had made the movement's political achievements possible. Former white supporters turned inward, turned conservative, turned to other causes. "Rights consciousness," popularized by the black-rights movement, ironically sparked a host of other movements for liberation and equality, which copied the tactics and slogans of the struggle for civil rights and captured much of the energy, resources, and media attention once devoted to the African-American struggle. Consequently, white women became the major beneficiary of the Equal Employment Opportunity Commission, which had been initiated to assist disadvantaged blacks.

With Martin Luther King's dream of a just and equal society fading, a discouraged African-American leadership, as it had a century earlier, asked less from white America and more from blacks themselves. It quoted Malcolm X: "It is not necessary to change the white man's mind. We have to change our own mind." It talked frequently of self-discipline and self-reliance, of responsibility and respectability, of staying in school and studying hard, of black investments to create jobs and end welfare dependency, of buying public-housing projects so that blacks can manage them, of the necessity to acquire middle-class values, of policing their own communities to rid them of drugs and gang violence. Self-help groups sprouted in every black ghetto. Forced back on themselves by the opposition and neglect of the white majority, African-Americans sought to develop the internal strengths of the black community. The movement's strategy of protest as the means of advancement gave way to a less confrontational quest for achievement within a racially inegalitarian and unjust American society.

In tandem with this transformation, with the magnified skepticism toward the possibility of significant reform from the federal government, a dismissive view of the civil-rights movement and its accomplishments gained credence. Black commentators disparaged it as "bourgeois" or elitist, and belittled the reforms of the 1960s for failing to produce major structural changes or to overturn racism. Only African-American professionals and entrepreneurs had gained, they argued, while the mass of blacks saw their status decline and their hopes dashed. Continuity, not change, was the chief characteristic of their interpretation of African-American history.

That view of the black struggle for equality and justice, of essentially *easy* and *inconsequential* triumphs, is not the perspective expressed in this book. However pressing the problems of today, however immutable the conditions of life appear, it is vital to assess alterations and transformations as well as constancy, to recall past barriers and to understand how and why they were overcome. Slavery was once almost universally assumed to be a permanent feature of American life. It was abolished. The Supreme Court once declared that African-Americans were not citizens of the United States, and would never be citizens; then, following recognition of their citizenship, it consigned blacks to a caste of subordinate, second-class citizens. Those rulings, in their day, also seemed irrevocable. They were not. Describing the plight of African-Americans prior to the *Brown* decision, Chief Justice Earl Warren recalled:

> They could not live where they desired, they could not work where white people worked. . . . They could not use the same rest rooms, drinking fountains, or telephone booths. They could not eat in the same restaurants, sleep in the same hotels, be treated in the same hospitals. . . . They were denied admission to any university attended by whites, whether public or private. They were denied the right to sit on juries even when their own lives, freedom, or property were involved. . . . They were segregated on buses, street cars, trains, ships, and airplanes and terminals of all kinds. They were not allowed to vote.

This, too, was believed to be unalterable. But persistent organized struggle by African-Americans, abetted by sympathetic whites, overcame Jim Crow. Battling within a political system highly resistant to rapid, definitive change, blacks in the decade after *Brown* vanquished the biracial caste system of the South and its legally sanctioned disenfranchisement, discrimination, and segregation. They paid a woeful price in pain and suffering; but they did overcome, and gained the rights of full, unqualified first-class citizenship. Because of that struggle and triumph, moreover, African-Americans today have the tools necessary to preserve and complete the Second Reconstruction. The struggle for first-class citizenship gained more than just constitutional rights. It brought African-Americans self-pride and respect. It reawakened black consciousness. It liberated millions of whites and blacks from prejudice and ignorance of one another. And, as a consequence of changed attitudes, nondiscrimination laws, and affirmative-action policies, African-Americans, as never before in history, are a signficant presence in public life. In numbers and influence, they have moved beyond tokenism in the workplace, the government, the society.

Their voice, their dollars, their votes cannot easily be disregarded. Although the civil-rights movement did not bring all the results it promised, it has given African-Americans the resources and strengths necessary to continue the struggle. However much it is now important to focus on the plight of the black underclass, to call attention to the crisis it poses, it must also be noted that even more African-Americans today are neither destitute nor slum-ridden, neither on drugs nor in prison, neither high-school dropouts nor third-generation welfare recipients.

While there are no easy answers for the problems that remain, we need to remember what President Johnson in 1965 said was necessary to overcome the deprivations caused by decades of racism:

> Jobs are part of the answer. They bring the income which permits a man to provide for his family. Decent homes in decent surroundings and a chance to learn—an equal chance to learn—are part of the answer. Welfare and social programs better designed to hold families together are part of the answer. Care for the sick is part of the answer. An understanding heart by all Americans is another big part of the answer.

We ought also to remember that a majority of whites once supported a "war on poverty," and that the provision of federal student loans, higher Social Security benefits, food stamps, job training programs, Head Start, Medicare and Medicaid, and affirmative-action policies cut the poverty rate by nearly 50 percent between the mid-1960s and the early 1970s, and very significantly improved the standard of living for millions of African-American families. And we must remember that Dr. King's dream was once not only the dream of African-Americans. The nonviolent black protest movement touched the conscience of white America, altered its values and thought, and resulted in a vast array of edicts and efforts, governmental and private, to begin to overcome the legacy of more than three centuries of slavery and white supremacy.

In the process, African-Americans proved their capacity to compel change. That, above all, should be remembered. Undue pessimism or fatalism never stimulated the struggles necessary for advancement. Hopefulness has. As President Franklin Roosevelt reminded the nation more than half a century ago, "when there is no vision, the people perish." It is necessary, says Jesse Jackson, to "keep hope alive." That is the key to continuing the struggle until it closes the gulf in the quality of lives lived by whites and by African-Americans. With that understanding, the struggle to complete the unfinished business of American democracy will endure until it is fulfilled.

# BIBLIOGRAPHICAL ESSAY

·······················

The literature on the modern black struggle is voluminous, and mostly of an ephemeral nature. To date, few significant historical monographs analyze racial events since 1954. The student of history must, accordingly, make judicious use of journalistic and participants' accounts, and works by social scientists. What follows is a selective sample of the books, and a few indispensable articles, I found most helpful in preparing this volume. Many of the specialized studies include comprehensive bibliographies, and these need to be consulted for the full range of materials on a given subject.

The most authoritative overviews of the movement are Rhoda Lois Blumberg, *Civil Rights: The 1960s Freedom Struggle* (1984); Manning Marable, *Race, Reform, and Rebellion: The Second Reconstruction in Black America, 1945–1982* (1984); Robert Weisbrot, *Freedom Bound, A History of America's Civil Rights Movement* (1990); and, especially for recent political developments, Steven F. Lawson, *Running for Freedom, Civil Rights and Black Politics in America Since 1941* (1991). Also see Thomas R. Brooks, *Walls Come Tumbling Down: A History of the Civil Rights Movement: 1940–1970* (1974); Anthony Lewis, *Portrait of a Decade: The Second American Revolution* (1964); and Benjamin Muse, *Ten*

*Years of Prelude: The Story of Integration Since the Supreme Court's 1954 Decision* (1964) and *The American Negro Revolution: From Nonviolence to Black Power, 1963–1967* (1968). Howell Raines, *My Soul Is Rested: Movement Days in the Deep South Remembered* (1977), and Clayborne Carson, et al., *The Eyes on the Prize Civil Rights Reader* (1991), are best for the words of those who participated in the struggle. Two indispensable collections of essays are Charles W. Eagles, ed., *The Civil Rights Movement in America* (1986), and Michael V. Namorato, ed., *Have We Overcome?* (1979). Also see Lerone Bennett, Jr., *Confrontation: Black and White* (1965); Robert H. Brisbane, *Black Activism: Racial Revolution in the United States, 1954–1970* (1974); Louis E. Lomax, *The Negro Revolt* (1962); and Edward Peeks, *The Long Struggle for Black Power* (1971).

Overall analyses of particular insight are Lerone Bennett, Jr., *The Negro Mood* (1965); Debbie Lewis, *And We Are Not Saved: A History of the Movement as People* (1970); and Pat Watters, *Down to Now: Reflections on the Southern Civil Rights Movement* (1971). Also useful: W. Heywood Burns, *The Voices of Negro Protest in America* (1963); Joseph S. Himes, *Racial Conflict in American Society* (1973); and James W. Vander Zanden, *Race Relations in Transition: The Segregation Crises within the South* (1965). Nat Hentoff's *The New Equality* (1964) and Charles E. Silberman's *Crisis in Black and White* (1964) brilliantly illuminate the difficulties of the struggle in Northern ghettos. Ruth P. Morgan's *The President and Civil Rights—Policy Making by Executive Order* (1970) and Allan Wolk's *The Presidency and Black Civil Rights: Eisenhower to Nixon* (1971) analyze executive decision-making. Important analytical articles are Kenneth B. Clark, "The Civil Rights Movement: Momentum and Organization," *Daedalus* XCV (Winter 1966); James A. Geschwender, "Social Structure of the Negro Revolt: An Examination of Some Hypotheses," *Social Forces* XLIII (Dec. 1964); and James H. Laue, "Power, Conflict and Social Change," in Louis Masotti and Don Bowen, eds., *Riots and Rebellion: Civil Violence in the Urban Community* (1968). The most helpful attitudinal studies are Angus Campbell, *White Attitudes toward Black People* (1971); Peter Goldman, *Report from Black America* (1970); Samuel Lubell, *White and Black: Test of a Nation* (1964); Richard Lemon, *The Troubled Americans* (1970); Gary Marx, *Protest and Prejudice: A Study of Belief in the Black Community* (rev. ed., 1969); and two compilations of poll data by William Brink and Louis Harris, *The Negro Revolution in America* (1964) and *Black and White* (1967).

The indispensable documents of the struggle can be found in Richard A. Bardolph, ed., *The Civil Rights Record: Black Americans and the Law, 1849–1970* (1970); Albert P. Blaustein and Robert L. Zangrando, eds., *Civil Rights and the American Negro: A Documentary History* (1968); Leon Friedman, ed., *The Civil Rights Reader: Basic Documents of the Civil Rights Movement* (1967); Joanne Grant, ed., *Black Protest: History, Documents and Analyses, 1619 to the Present* (1968); August Meier, Elliott Rudwick, and Francis L. Broderick, eds., *Black Protest Thought in the Twentieth Century* (rev. ed., 1971); and Lester A. Sobel, ed., *Civil Rights, 1960–66* (1967).

The best collections of articles on the struggle are John H. Bracey, Jr., August Meier, and Elliott Rudwick, eds., *Conflict and Competition: Studies in the Recent Black Protest Movement* (1971); Kenneth B. Clark, ed., *The Negro Protest* (1963); John Hope Franklin and Isidore Starr, eds., *The Negro in Twentieth Century America: A Reader on the Struggle for Civil Rights* (1967); August Meier and Elliott Rudwick, eds., *Black Protest in the Sixties* (1970); and Alan F. Westin, ed., *Freedom Now! The Civil Rights Struggle in America* (1964). The two most useful journals are *Freedomways* and *New South*, a publication of the Southern Regional Council. Much can also be gleaned from *Race Relations Law Reporter* and *The Civil Rights Digest*, a quarterly of the U.S. Commission on Civil Rights.

Germinal developments leading to the emergence of the modern black struggle have been studied by numerous historians. For analyses focusing on three different decades, see Raymond Wolters, *The*

*New Negro on Campus: Black College Rebellions of the 1920s* (1975); Harvard Sitkoff, *A New Deal for Blacks: The Emergence of Civil Rights as a National Issue,* Vol. I: *Depression Decade* (1978); and Richard M. Dalfiume, *Desegregation of the U.S. Armed Forces: Fighting on Two Fronts, 1939–1953* (1969). Civil-rights organizations in the second quarter of the twentieth century are the subject of Langston Hughes, *Fight for Freedom: The Story of the NAACP* (1962); Herbert Garfinkel, *When Negroes March: The March on Washington Movement in the Organization's Politics for FEPC* (1959); Louis C. Kesselman, *The Social Politics of FEPC: A Study in Reform Movements* (1948); Thomas A. Krueger, *And Promises to Keep: The Southern Conference for Human Welfare, 1938–1948* (1968); B. Joyce Ross, *J. E. Spingarn and the Rise of the N.A.A.C.P.* (1972); and Nancy Weiss, *The National Urban League, 1910–1940* (1974). Other key monographs are Catherine A. Barnes, *Journey from Jim Crow: The Desegregation of Southern Transit* (1983); Darlene Clark Hine, *Black Victory: The Rise and Fall of the White Primary in Texas* (1979); Merl E. Reed, *Seedtime for the Modern Civil Rights Movement: The President's Committee on Fair Employment Practice, 1941–1946* (1991); Linda Reed, *Simple Decency & Common Sense, The Southern Conference Movement, 1938–1963* (1991); and Jules Tygiel, *Baseball's Great Experiment: Jackie Robinson and His Legacy* (1983). Also see Robert Korstad and Nelson Lichtenstein, "Opportunities Found and Lost: Labor, Radicals, and the Early Civil Rights Movement," *Journal of American History* LXXV (Dec. 1988). Charles Abrams, *Forbidden Neighbors* (1955); E. Franklin Frazier, *Black Bourgeoisie: The Rise of a New Middle Class in the United States* (1957); Eli Ginzberg, *The Negro Potential* (1956); Spencer Logan, *A Negro's Faith in America* (1946); and Ray Sprigle, *In the Land of Jim Crow* (1949) reveal much about African-American attitudes and problems at mid-century. Four sociological analyses of very special importance are Doug McAdam, *Political Process and the Development of Black Insurgency* (1982); Aldon D. Morris, *The Origins of the*

*Civil Rights Movement* (1984); Jack M. Bloom, *Class, Race, and the Civil Rights Movement* (1987); and Herbert H. Haines, *Black Radicals and the Civil Rights Mainstream, 1954–1970* (1988).

No civil-rights topic has been more written about than the school-desegregation decision. In a class by itself, Richard Kluger's *Simple Justice: The History of Brown v. Board of Education: Black America's Struggle for Equality* (1976) is magisterial. Not to be overlooked are Daniel M. Berman, *It Is So Ordered: The Supreme Court Rules on School Segregation* (1966); Albert P. Blaustein and Clarence C. Ferguson, Jr., *Desegregation and the Law: The Meaning and Effect of the School Segregation Cases* (rev. ed., 1962); and Robert V. Harris, *The Quest for Equality: The Constitution, Congress and the Supreme Court* (1960). For a dissenting view, see Lino S. Graglia, *Disaster by Decree: The Supreme Court Decision on Race and the Schools* (1976). NAACP strategy is treated in Randall W. Bland, *Private Pressure and Public Law: The Legal Career of Justice Thurgood Marshall* (1973), and Jack Greenberg, *Race Relations and American Law* (1959). A key article is Michael Mayer, "With Much Deliberation and Some Speed," *Journal of Southern History* 52 (Feb. 1986).

Post-*Brown* developments are the subject of Numan V. Bartley, *The Rise of Massive Resistance: Race and Politics in the South during the 1950's* (1969); Earl Black, *Southern Governors and Civil Rights: Racial Segregation as a Campaign Issue in the Second Reconstruction* (1976); Neil R. McMillen, *The Citizens' Council: Organized Resistance to the Second Reconstruction, 1954–64* (1971); and Francis M. Wilhoit, *The Politics of Massive Resistance* (1973). Contemporary conservative opposition to the Court is expressed in Tom Brady, *Black Monday* (1955); James J. Kilpatrick, *The Southern Case for School Segregation* (1962); and William D. Workman, *The Case for the South* (1960). Liberal rejoinders are Harry Ashmore, *The Negro and the Schools* (1954) and *Epitaph for Dixie* (1958), and John B. Martin, *The Deep South Says "Never"* (1957). Additional information on Little Rock is in Virgil T. Blossom, *It*

*Has Happened Here* (1959); Brooks Hays, *A Southern Moderate Speaks* (1959); and Wilson and Jane C. Record, eds., *Little Rock U.S.A.: Materials for Analysis* (1960).

The politics of civil rights during the Eisenhower years is covered by J. W. Anderson, *Eisenhower, Brownell and the Congress: The Tangled Origins of the Civil Rights Bill of 1956–1957* (1964); Daniel M. Berman, *A Bill Becomes a Law: The Civil Rights Act of 1960* (1962); and Foster Rhea Dulles, *The Civil Rights Commission: 1957–1965* (1968). Excellent analyses of this Administration and the two subsequent ones are Steven F. Lawson, *Black Ballots: Voting Rights in the South, 1944–1969* (1976), and James L. Sundquist, *Politics and Policy: The Eisenhower, Kennedy, and Johnson Years* (1968). A negative "insider" account is E. Frederic Morrow's *Black Man in the White House* (1963). More scholarly and equally unfavorable is Robert Frederick Burk, *The Eisenhower Administration and Black Civil Rights* (1984). One should also see Gary W. Reichard, "Democrats, Civil Rights, and Electoral Strategies in the 1950s," *Congress and the Presidency* XIII (Spring 1986).

Numerous biographies of King have been published. The two indispensable, most comprehensive, are David J. Garrow, *Bearing the Cross: Martin Luther King, Jr., and the Southern Christian Leadership Conference* (1986), and Taylor Branch, *Parting the Waters: America in the King Years, 1954–1963* (1988). Somewhat dated, yet still offering significant insight, is David Lewis, *King: A Biography* (2nd ed., 1978). Also of value are Lerone Bennett, Jr., *What Manner of Man* (rev. ed., 1968); William Robert Miller, *Martin Luther King, Jr.* (1968); and Lawrence D. Reddick, Jr., *Crusader without Violence* (1959). August Meier's "On the Role of Martin Luther King," *New Politics* IV (Winter 1965), is particularly enlightening. Further details on the bus boycott are provided by Martin Luther King, Jr., *Stride toward Freedom* (1958). The best history of the SCLC is Adam Fairclough, *To Redeem the Soul of America: The Southern Christian Leadership Conference and Martin Luther King, Jr.* (1987). Also see David J. Garrow, ed., *The Montgomery Bus Boycott and the Women Who Started It: The*

*Memoir of Jo Ann Gibson Robinson* (1987); J. Mills Thornton, "Challenge and Response in the Montgomery Bus Boycott of 1955–56," *Alabama Review* XXXIII (July 1989); and Preston Valien, "The Montgomery Bus Protest as a Social Movement," in Jitsuichi Masouka and Valien, eds., *Race Relations: Problems and Theory* (1961).

The Student Non-Violent Coordinating Committee's history is superbly covered in Clayborne Carson, *In Struggle: SNCC and the Black Awakening of the 1960s* (1981). Other penetrating analyses appear in Mary King, *Freedom Song: A Personal Story of the 1960s Civil Rights Movement* (1987); Howard Zinn, *SNCC: The New Abolitionists* (1964); Jack Newfield, *A Prophetic Minority* (1966); and Cleveland Sellers, *River of No Return: The Autobiography of a Black Militant and the Life and Death of SNCC* (1973). William H. Chafe's *Civilities and Civil Rights: Greensboro, North Carolina and the Black Struggle for Freedom* (1980) is the best case study of a sit-in and description of the evolving nature of the movement in a single city. Also see Miles Wolff, *Lunch at the Five and Ten: The Greensboro Sit-ins: A Contemporary History* (1970); Merrill Proudfoot, *Diary of a Sit-in* (1962); Jack L. Walker, *Sit-ins in Atlanta: A Study in the Negro Revolt* (1964); and Donald R. Matthews and James W. Prothro, *Negroes and the New Southern Politics* (1966), particularly chapter 14. Of special value are J. Allen Williams, "Negro College Students Participation in Sit-ins," *Social Forces* XL (March 1962), and Emily Stoper, "The Student Non-violent Coordinating Committee: Rise and Fall of a Redemptive Organization," *Journal of Black Studies* VIII (Sept. 1977).

The history of the Congress of Racial Equality is comprehensively and judiciously treated by August Meier and Elliott Rudwick, *CORE: A Study in the Civil Rights Movement, 1942–1968* (1973). Also see Inge Powell Bell, *CORE and the Strategy of Nonviolence* (1968), and a case study of CORE in Chapel Hill, John Ehle, *The Free Men* (1965). Two personal views of the Freedom Rides are James Farmer, *Freedom—When?* (1965), and James Peck, *Freedom Ride* (1962). Indispensable for the voter-registration campaigns and the meaning of Albany are Pat Watters and Reese Cleghorn, *Climbing Jacob's Ladder: The Arrival of Negroes in Southern Politics* (1967), and Howard Zinn, *The Southern Mystique* (1964). Also essential for an understanding of the movement is Gerald McWorter and Robert Crain, "Subcommunity Gladiatorial Competition: Civil Rights Leadership as a Competitive Process," *Social Forces* XLVI (Sept. 1967); James W. Vander Zanden, "The Non-Violent Movement Against Segregation," *American Journal of Sociology* LXVIII (March 1963); and Archie E. Ellen, "John Lewis—Keeper of the Dream," *New South* XXVI (Spring 1971). For Farmer's insights, see James Farmer, *Lay Bare the Heart: An Autobiography of the Civil Rights Movement* (1985). Roy Wilkins, with Tom Matthews, *Standing Fast* (1982) presents the views of the NAACP's longtime leader.

Events in Birmingham are described by Michael Dorman, *We Shall Overcome* (1964); Marshall Frady, *Wallace* (1970); Martin Luther King, Jr., *Why We Can't Wait* (1964); and Charles Morgan, Jr., *A Time to Speak* (1964). Vincent Harding's "A Beginning in Birmingham," *The Reporter* (June 6, 1963), and Bayard Rustin's "The Meaning of Birmingham," *Liberation* VIII (June 1963), are perceptive statements by advisors to King. President Kennedy's response to the black struggle is favorably evaluated in Carl M. Brauer, *John F. Kennedy and the Second Reconstruction* (1977). More critical is Victor S. Navasky, *Kennedy Justice* (1971). Also see James C. Harvey, *Civil Rights during the Kennedy Administration* (1971), and Doris E. Saunders, ed., *The Kennedy Years and the Negro* (1964). On the March on Washington, see Anna Arnold Hedgeman, *The Trumpet Sounds: A Memoir of Negro Leadership* (1964), chapter 9, and the photographic survey by Doris E. Saunders, *The Day They Marched* (1963). Clifford M. Lytle's "The History of the Civil Rights Bill of 1964," *Journal of Negro History* LI (Oct. 1966), and Charles and Barbara Whalen's *The Longest Debate: A Legislative History of the 1964 Civil Rights Act* (1986) record the legislative battle.

Participants in the struggle in Mississippi best convey the critical events of 1964. See Sally Belfrage, *Freedom Summer* (1965); Len Holt, *The Summer That Didn't End* (1968); Ann Moody, *Coming of Age in Mississippi* (1968); Tracy Sugerman, *Stranger at the Gates* (1966); Elizabeth Sutherland, ed., *Letters from Mississippi* (1965); and Nicholas Von Hoffman, *Mississippi Notebook* (1964). Further analysis is provided by Paul Good, *The Trouble I've Seen* (1975), and William McCord, *Mississippi: The Long Hot Summer* (1965). William Bradford Huie's *Three Lives for Mississippi* (1965) graphically depicts the murder of the civil-rights workers. Also see Walter Lord, *The Past That Would Not Die* (1965); James Meredith, *Three Years in Mississippi* (1966); and Frank Smith, *Congressmen from Mississippi* (1964). James Silver's *Mississippi: The Closed Society* (1964); Doug McAdam, *Freedom Summer* (1988); Seth Cagin and Philip Dray, *We Are Not Afraid: The Story of Goodman, Schwerner, and Chaney and the Civil Rights Campaign for Mississippi* (1988); Mary Aickin Rothschild, *A Case of Black and White: Northern Volunteers and the Southern Freedom Summer* (1982); and Michael Belknap, *Federal Law and Southern Order: Racial Violence and Constitutional Conflict in the Post-Brown South* (1987) are indispensable.

The Selma campaign is analyzed in David J. Garrow, *Protest at Selma, Martin Luther King, Jr., and the Voting Rights Act of 1965* (1978). Conflicting interpretations are presented by James G. Clark, Jr., *The Jim Clark Story—"I Saw Selma Raped"* (1966), and Charles E. Fager, *Selma 1965* (1974). The President's view is best stated in Lyndon B. Johnson, *The Vantage Point: Perspectives of the Presidency, 1963–1969* (1969), and that of young Selma African-Americans in Sheyanne Webb and Rachel West Nelson, *Selma, Lord, Selma* (1980). Further documentary and statistical material can be found in James C. Harvey, *Black Civil Rights during the Johnson Administration* (1973). The consequences of the laws passed in the Johnson years are described in Frances R. Cousens, *Public Civil Rights Agencies and Fair Employment: Promise vs. Performance* (1969); William R. Keech, *The Impact of Negro Voting: The Role of the Vote in the Quest for Equality* (1968); Gary

Orfield, *The Reconstruction of Southern Education: The Schools and the 1964 Civil Rights Act* (1969); Harrell R. Rodgers and Charles S. Bullock III, *Law and Social Change: Civil Rights Laws and Their Consequences* (1972); Frederick W. Wirt, *Politics of Southern Equality: Law and Change in a Mississippi County* (1970); and particularly Hugh Davis Graham, *The Civil Rights Era* (1990), and Steven F. Lawson, *In Pursuit of Power: Southern Blacks & Electoral Politics, 1965–1982* (1985). Also see Lawrence J. Hanks, *The Struggle for Black Political Empowerment in Three Georgia Counties* (1987); Minion Morrison, *Black Political Mobilization* (1987); and Harold W. Stanley, *Voter Mobilization and the Politics of Race* (1987).

The transformation and demise of the movement is best told by Vincent Harding, "Black Radicalism: The Road from Montgomery," in Alfred Young, ed., *Dissent: Explorations in the History of American Radicalism* (1968); John Herbers, *The Lost Priority: What Happened to the Civil Rights Movement in America* (1970); Allen J. Matusow, "From Civil Rights to Black Power: The Case of SNCC, 1960–1966," in Barton J. Bernstein and Matusow, eds., *Twentieth Century America: Recent Interpretations* (1969); and Pat Watters, *Down to Now, Reflections on the Southern Civil Rights Movement* (1971). C. Vann Woodward's "What Happened to the Civil Rights Movement?" *Harper's* CCXXIV (Jan. 1967), should be read in conjunction with his *The Strange Career of Jim Crow* (rev. ed., 1966), chapter 5.

Most manifestations of racial violence in the 1960s were extensively reported and analyzed. The best studies of single riots are Sidney Fine, *Violence in the Model City: Race Relations, the Cavanagh Administration, and the Detroit Race Riot of 1967* (1989); Robert Conot, *Rivers of Blood, Years of Darkness* (1968); Tom Hayden, *Rebellion in Newark: Official Violence and Ghetto Response* (1967); and John Hersey, *The Algiers Motel Incident* (1968). Joe R. Feagin and Harlan Hahn's *Ghetto Revolts: The Politics of Violence in American Cities* (1973) and Robert Fogelson's *Violence as Protest: A Study of Riots and Ghettos* (1971) are especially discerning. Martin Oppenheimer's *The Urban Guerilla* (1969) and Garry Wills's *The Second Civil War: Arming for Armageddon* (1968) are chilling speculations. The most useful anthologies are David Boesal and Peter H. Rossi, eds., *Cities under Siege: An Anatomy of the Ghetto Riots, 1964–1968* (1971); Robert H. Connery, ed., *Urban Riots: Violence and Social Change* (1968); and Louis H. Masotti and Don R. Bowen, eds., *Riots and Rebellion: Civil Violence in the Urban Community* (1968). Also see James W. Button, *Black Violence: Political Impact of the 1960s Riots* (1978).

Essential to an understanding of the riots are Kenneth B. Clark, *Dark Ghetto: Dilemmas of Social Power* (1965); Charles Grier and Price M. Cobbs, *Black Rage* (1968); James A. Geschwender, "Civil Rights Protest and Riots: A Disappearing Distinction," *Social Science Quarterly* XLIX (Dec. 1968); and T. M. Tomlinson, "Determinants of Black Politics: Riots and the Growth of Militancy," *Psychiatry* XXXIII (May 1970).

The starting point for understanding Black Power is Stokely Carmichael and Charles V. Hamilton, *Black Power: The Politics of Liberation in America* (1967). Two prominent interpretations are Julius Lester, *Look Out Whitey! Black Power's Gon' Get Your Mama* (1968), and Nathan Wright, Jr., *Black Power and Urban Unrest* (1967). Its diversity is best sampled in Floyd Barbour, ed., *The Black Power Revolt* (1968), and LeRoi Jones and Larry Neal, eds., *Black Fire: An Anthology of Afro-American Writing* (1968). King's critique is stated in Martin Luther King, Jr., *Where Do We Go from Here: Chaos or Community* (1967). Perceptive explanations for the emergence of the slogan are contained in Thomas L. Blair, *Retreat to the Ghetto* (1977), and Lewis Killian, *The Impossible Revolution: Black Power and the American Dream* (1968). Also worth consulting are the views of Harold Cruse, *The Crisis of the Negro Intellectual* (1967) and *Rebellion or Revolution* (1968).

A personal account of radicalization within the movement is

James Forman, *Sammy Younge, Jr.* (1968) and *The Making of Black Revolutionaries* (1972). H. Rap Brown's *Die Nigger Die* (1969); Stokely Carmichael's *Stokely Speaks* (1971); Eldridge Cleaver's *Soul on Ice* (1968); and Floyd McKissick's *Genocide USA: A Blueprint for Black Survival* (1967) express the changed mood. The influence of Malcolm X is the subject of Archie Epps, *Malcolm X and the American Negro Revolution* (1969). Also see George Breitman, ed., *Malcolm X Speaks* (1965); Peter Goldman, *The Death and Life of Malcolm X* (1973); and Malcolm X, with Alex Haley, *The Autobiography of Malcolm X* (1965). James Baldwin's *The Fire Next Time* (1963) is prophetic on the appeal of Malcolm X and the transformation of the black struggle.

Leon E. Panetta and Peter Gall's *Bring Us Together—The Nixon Team and the Civil Rights Retreat* (1971) pinpoints the direction of the politics of civil rights in the 1970s. Also see Milton D. Morris, *The Politics of Black America* (1975). Changing attitudes on the high court are explained in J. Harvie Wilkinson III, *From Brown to Bakke: The Supreme Court and School Integration, 1954–1978* (1979). Continuing instances of white racism are documented by Michael N. Danielson, *The Politics of Exclusion* (1976); Orlando Patterson, *Ethnic Chauvinism: The Reactionary Impulse* (1977); Alan Anderson and George Pickering, *Confronting the Color Line: The Broken Promise of the Civil Rights Movement in Chicago* (1986); J. Anthony Lukas, *Common Ground* (1985); Rufus Browning, et al., *Protest Is Not Enough: The Struggle of Blacks and Hispanics for Equality in Urban Politics* (1984); and Jonathan Kaufman, *Broken Alliance* (1988). Two most perceptive studies of the movement's successes and failures are David R. Colburn, *Racial Change and Community Crisis: St. Augustine, Florida, 1877–1980* (1985), and Robert J. Norrell, *Reaping the Whirlwind: The Civil Rights Movement in Tuskegee* (1985).

Recent political developments are covered in Sheila D. Collins, *The Rainbow Challenge: The Jackson Campaign and the Future of U.S. Politics* (1986); Margaret Edds, *Free at Last: What Really*

*Happened When Civil Rights Came to Southern Politics* (1987); Michael B. Preston, et al., eds., *The New Black Politics: The Search for Political Power* (1982); Manning Marable, *Black American Politics: From the Washington Marches to Jesse Jackson* (1985); Adolph L. Reed, Jr., *The Jesse Jackson Phenomenon: The Crisis of Purpose in Afro-American Politics* (1986); and Ronald W. Walters, *Black Presidential Politics in America* (1988).

Indispensable for understanding the current status of African-Americans are Elijah Anderson, *Streetwise: Race, Class, and Change in an Urban Community* (1992); Lois Benjamin, *The Black Elite: Facing the Color Line in the Twilight of the Twentieth Century* (1992); James W. Button, *Blacks and Social Change* (1989); Andrew Hacker, *Two Nations: Black and White, Separate, Hostile, Unequal* (1992); Christopher Jencks, *Rethinking Social Policy: Race, Poverty, and the Underclass* (1992); L. Bart Landry, *The New Black Middle Class* (1987); Lisbeth B. Schorr, *Within Our Reach* (1991); Jim Sleeper, *The Closest of Strangers* (1990); Robin Williams, et al., *A Common Destiny: Blacks and American Society* (1989); and William Julius Wilson, *The Truly Disadvantaged: The Inner City, the Underclass, and Public Policy* (1987). Compare with Leonard Broom and Norval Glenn, *Transformation of the Negro American* (1965); Sar Levitan, William B. Johnson, and Robert Taggart, *Still a Dream: The Changing Status of Blacks Since 1960* (1978); Mabel M. Smythe, ed., *The Black American Reference Book* (1976); and William J. Wilson, *The Declining Significance of Race: Blacks and Changing American Institutions* (1978). Also see Reynolds Farley, "Trends in Racial Inequalities: Have the Gains of the 1960s Disappeared in the 1970s?" *American Sociological Review* XLII (April 1977), and Elliot Zashin, "The Progress of Black Americans in Civil Rights: The Past Two Decades Assessed," *Daedalus* CVII (Winter 1978). Their assessments should be balanced with Earl Black and Merle Black, *Politics and Society in the South* (1987); Gertrude Ezorsky, *Racism and Justice: The Case for Affirmative Action* (1992); Paula Giddings, *When and Where I Enter: The*

*Impact of Black Women on Race and Sex in America* (1984); Vincent Harding, *The Other American Revolution* (1981); Studs Terkel, *Race: How Blacks and Whites Think and Feel about the American Obsession* (1992); and Hanes Walton, *When the Marching Stopped: The Politics of Civil Rights Regulatory Agencies* (1988).

# INDEX

........................

251